Ruth C. Gerrard.

POETRY OF THE PEOPLE

COMPRISING

*POEMS ILLUSTRATIVE OF THE HISTORY
AND NATIONAL SPIRIT OF ENGLAND,
SCOTLAND, IRELAND, AND AMERICA*

Selected and Arranged with Notes

BY

CHARLES MILLS GAYLEY
AND
MARTIN C. FLAHERTY

Of the University of California

GINN & COMPANY
BOSTON · NEW YORK · CHICAGO · LONDON

COPYRIGHT, 1903, BY
CHARLES MILLS GAYLEY AND MARTIN C. FLAHERTY

ALL RIGHTS RESERVED

215.1

The Athenæum Press
GINN & COMPANY · PRO-
PRIETORS · BOSTON · U.S.A.

A BALLAD OF HEROES

Because you passed, and now are not, —
    Because, in some remoter day,
Your sacred dust from doubtful spot
    Was blown of ancient airs away, —
    Because you perished, — must men say
Your deeds were naught, and so profane
    Your lives with that cold burden? Nay,
The deeds you wrought are not in vain!

Though it may be, above the plot
    That hid your once imperial clay,
No greener than o'er men forgot
    The unregarding grasses sway; —
    Though there no sweeter is the lay
Of careless bird, — though you remain
    Without distinction of decay, —
The deeds you wrought are not in vain!

No. For while yet in tower or cot
    Your story stirs the pulses' play;
And men forget the sordid lot —
    The sordid care, of cities gray; —
    While yet, be-set in homelier fray,
They learn from you the lesson plain
    That Life may go, so Honor stay, —
The deeds you wrought are not in vain!

ENVOY

Heroes of old! I humbly lay
    The laurel on your graves again;
Whatever men have done, men may, —
    The deeds you wrought are not in vain.

AUSTIN DOBSON

PREFACE

THIS little volume has a very modest but distinct and, we think, unique purpose,— to supply the reading public and the schools with a compact body not necessarily of the most highly polished or artistic poems in the English tongue, but of those which are at once most simple, most hearty, most truly characteristic of the people, their tradition, history, and spirit. By Poetry of the People we do not mean only ballads of countryside or battlefield, or of street or village, hearth or market, not only the production of the folk-improviser or his succeeding bard long ago buried behind the hills of anonymity: but poetry that the people possess and occupy (or should occupy) because it is of their blood and bone and sinew: poetry sometimes by, and sometimes not, but always for, the people; poems that were household words with our fathers and mothers, and lay close to the heart because *of* the heart; poems that even now beat in the bosom of the Folk and find utterance in the hour of stress; poems which more often than not are all the truer art because they are not artful.

It may have appeared to others, as it has to us, that literature in verse is not learned nor enjoyed nor even read by young or old as much as it used to be. One explanation of this neglect is very probably that in the place of unsophisticated poetry, such as generations of our forefathers loved, there have been too frequently introduced into the schools, and at too early a period, the masterpieces of our consciously artistic, highly intellectual, and even subjective verse. Of this illogical procedure the inevitable corollary is that not a few well-meaning but theory-ridden teachers — in their efforts to fix a youthful mind upon things literary designed for grown-ups, highly cultivated at that — are driven to rhetorical, gerund-grinding, analytical, or — *horresco referens* — quasi-philosophical, pseudo-scientific devices in handling that which should be the simplest of ideal devotions and delights. Now everybody who has not been spoiled by vagaries knows that the natural and healthy taste of the growing boy, when it is for literature at all, is for the literature that while it informs manages to entertain — for the poetry that interprets *because it delights;* that is to say, for the spontaneous and healthy poetry of the Folk when it was a boy, or of that element in the Folk that preserves always the vigor and push of youth.

If this little book can contribute somewhat toward exploding the fallacy that poetry is something other than poetry, — material, forsooth, for translation, parsing, trope-hunting, rhetorical exercises, platitudinous preaching, or anything else extraneous to art, — it will have accomplished at least half the purpose of the editors. Of course good poetry has a lesson for him who can *feel* it. Like all good things it can't help blessing those who take it on faith. Its favors are not for those who would conquer but for those who surrender. The best way to study it is not to study but to enjoy. And this should be especially true of the poetry which we place in the hands of our ingenuous youth; if it cannot captivate it is an offense, a folly, — worse than that, a bore. Such poetry must be chiefly of an objective cast, of genuine sentiment, and of simple style. It must neither bewilder nor deliberately instruct. It must have the quality of charming, of winning the reader to repeat and to murmur, and to learn because it is easier to do so than to forget.

Here are ballads of the olden time, direct and naïve, easy to understand, — save where some antiquated word or phrase may intervene, and then glossary and notes stand ready to help out, — ballads made to say and to sing; stories of heroic adventure, romantic and supernatural; whilom fyttes and modern instances of patriotism and devotion; songs of homely sentiment, popular spirit, and nationality; themes mostly external and concrete, — the poetry of history, such as appealed naïvely to the listening and consentaneous crowd. And if occasionally there is here to be found the poetry also of suggestion for the individual who reads and reflects, it is always of emotions simple and unsophisticated, universal, abiding, and sincere. Here, too, are manly ideals, ancient but ever-living.

If this little bark succeeds in making the haven of the heart, it may also, perchance, succeed in unlading the hope with which it is fraught. Who can estimate the gain to the American spirit, — and by that we mean the spirit of rational freedom expressed in terms of nationality, — the gain that would ensue, if our youth would but occupy and prize the literary heritage that is theirs? The poetry of the people of England, Ireland, Scotland, and America has for us a certain scriptural worth as well as historic. Is it not the immemorial record of sentiment, sacrifice, and ideal — the most enduring and the noblest of our forefathers; is it not the conserver of that experience whence proceed our present prestige and security? Now, naturally effective in the development and discipline of the national pride as is an intimate acquaintance with national history, more effective still is the possession of that which, as Aristotle has said, is truer than history, — the speaking soul of its events, its poetry. Young men and women for whom that voice continues to haunt the corridors of the present cannot but honor our national forebears, cannot but emulate their love of liberty, their endurance and orderly restraint, their manliness, their devotion to duty and to country, and so cannot but cultivate in perpetuity those ideals that go to make a noble people.

Since, however, there is a difference — a gulf fixed — between the sense of nationality of which we speak, dignified, legitimate, and effective, and the provincialism that often parades in its place, we have tried in these excerpts from the Poetry of the People to emphasize the deeper and wider justification of our national pride — the justification that lies in the blood and speech of generations overseas who knew what patriotism meant long before their children, our immediate ancestors, founded here the liberties which we enjoy. A parochial spirit which ignores the transatlantic conditions from which we proceed sacrifices more in meaning than it makes in show. If we would appreciate our national purport we must insist upon our proprietorship in the thousand-year roots of the racial oak; we must continue to possess the stately green and spread of the lower foliage, the common antecedent of the Anglo-Celto-American ramifications that stir the upper air to-day. We must rejoice as by community of birthright, in the outgrowth, overseas as well as here at home, of that poetry that expresses the spirit and sap of our common stock. While, therefore, this book contains a liberal supply of poems illustrative of our American history and national spirit, so arranged as to be readily perused in connection with the narrative of the growth of the nation, it prefaces the poems of America, not simply for chronological reason, with those of the motherlands — poetry of event and sentiment, ours by inheritance as much as theirs.

It will of course be remarked that a few of the songs included in the collection, like *Yankee Doodle*, for instance, and *The British Grenadiers*, are devoid of literary merit. These few were inserted because of their historical importance. The inclusion of others, like *Annie Laurie, The Lass of Richmond Hill, The Coolun, Bells of Shandon*, and *Ben Bolt*, though not in any sense expressive of public, but of personal, emotion, calls for no justification. It is a matter of regret that golden songs, stately in their simplicity, which are as much a part of our literary heritage and as indicative of the spirit of the people as the more studied contributions of our great poets, should be elbowed out of school and home in favor of ready-made jingles, mediocre, mawkish, vapid, trumped up for the trick of the music hall or the trade of secondary education. There is, surely, a mean between verses that are cabbage and verses that are *caviare*. We think that it may be found in that Poetry of the People which grows never old because it is sturdy, sweet, and true — sufficient to the needs of to-morrow as of yesterday.

CHARLES MILLS GAYLEY

UNIVERSITY OF CALIFORNIA
    October 7, 1903

COPYRIGHT NOTICE

It remains to acknowledge the courtesy of publishers and authors. The selections from the writings of Henry W. Longfellow, Ralph Waldo Emerson, Oliver Wendell Holmes, Julia Ward Howe, Bret Harte, E. C. Stedman, John Greenleaf Whittier, James Russell Lowell, and Bayard Taylor are used by permission of, and by special arrangement with, Houghton, Mifflin and Company, the authorized publishers of their works. We are similarly indebted to Harper and Brothers for the selections from the poetry of G. W. Carryl (in *Harper's Weekly*), J. B. Gilder, and Miss Kate Putnam Osgood; to the J. B. Lippincott Company for the selections from T. Buchanan Read; to the B. F. Johnson Publishing Company for Timrod's *Ode*; to Mr. P. J. Kennedy, New York, for Father Ryan's *The Conquered Banner*; to the *Youth's Companion* for Bennett's *The Flag Goes By*; to the Century Company for the selections from Riley and Meredith; to Mrs. George Boker for George H. Boker's *Dirge*; to D. Appleton and Company for the selections from Bryant and Stanton; to the Whitaker and Ray Company, publishers of the Complete Works of Joaquin Miller, for the two poems by that author; to Mr. C. Eliot Beers for his mother's *All Quiet along the Potomac*; to Charles Scribner's Sons for the selection from G. P. Lathrop; to the New England Publishing Company for Butterworth's *Thanksgiving*; to the Lothrop Publishing Company for Hayne's *Vicksburg*; to Dodd, Mead and Company for the prologue from Austin Dobson; to the *Philadelphia Record* for *The Warship of 1812*; to Small, Maynard and Company for the selection from Whitman. We are also under especial obligation for individual permission to use their poems, and, in several cases for kind assistance, to Messrs. Joseph I. C. Clarke, Henry Holcomb Bennett, James Whitcomb Riley, William T. Meredith, Joseph B. Gilder, Guy Wetmore Carryl, Hezekiah Butterworth, John Albee, James Jeffrey Roche, and Albert Bigelow Paine.

If in any case publisher or author should fail to find here due acknowledgment of his proprietorship, we shall welcome information of the fact and attempt to remedy the deficiency. We should, for instance, have been glad to know the addresses of Robert Mowry Bell and John Jerome Rooney, to each of whom we are indebted for a selection.

CONTENTS

BOOK FIRST — OLDER BALLADS

HEROIC

	PAGE
Sir Patrick Spens	1
The Battle of Otterbourne	3
The Hunting of the Cheviot	8
Edom o' Gordon	18

OF ROBIN HOOD

Robin Hood and Little John	24
Robin Hood Rescuing the Widow's Three Sons	29
Robin Hood and Allin a Dale	34
Robin Hood and the King	38
Robin Hood's Death and Burial	47

ROMANTIC AND DOMESTIC

The Douglas Tragedy	50
Lord Randal	53
Bonnie George Campbell	54
Bessie Bell and Mary Gray	55
The Twa Corbies	56
Helen of Kirconnell	57

OF THE SUPERNATURAL

The Wife of Usher's Well	58
The Demon Lover	60

BOOK SECOND — POEMS OF ENGLAND

HISTORICAL AND PATRIOTIC

	PAGE
God Save the King. Attributed to *Henry Carey*	65
England. *Shakespeare*	66
Henry the Fifth's Address to his Soldiers before Harfleur. *Shakespeare*	67
King Henry the Fifth before Agincourt. *Shakespeare*	68
The Ballad of Agincourt. *Drayton*	70
The "Revenge," a Ballad of the Fleet. *Tennyson*	74
Give a Rouse. *Browning*	80
The Sally from Coventry. *Thornbury*	81
The Battle of Naseby. *Macaulay*	82
The Three Troopers. *Thornbury*	85
The British Grenadiers. *Anon.*	87
Rule, Britannia. *Thomson*	88
Ode, Written in the Year 1746. *Collins*	90
Battle of the Baltic. *Campbell*	90
Ye Mariners of England. *Campbell*	93
Character of the Happy Warrior. *Wordsworth*	94
The Burial of Sir John Moore. *Wolfe*	97
The Field of Waterloo. *Byron*	98
The Lost Leader. *Browning*	101
Memorial Verses on the Death of Wordsworth. *Matthew Arnold*	102
Ode on the Death of the Duke of Wellington. *Tennyson*	105
The Loss of the "Birkenhead." *Doyle*	114
The Charge of the Light Brigade. *Tennyson*	116
Santa Filomena. *Longfellow*	118
The Song of the Camp. *Bayard Taylor*	119
The Relief of Lucknow. *R. T. S. Lowell*	121
The March of the Workers. *William Morris*	124
Recessional. *Kipling*	126

MISCELLANEOUS SONGS AND BALLADS

Barbara Allen. *Anon.*	128
The Bailiff's Daughter of Islington. *Anon.*	129
My True-Love hath my Heart. *Sir Philip Sidney*	131

Contents

	PAGE
Who is Silvia? *Shakespeare*	132
Take, O, Take those Lips Away. *Shakespeare*	132
Blow, Blow, Thou Winter Wind. *Shakespeare*	133
To Celia. *Jonson*	133
You Gentlemen of England. Altered from *Martin Parker*	134
Sally in our Alley. *Carey*	136
The Vicar of Bray. *Anon.*	138
The Lass of Richmond Hill. *McNally*	140
A Wet Sheet and a Flowing Sea. *Cunningham*	141
Poor Tom Bowling. *Dibdin*	142

BOOK THIRD — POEMS OF SCOTLAND

HISTORICAL AND PATRIOTIC

✗ This is my Own, my Native Land. *Scott*	143
✗ Bannockburn. *Burns*	144
Gathering Song of Donald the Black. *Scott*	145
The Flowers of the Forest; or, The Battle of Floden. *Jane Elliott* and *Alison Rutherford*	146
Blue Bonnets over the Border. *Scott*	149
The Execution of Montrose. *Aytoun*	150
The Bonnets o' Bonnie Dundee. *Scott*	157
The Old Scottish Cavalier. *Aytoun*	159
The Lament of Flora Macdonald. *Hogg*	162
Wae's Me for Prince Charlie. *William Glen*	163
The Campbells are Comin'. *Anon.*	164
✗ The Blue Bell of Scotland. *Anon.*	165

MISCELLANEOUS SONGS AND BALLADS

Annie Laurie. *William Douglas* and *Lady John Scott*	166
Lochaber No More. *Ramsay*	167
There's Nae Luck about the House. *Mickle* and *Beattie*	168
A Red, Red Rose. *Burns*	171
For a' that, and a' that. *Burns*	171
John Anderson, my Jo. *Burns*	173
Afton Water. *Burns*	174
Ye Banks and Braes o' Bonnie Doon. *Burns*	175

	PAGE
My Heart's in the Highlands. *Burns*	176
Jock of Hazeldean. *Scott*	176
Lochinvar. *Scott*	178
When the Kye Comes Hame. *Hogg*	180
Jessie, the Flower of Dumblane. *Tannahill*	182
The Bonnie Banks o' Loch Lomond. *Anon.*	183
The Land o' the Leal. *Lady Nairne*	184
Auld Lang Syne. *Burns*	185

BOOK FOURTH — POEMS OF IRELAND

HISTORICAL AND PATRIOTIC

The Green Little Shamrock of Ireland. *Cherry*	187
The Irish Wife. *McGee*	188
Dark Rosaleen. *Mangan*	190
The Battle of the Boyne. Attributed to *Blacker*	193
After Aughrim. *Geoghegan*	195
The Shan Van Vocht. *Anon.*	196
The Wearing of the Green. Street Ballad. Attributed to *Boucicault*	198
The Memory of the Dead. *Ingram*	200
The Geraldines. *Davis*	202
Soggarth Aroon. *Banim*	205
The Girl I Left behind Me. *Anon.*	207

MISCELLANEOUS SONGS AND BALLADS

The Harp that once through Tara's Halls. *Moore*	209
The Meeting of the Waters. *Moore*	209
Believe me, if all those endearing young charms. *Moore*	210
The Last Rose of Summer. *Moore*	211
Oft, in the Stilly Night. *Moore*	212
The Coolun. *Ferguson*	213
The Bells of Shandon. *Mahony*	214
Kathleen Mavourneen. *Mrs. Crawford*	215
The Lament of the Irish Emigrant. *Lady Dufferin*	216
Dear Land. *Sliabh Cuilinn*	218
O Bay of Dublin. *Lady Dufferin*	220

Contents

	PAGE
Killarney. *O'Rourke*. Edmund	221
Song from the Backwoods. *Sullivan*	223
To God and Ireland True. *Ellen O'Leary*	225

BOOK FIFTH — POEMS OF AMERICA

HISTORICAL AND PATRIOTIC

America. *Smith*	227
Columbus. *Miller*	228
The Landing of the Pilgrims. *Hemans*	230
The Pilgrim Fathers. *Pierpont*	231
The Thanksgiving in Boston Harbor. *Butterworth*	233
The Concord Hymn. *Emerson*	236
Warren's Address. *Pierpont*	237
The Maryland Battalion. *Palmer*	238
"Columbia, Columbia, to Glory Arise." *Dwight*	240
Song of Marion's Men. *Bryant*	241
Eutaw Springs. *Freneau*	244
Carmen Bellicosum. *McMaster*	245
The Sword of Bunker Hill. *Wallace*	247
Washington's Statue. *Tuckerman*	248
Hail, Columbia. *Hopkinson*	249
The "Constitution's" Last Fight. *Roche*	251
"Old Ironsides." *Holmes*	254
The Warship of 1812. *Philadelphia Record*	255
The Star-Spangled Banner. *Key*	256
Columbia, the Gem of the Ocean. *Shaw*	258
The American Flag. *Drake*	259
God Bless our Native Land. *Brooks* and *Dwight*	261
The Defence of the Alamo. *Miller*	262
The Bivouac of the Dead. *O'Hara*	263
John Brown's Body. *Anon.*	267
Battle-Hymn of the Republic. *Howe*	268
The Battle-Cry of Freedom. *Root*	269
The Reveille. *Harte*	270
The "Cumberland." *Longfellow*	271
Kearney at Seven Pines. *Stedman*	273

Contents

	PAGE
Barbara Frietchie. *Whittier*	274
Vicksburg. *Hayne*	277
Keenan's Charge. *Lathrop*	279
Gettysburg. *Stedman*	282
Three Hundred Thousand More. *Gibbons*	288
Tramp, Tramp, Tramp. *Root*	290
Farragut. *Meredith*	291
Marching through Georgia. *Work*	293
Sheridan's Ride. *Read*	294
The Old Man and Jim. *Riley*	296
Roll-Call. *Shepherd*	299
Dixie, *Pike;* Dixie's Land, *Emmett*	300, 354
My Maryland. *Randall*	302
The Bonnie Blue Flag. *McCarthy* or *Ketchum*	305
A Georgia Volunteer. *Townsend*	306
Stonewall Jackson's Way. *Palmer*	308
The Conquered Banner. *Ryan*	310
Ode to the Confederate Dead. *Timrod*	312
Dirge for a Soldier. *Boker*	313
A Soldier's Grave. *Albee*	314
Driving Home the Cows. *Osgood*	315
The Brave at Home. *Read*	317
The Blue and the Gray. *Finch*	318
Abraham Lincoln. *Bryant*	320
O Captain! My Captain! *Whitman*	320
Lincoln. *Lowell*	322
The Republic. *Longfellow* (From "The Building of the Ship")	324
Centennial Hymn. *Whittier*	325
America. *Bayard Taylor*	327
For Cuba. *Bell*	328
Answering to Roll-Call. *Stanton*	329
The Men behind the Guns. *Rooney*	330
The War-Ship "Dixie." *Stanton*	331
The Fighting Race. *Clarke*	332
The New Memorial Day. *Paine*	335
The Flag Goes By. *Bennett*	336
When the Great Gray Ships Come In. *Carryl*	337
The Parting of the Ways. *J. B. Gilder*	339

MISCELLANEOUS SONGS AND BALLADS

	PAGE
Yankee Doodle. *Anon.*	340
Nathan Hale. *Anon.*	342
All Quiet along the Potomac. *Ethelinda Beers*	344
Tenting on the Old Camp Ground. *Kittredge*	346
Home, Sweet Home. *Payne*	347
A Life on the Ocean Wave. *Sargent*	348
Ben Bolt. *English*	349
My Old Kentucky Home, Good-Night. *Foster*	351
Massa's in de Cold Ground. *Foster*	352
Old Folks at Home. *Foster*	353
Dixie's Land. *Emmett*	354
PROLOGUE. A Ballad of Heroes. *Dobson*	iii
EPILOGUE. Sons of the Self-Same Race. *Austin*	356
NOTES	357
GLOSSARY	383
INDEX OF AUTHORS AND POEMS	389
INDEX OF TITLES AND FIRST LINES	397

Poetry of the People

BOOK FIRST — OLDER BALLADS

I

Sir Patrick Spens

The king sits in Dumferling toune,
    Drinking the blude-reid wine:
"O whar will I get guid sailor,
    To sail this schip of mine?"

Up and spak an eldern knicht,
    Sat at the kings richt kne:
"Sir Patrick Spence is the best sailor,
    That sails upon the se."

The king has written a braid letter,
    And signd it wi his hand,
And sent it to Sir Patrick Spence,
    Was walking on the sand.

The first line that Sir Patrick red,
    A loud lauch lauched he;
The next line that Sir Patrick red,
    The teir blinded his ee.

"O wha is this has don this deid,
  This ill deid don to me,
To send me out this time o' the yeir,
  To sail upon the se!

"Mak hast, mak haste, my mirry men all,
  Our guid schip sails the morne:"
"O say na sae, my master deir,
  For I feir a deadlie storme.

"Late late yestreen I saw the new moone,
  Wi the auld moone in hir arme,
And I feir, I feir, my deir master,
  That we will cum to harme."

O our Scots nobles wer richt laith
  To weet their cork-heild schoone;
Bot lang owre a' the play wer playd,
  Thair hats they swam aboone.

O lang, lang may their ladies sit,
  Wi thair fans into their hand,
Or eir they se Sir Patrick Spence
  Cum sailing to the land.

O lang, lang may the ladies stand,
  Wi thair gold kems in their hair,
Waiting for thair ain deir lords,
  For they'll se thame na mair.

Haf owre, half owre to Aberdour,
  It's fiftie fadom deip,
And thair lies guid Sir Patrick Spence,
  Wi the Scots lords at his feit.

II

The Battle of Otterbourne
1388

It fell about the Lammas tide,
    When the muir-men win their hay,
The doughty Douglas bound him to ride
    Into England to drive a prey.

He chose the Gordons and the Graemes
    With them the Lindsays light and gay;
But the Jardines wad not with him ride,
    And they rue it to this day.

And he has burned the dales o' Tyne,
    And part o' Bambrough shire,
And three good towers on Reidswire fells,
    And left them a' on fire.

And he marched up to Newcastel
    And rade it round about:
" O wha 's the lord of this castel
    Or wha 's the lady o 't? "

But up spake proud Lord Percy then,
    And O but he spake hie!
" I am the lord of this castel,
    My wife 's the lady gay."

" If thou 'rt the lord of this castel,
    Sae weel it pleases me!
For, ere I cross the Border fells,
    The tane of us shall dee." —

He took a lang spear in his hand,
   Shod with the metal free;
And for to meet the Douglas there
   He rade richt furiouslie.

But O how pale his lady lookd
   Frae aff the castel wa',
As doun before the Scottish spear
   She saw proud Percy fa'!

"Had we twa been upon the green,
   And never an eye to see,
I wad hae had you, flesh and fell,
   But your sword sall gae wi' me."

"But gae ye up to Otterbourne,
   And bide there dayis three,
And gin I come not ere three dayis end,
   A fause knight ca' ye me!"

"The Otterbourne's a bonnie burn,
   'T is pleasant there to be;
But there is nought at Otterbourne
   To feed my men and me.

"The deer rins wild on hill and dale,
   The birds fly wild frae tree to tree;
But there is neither bread nor kale,
   To fend my men and me.

"Yet I will stay at the Otterbourne,
   Where you shall welcome be;
And, if ye come not at three dayis end,
   A fause lord I'll ca' thee."

The Battle of Otterbourne

"Thither will I come," proud Percy said,
    "By the might of our Ladye!"
"There will I bide thee," said the Douglas,
    "My troth I plight to thee!"

They lichted high on Otterbourne,
    Upon the bent sae broun;
They lichted high on Otterbourne,
    And threw their pallions doun.

And he that had a bonnie boy,
    Sent out his horse to grass;
And he that had not a bonnie boy,
    His ain servant he was.

But up then spake a little page,
    Before the peep of dawn:
"O, waken ye, waken ye, my good lord,
    For Percy 's hard at hand."

"Ye lee, ye lee, ye leear loud!
    Sae loud I hear ye lee:
For Percy had not men yestreen
    To dight my men and me.

"But I hae dreamed a dreary dream,
    Beyond the Isle o' Sky;
I saw a deid man win a fight,
    And I think that man was I."

He belted on his guid braidsword,
    And to the field he ran;
But he forgot the helmet good,
    That should have kept his brain.

When Percy wi' the Douglas met,
   I wot he was fu' fain:
They swakked their swords, till sair they swat,
   And the blude ran down like rain.

But Percy wi' his guid braidsword,
   That could sae sharply wound,
Has wounded Douglas on the brow,
   Till he fell to the ground.

And then he calld on his little foot-page,
   And said — "Run speedilie,
And fetch my ain dear sister's son,
   Sir Hugh Montgomery.

"My nephew guid!" the Douglas said,
   "What recks the death of ane?
Last night I dreamed a dreary dream,
   And I ken the day's thy ain!

"My wound is deep; I fain wad sleep!
   Tak' thou the vanguard o' the three,
And hide me by the bracken bush,
   That grows on yonder lilye lee.

"O bury me by the bracken bush,
   Beneath the blooming brier;
Let never living mortal ken
   That ere a kindly Scot lies here!"

He lifted up that noble lord,
   Wi' the saut tear in his ee;
And he hid him in the bracken bush,
   That his merrie men might not see.

The moon was clear, the day drew near,
  The spears in flinders flew;
But mony a gallant Englishman
  Ere day the Scotsmen slew.

The Gordons good, in English blude
  They steepd their hose and shoon;
The Lindsays flew like fire about,
  Till a' the fray was done.

The Percy and Montgomery met,
  That either of other was fain;
They swapped swords, and they twa swat,
  And aye the blude ran doun between.

"Now yield thee, yield thee, Percy!" he said,
  Or else I vow I'll lay thee low!"
"To whom maun I yield," quoth Earl Percy,
  "Now that I see it maun be so?"

"Thou shalt not yield to lord nor loun,
  Nor yet shalt thou yield to me;
But yield thee to the bracken-bush
  That grows upon yon lilye lee!"

"I will not yield to a bracken-bush
  Nor yet will I yield to a brier;
But I wad yield to Earl Douglas,
  Or Sir Hugh the Montgomery, if he were here."

As soon as he knew it was Montgomery
  He struck his sword's point in the gronde;
The Montgomery was a courteous knight,
  And quickly took him by the honde.

This deed was done at the Otterbourne
  About the breaking o' the day;
Earl Douglas was buried at the bracken-bush,
  And the Percy led captive away.

III

The Hunting of the Cheviot

The Persë owt off Northombarlonde,
  and a vowe to God mayd he
That he wold hunte in the mowntayns
  off Chyviat within days thre,
In the magger of doughtë Dogles,
  and all that ever with him be.

The fattiste hartes in all Cheviat
  he sayd he wold kyll, and cary them away:
"Be my feth," sayd the dougheti Doglas agayn,
  "I wyll let that hontyng yf that I may."

Then the Persë owt off Banborowe cam,
  with him a myghtee meany,
With fifteen hondrith archares bold off blood and
    bone;
  the wear chosen owt of shyars thre.

This begane on a Monday at morn,
  in Cheviat the hillys so he;
The chylde may rue that ys unborn,
  it wos the more pittë.

The dryvars thorowe the woodës went,
    for to reas the dear;
Bomen byckarte uppone the bent
    with ther browd aros cleare.

Then the wyld thorowe the woodës went,
    on every sydë shear;
Greahondës thorowe the grevis glent,
    for to kyll thear dear.

This begane in Chyviat the hyls abone,
    yerly on a Monnyn-day;
Be that it drewe to the oware off none,
    a hondrith fat hartës ded ther lay.

The blewe a morte uppone the bent,
    the semblyde on sydis shear;
To the quyrry then the Persë went,
    to se the bryttlynge off the deare.

He sayd, "It was the Duglas promys
    this day to met me hear;
But I wyste he wolde faylle, verament;"
    a great oth the Persë swear.

At the laste a squyar off Northomberlonde
    lokyde at his hand full ny;
He was war a the doughetie Doglas commynge,
    with him a myghttë meany.

Both with spear, bylle, and brande,
    yt was a myghtti sight to se;
Hardyar men, both off hart nor hande,
    wear not in Cristiantë.

The wear twenti hondrith spear-men good,
   withoute any feale;
The wear borne along be the watter a Twyde,
   yth bowndës of Tividale.

"Leave of the brytlyng of the dear," he sayd,
   "and to your boÿs lock ye tayk good hede;
For never sithe ye wear on your mothars borne
   had ye never so mickle nede."

The dougheti Dogglas on a stede,
   he rode alle his men beforne;
His armor glytteryde as dyd a glede;
   a boldar barne was never born.

"Tell me whos men ye ar," he says,
   "or whos men that ye be:
Who gave youe leave to hunte in this Chyviat chays,
   in the spyt of myn and of me."

The first name that ever him an answear mayd,
   yt was the good lord Persë:
"We wyll not tell the whoys men we ar," he says,
   "nor whos men that we be;
But we wyll hounte hear in this chays,
   in the spyt of thyne and of the.

"The fattiste hartës in all Chyviat
   we have kyld, and cast to carry them away:
"Be my troth," sayd the doughetë Dogglas agayn,
   "therfor the ton of us shall de this day."

Then sayd the doughtë Doglas
   unto the lord Persë:

"To kyll alle thes giltles men,
 alas, it wear great pittë!

"But, Persë, thowe art a lord of lande,
 I am a yerle callyd within my contrë;
Let all our men uppone a parti stande,
 and do the battell off the and of me."

"Nowe Cristes cors on his crowne," sayd the lord Persë,
 "who-so-ever ther-to says nay;
Be my troth, doughttë Doglas," he says,
 "thow shalt never se that day.

"Nethar in Ynglonde, Skottlonde, nar France,
 nor for no man of a woman born,
But, and fortune be my chance,
 I dar met him, on man for on."

Then bespayke a squyar off Northombarlonde,
 Richard Wytharyngton was his nam:
"It shall never be told in Sothe-Ynglonde," he says,
 "to Kyng Herry the Fourth for sham.

"I wat youe byn great lordës twaw,
 I am a poor squyar of lande:
I wylle never se my captayne fyght on a fylde,
 and stande my selffe and loocke on,
But whylle I may my weppone welde,
 I wylle not fayle both hart and hande."

That day, that day, that dredfull day!
 the first fit here I fynde;

And youe wyll here any mor a the hountyng a the
  Chyviat,
 yet ys ther mor behynde.

The Yngglyshe men hade ther bowys yebent,
 ther hartes wer good yenoughe;
The first off arros that the shote off,
 seven skore spear-men the sloughe.

Yet byddys the yerle Doglas uppon the bent,
 a captayne good yenoughe,
And that was sene verament,
 for he wrought hom both woo and wouche.

The Dogglas partyd his ost in thre,
 lyk a cheffe cheften off pryde;
With suar spears off myghttë tre,
 the cum in on every syde:

Thrughe our Yngglyshe archery
 gave many a wounde fulle wyde;
Many a doughetë the garde to dy,
 which ganyde them no pryde.

The Ynglyshe men let ther boÿs be,
 and pulde owt brandes that wer brighte;
It was a hevy syght to se
 bryght swordes on basnites lyght.

Thorowe ryche male and myneyeple,
 many sterne the strocke done streght;
Many a freyke that was fulle fre,
 ther undar foot dyd lyght.

At last the Duglas and the Persë met,
 lyk to captayns of myght and of mayne;

An arow, that a cloth-yarde was lang,
  to the harde stele halyde he;
A dynt that was both sad and soar
  he sat on Ser Hewe the Monggombyrry.

The dynt yt was both sad and sar,
  that he of Monggomberry sete;
The swane-fethars that his arrowe bar
  with his hart-blood the wear wete.

Ther was never a freake wone foot wolde fle,
  but still in stour dyd stand,
Heawyng on yche othar, whylle the myghte dre,
  with many a balfull brande.

This battell begane in Chyviat
  an owar befor the none,
And when even-songe bell was rang,
  The battell was nat half done.

The tocke . . . on ethar hande
  be the lyght off the mone;
Many hade no strenght for to stande,
  in Chyviat the hillys abon.

Of fifteen hondrith archars of Ynglonde
  went away but seventi and thre;
Of twenti hondrith spear-men of Skotlonde,
  but even five and fifti.

But all wear slayne Cheviat within;
  the hade no strengthe to stand on hy;
The chylde may rue that ys unborne,
  it was the mor pittë

Thear was slayne, withe the lord Persë,
　　Sir Johan of Agerstone,
Ser Rogar, the hinde Hartly,
　　Ser Wyllyam, the bolde Hearone.

Ser Jorg, the worthë Loumle,
　　a knyghte of great renowen,
Ser Raff, the ryche Rugbe,
　　with dyntes wear beaten dowene.

For Wetharryngton my harte was wo,
　　that ever he slayne shulde be;
For when both his leggis wear hewyne in to,
　　yet he knyled and fought on hys kny.

Ther was slayne, with the dougheti Duglas,
　　Ser Hewe the Monggombyrry,
Ser Davy Lwdale, that worthë was,
　　his sistar's son was he.

Ser Charls a Murrë in that place,
　　that never a foot wolde fle;
Ser Hewe Maxwelle, a lorde he was,
　　with the Doglas dyd he dey.

So on the morrowe the mayde them byears
　　off birch and hasell so gray;
Many wedous, with wepyng tears,
　　cam to fache ther makys away.

Tivydale may carpe off care,
　　Northombarlond may mayk great mon,
For towe such captayns as slayne wear thear,
　　on the March-parti shall never be non.

Word ys commen to Eddenburrowe,
   to Jamy the Skottische kynge,
That dougheti Duglas, lyff-tenant of the Marches,
   he lay slean Chyviot within.

His handdës dyd he weal and wryng,
   he sayd, "Alas, and wo ys me!
Such an othar captayn Skotland within,"
   he sayd, "ye-feth shuld never be."

Worde ys commyn to lovly Londone,
   till the fourth Harry our kynge,
That lord Persë, leyff-tenante of the Marchis,
   he lay slayne Chyviat within.

"God have merci on his solle," sayde Kyng Harry,
   "good lord, yf thy will it be!
I have a hondrith captayns in Ynglonde," he sayd,
   "as good as ever was he:
But, Persë, and I brook my lyffe,
   thy deth well quyte shall be."

As our noble kynge mayd his avowe,
   lyke a noble prince of renowen,
For the deth of the lord Persë
   he dyde the battell of Hombyll-down;

Wher syx and thrittë Skottishe knyghtes
   on a day wear beaten down:
Glendale glytteryde on ther armor bryght,
   over castille, towar, and town.

This was the hontynge off the Cheviat,
   that tear begane this spurn;

Old men that knowen the grownde well yenoughe
    call it the battell of Otterburn.

At Otterburn begane this spurne
    uppone a Monnynday;
Ther was the doughtë Doglas slean,
    the Persë never went away.

Ther was never a tym on the Marche-partës
    sen the Doglas and the Persë met,
But yt ys mervele and the rede blude ronne not,
    as the reane doys in the stret.

Jhesue Crist our balys bete,
    and to the blys us brynge!
Thus was the hountynge of the Chivyat:
    God send us alle good endyng!

IV

Edom o' Gordon

It fell about the Martinmas,
    When the wind blew shrill and cauld,
Said Edom o' Gordon to his men,
    "We maun draw to a hauld.

"And whatna hauld sall we draw to,
    My merry men and me?
We will gae to the house o' the Rodes,
    To see that fair ladie."

Edom o' Gordon

The ladie stude on her castle wa',
    Beheld baith dale and doun,
There she was ware of a host o' men
    Cam riding towards the toun.

"O see ye not, my merry men a',
    O see ye not what I see?
Methinks I see a host of men —
    I marvel wha' they be."

She ween'd it had been her ain dear lord
    As he cam riding hame;
It was the traitor, Edom o' Gordon,
    Wha recked nor sin nor shame.

She had nae suner buskit hersel,
    Nor putten on her goun,
Till Edom o' Gordon and his men
    Were round about the toun.

They had nae suner supper set,
    Nae suner said the grace,
Till Edom o' Gordon and his men
    Were light about the place.

The ladie ran to her tower head,
    As fast as she could hie,
To see if, by her fair speeches,
    She could with him agree.

As sune as he saw the ladie fair,
    And her yetts a' lockit fast,
He fell into a rage o' wrath,
    And his look was all aghast.

"Come doun to me, ye ladye gay,
  Come doun, come doun to me;
This nicht sall ye lie within my arms,
  The morn my bride sall be."

"I winna come doun, ye fause Gordon,
  I winna come doun to thee;
I winna forsake my ain dear lord,
  That is sae far frae me."

"Gie owre your house, ye ladie fair,
  Gie owre your house to me;
Or I sall burn yoursell therein,
  But and your babies three."

"I winna gie owre, ye false Gordon,
  To nae sic traitor as thee;
And if ye burn my ain dear babes,
  My lord sall mak ye dree!

"But reach my pistol, Glaud, my man,
  And charge ye weel my gun;
For, but an I pierce that bluidy butcher,
  We a' sall be undone."

She stude upon the castle wa',
  And let twa bullets flee;
She miss'd that bluidy butcher's heart,
  And only razed his knee.

"Set fire to the house!" quo the fause Gordon,
  All wude wi' dule and ire;
"Fause ladie! ye sall rue that shot,
  As ye burn in the fire."

"Wae worth, wae worth ye, Jock, my man!
　I paid ye weel your fee;
Why pu' ye out the grund-wa-stane,
　Lets in the reek to me?

"And e'en wae worth ye, Jock, my man!
　I paid ye weel your hire;
Why pu' ye out my grund-wa-stane,
　To me lets in the fire?"

"Ye paid me weel my hire, lady,
　Ye paid me weel my fee;
But now I'm Edom o' Gordon's man,
　Maun either do or dee."

O then outspak her youngest son,
　Sat on the nourice' knee;
Says, "Mither dear, gie owre this house,
　For the reek it smithers me."

"I wad gie a' my gowd, my bairn,
　Sae wad I a' my fee,
For ae blast o' the westlin' wind,
　To blaw the reek frae thee!"

O then outspak her daughter dear —
　She was baith jimp and sma' —
"O row me in a pair o' sheets,
　And tow me owre the wa'."

They row'd her in a pair o' sheets,
　And tow'd her owre the wa';
But on the point o' Gordon's spear
　She gat a deadly fa'.

O bonnie, bonnie was her mouth,
  And cherry were her cheeks;
And clear, clear was her yellow hair,
  Whereon the red bluid dreeps.

Then wi' his spear he turned her owre,
  O gin her face was wan!
He said, "You are the first that e'er
  I wish'd alive again."

He turned her owre and owre again,
  O gin her skin was white!
"I might hae spared that bonnie face,
  To hae been some man's delight.

"Busk and boun, my merry men a',
  For ill dooms I do guess;
I canna look on that bonnie face,
  As it lies on the grass!"

"Wha looks to freits, my master deir,
  It's freits will follow them;
Let it ne'er be said that Edom o' Gordon
  Was dauntit by a dame."

But when the lady saw the fire
  Come flaming owre her head,
She wept, and kiss'd her children twain,
  Says, "Bairns, we been but dead."

The Gordon then his bugle blew,
  And said, "Awa', awa';
The house o' the Rodes is a' in a flame,
  I hauld it time to ga'."

O then bespied her ain dear lord,
   As he came owre the lea;
He saw his castle a' in a lowe,
   Sae far as he could see.

Then sair, O sair, his mind misgave,
   And a' his heart was wae;
"Put on, put on, my wichty men,
   As fast as ye can gae.

"Put on, put on, my wichty men,
   As fast as ye can dri'e;
For he that is hindmost of the thrang,
   Shall ne'er get gude o' me!"

Then some they rade, and some they ran,
   Fu' fast out owre the bent;
But ere the foremost could win up,
   Baith lady and babes were brent.

He wrang his hands, he rent his hair,
   And wept in teenfu' mood;
"Ah, traitors! for this cruel deed,
   Ye shall weep tears of bluid."

And after the Gordon he has gane,
   Sae fast as he might dri'e,
And soon i' the Gordon's foul heart's bluid,
   He 's wroken his fair ladie.

V

Robin Hood and Little John

When Robin Hood was about twenty years old,
   With a hey down, down, and a down;
He happen'd to meet Little John,
A jolly brisk blade, right fit for the trade,
   For he was a lusty young man.

Though he was call'd Little, his limbs they were large,
   And his stature was seven foot high;
Wherever he came, they quaked at his name,
   For soon he would make them to fly.

How they came acquainted, I'll tell you in brief,
   If you would but listen awhile;
For this very jest, among all the rest,
   I think it may cause you to smile.

For Robin Hood said to his jolly bowmen,
   "Pray tarry you here in this grove;
And see that you all observe well my call,
   While thorough the forest I rove.

"We have had no sport for these fourteen long days,
   Therefore now abroad will I go;
Now should I be beat, and cannot retreat,
   My horn I will presently blow."

Then did he shake hands with his merry men all,
   And bid them at present good-by:
Then, as near the brook his journey he took,
   A stranger he chanced to espy.

They happened to meet on a long narrow bridge,
  And neither of them would give way ;
Quoth bold Robin Hood, and sturdily stood,
  " I 'll shew you right Nottingham-play."

With that from his quiver an arrow he drew,
  A broad arrow with a goose-wing.
The stranger reply'd, " I 'll liquor thy hide,
  If thou offerst to touch the string."

Quoth bold Robin Hood, "Thou dost prate like an ass,
  For were I to bend but my bow,
I could send a dart, quite thro' thy proud heart,
  Before thou couldst strike me one blow."

" Thou talkst like a coward," the stranger reply'd ;
  " Well arm'd with a long bow you stand,
To shoot at my breast, while I, I protest,
  Have nought but a staff in my hand."

" The name of a coward," quoth Robin, " I scorn,
  Wherefore my long bow I 'll lay by,
And now, for thy sake, a staff will I take,
  The truth of thy manhood to try."

Then Robin Hood stept to a thicket of trees,
  And chose him a staff of ground oak ;
Now this being done, away he did run
  To the stranger, and merrily spoke :

" Lo ! see my staff is lusty and tough,
  Now here on the bridge we will play ;
Whoever falls in, the other shall win,
  The battle, and so we 'll away."

"With all my whole heart," the stranger reply'd,
  "I scorn in the least to give out";
This said, they fell to 't without more dispute,
  And their staffs they did flourish about.

At first Robin he gave the stranger a bang,
  So hard that he made his bones ring:
The stranger he said, "This must be repaid,
  I 'll give you as good as you bring.

"So long as I am able to handle a staff,
  To die in your debt, friend, I scorn."
Then to it each goes, and followed their blows,
  As if they 'd been threshing of corn.

The stranger gave Robin a crack on the crown,
  Which caused the blood to appear;
Then Robin enraged, more fiercely engaged,
  And followed his blows more severe.

So thick and so fast did he lay it on him,
  With a passionate fury and ire;
At every stroke he made him to smoke,
  As if he had been all on fire.

O then into fury the stranger he grew,
  And gave him a damnable look,
And with it a blow, that laid him full low,
  And tumbled him into the brook.

"I prithee, good fellow, where art thou now?"
  The stranger, in laughter, he cried.
Quoth bold Robin Hood, "Good faith, in the flood,
  And floating along with the tide.

"I needs must acknowledge thou art a brave soul,
  With thee I'll no longer contend;
For needs must I say, thou hast got the day,
  Our battle shall be at an end."

Then unto the bank he did presently wade,
  And pulled himself out by a thorn;
Which done, at the last he blowed a loud blast
  Straightway on his fine bugle-horn:

The echo of which through the valleys did fly,
  At which his stout bowmen appeared,
All clothed in green, most gay to be seen,
  So up to their master they steered.

"O, what's the matter?" quoth William Stutly,
  "Good master you are wet to the skin."
"No matter," quoth he, "the lad which you see
  In fighting hath tumbled me in."

"He shall not go scot-free," the others reply'd.
  So straight they were seizing him there,
To duck him likewise: but Robin Hood cries,
  "He is a stout fellow; forbear.

"There's no one shall wrong thee, friend, be not afraid;
  These bowmen upon me do wait;
There's three score and nine; if thou wilt be mine,
  Thou shalt have my livery straight,

"And other accoutrements fit for a man;
  Speak up, jolly blade, never fear:
I'll teach you also the use of the bow,
  To shoot at the fat fallow deer."

"O, here is my hand," the stranger reply'd,
  "I 'll serve you with all my whole heart;
My name is John Little, a man of good mettle;
  Ne'er doubt me, for I 'll play my part."

"His name shall be alter'd," quoth William Stutly,
  "And I will his godfather be:
Prepare then a feast, and none of the least
  For we will be merry," quoth he.

They presently fetched him a brace of fat does,
  With humming strong liquor likewise;
They loved what was good; so in the green wood,
  This pretty sweet babe they baptize.

He was, I must tell you, but seven foot high,
  And, may be, an ell in the waist;
A sweet pretty lad: much feasting they had;
  Bold Robin the christening graced,

With all his bowmen, which stood in a ring,
  And were of the Nottingham breed;
Brave Stutly came then, with seven yeomen,
  And did in this manner proceed:

"This infant was called John Little," quoth he;
  "Which name shall be changed anon:
The words we'll transpose; so wherever he goes,
  His name shall be called Little John."

They all with a shout made the elements ring;
  So soon as the office was o'er,
To feasting they went, with true merriment,
  And tippled strong liquor gillore.

Then Robin he took the pretty sweet babe,
  And clothed him from top to the toe,
In garments of green, most gay to be seen,
  And gave him a curious long bow.

"Thou shalt be an archer as well as the best,
  And range in the green wood with us;
Where we'll not want gold nor silver, behold,
  While bishops have ought in their purse.

"We live here like 'squires, or lords of renown,
  Without e'er a foot of free land;
We feast on good cheer, with wine, ale, and beer,
  And everything at our command."

Then music and dancing did finish the day;
  At length, when the sun waxed low,
Then all the whole train the grove did refrain,
  And unto their caves they did go.

And so, ever after, as long as he liv'd,
  Although he was proper and tall,
Yet, nevertheless, the truth to express,
  Still Little John they did him call.

VI

Robin Hood Rescuing the Widow's Three Sons

There are twelve months in all the year,
  As I hear many men say,
But the merriest month in all the year
  Is the merry month of May.

Now Robin Hood is to Nottingham gone,
  With a link a down and a day,
And there he met a silly old woman,
  Was weeping on the way.

"What news? what news, thou silly old woman?
  What news hast thou for me?"
Said she, "There's my three sons in Nottingham town
  To-day condemned to die."

"O, have they parishes burnt?" he said,
  "Or have they ministers slain?
Or have they robbed any virgin?
  Or other men's wives have ta'en?"

"They have no parishes burnt, good sir,
  Nor yet have ministers slain,
Nor have they robbed any virgin,
  Nor other men's wives have ta'en."

"O, what have they done?" said Robin Hood,
  "I pray thee tell to me."
"It's for slaying of the king's fallow-deer,
  Bearing their long bows with thee."

"Dost thou not mind, old woman," he said,
  "How thou madest me sup and dine?
By the truth of my body," quoth bold Robin Hood,
  "You could not tell it in better time."

Now Robin Hood is to Nottingham gone,
  With a link a down and a day,
And there he met with a silly old palmer,
  Was walking along the highway.

"What news? what news, thou silly old man?
  What news, I do thee pray?"
Said he, "Three squires in Nottingham town
  Are condemned to die this day."

"Come change thy apparel with me, old man,
  Come change thy apparel for mine;
Here is forty shillings in good silvèr,
  Go drink it in beer or wine."

"O, thine apparel is good," he said,
  "And mine is ragged and torn;
Wherever you go, wherever you ride,
  Laugh not an old man to scorn."

"Come change thy apparel with me, old churl,
  Come change thy apparel with mine;
Here are twenty pieces of good broad gold,
  Go feast thy brethren with wine."

Then he put on the old man's hat,
  It stood full high on the crown:
"The first bold bargain that I come at,
  It shall make thee come down."

Then he put on the old man's cloak,
  Was patched black, blew, and red;
He thought it no shame all the day long,
  To wear the bags of bread.

Then he put on the old man's breeks,
  Was patched from leg to side:
"By the truth of my body," bold Robin can say,
  "This man loved little pride."

Then he put on the old man's hose,
  Were patched from knee to wrist:
"By the truth of my body," said bold Robin Hood,
  "I 'd laugh if I had any list."

Then he put on the old man's shoes,
  Were patched both beneath and aboon;
Then Robin Hood swore a solemn oath,
  "It 's good habit that makes a man."

Now Robin Hood is to Nottingham gone,
  With a link a down and a down,
And there he met with the proud sheriff,
  Was walking along the town.

"Save you, save you, sheriff!" he said;
  "Now heaven you save and see!
And what will you give to a silly old man
  To-day will your hangman be?"

"Some suits, some suits," the sheriff he said,
  "Some suits I 'll give to thee;
Some suits, some suits, and pence thirteen,
  To-day 's a hangman's fee."

Then Robin he turns him round about,
  And jumps from stock to stone:
"By the truth of my body," the sheriff he said,
  "That 's well jumpt, thou nimble old man."

"I was ne'er a hangman in all my life,
  Nor yet intends to trade;
But curst be he," said bold Robin,
  "That first a hangman was made!

Robin Hood Rescuing the Widow's Three Sons

"I 've a bag for meal, and a bag for malt,
   And a bag for barley and corn;
A bag for bread, and a bag for beef,
   And a bag for my little small horn.

"I have a horn in my pockèt,
   I got it from Robin Hood,
And still when I set it to my mouth,
   For thee it blows little good."

"O, wind thy horn, thou proud fellòw,
   Of thee I have no doubt.
I wish that thou give such a blast,
   Till both thy eyes fall out."

The first loud blast that he did blow,
   He blew both loud and shrill;
A hundred and fifty of Robin Hood's men
   Came riding over the hill.

The next loud blast that he did give,
   He blew both loud and amain,
And quickly sixty of Robin Hood's men
   Came shining over the plain.

"O, who are these," the sheriff he said,
   "Come tripping over the lee?"
"They 're my attendants," brave Robin did say;
   "They 'll pay a visit to thee."

They took the gallows from the slack,
   They set it in the glen,
They hanged the proud sherìff on that,
   Released their own three men.

VII

Robin Hood and Allin a Dale

Come listen to me, you gallants so free,
   All you that loves mirth for to hear,
And I will tell you of a bold outlaw,
   That lived in Nottinghamshire.

As Robin Hood in the forest stood,
   All under the green-wood tree,
There he was ware of a brave young man,
   As fine as fine might be.

The youngster was clothed in scarlet red,
   In scarlet fine and gay;
And he did frisk it over the plain,
   And chanted a roundelay.

As Robin Hood next morning stood,
   Amongst the leaves so gay,
There did he espy the same young man
   Come drooping along the way.

The scarlet he wore the day before,
   It was clean cast away;
And at every step he fetcht a sigh,
   "Alack and a well a day!"

Then stepped forth brave Little John,
   And Nick the miller's son,
Which made the young man bend his bow,
   When as he see them come.

"Stand off, stand off," the young man said,
  "What is your will with me?"
"You must come before our master straight,
  Under yon green-wood tree."

And when he came bold Robin before,
  Robin askt him courteously,
"O hast thou any money to spare
  For my merry men and me?"

"I have no money," the young man said,
  "But five shillings and a ring;
And that I have kept this seven long years,
  To have it at my wedding.

"Yesterday I should have married a maid,
  But she is now from me tane,
And chosen to be an old knight's delight,
  Whereby my poor heart is slain."

"What is thy name?" then said Robin Hood,
  "Come tell me, without any fail:"
"By the faith of my body," then said the young man,
  "My name it is Allin a Dale."

"What wilt thou give me," said Robin Hood,
  "In ready gold or fee,
To help thee to thy true love again,
  And deliver her unto thee?"

"I have no money," then quoth the young man,
  "No ready gold nor fee,
But I will swear upon a book
  Thy true servant for to be."

"How many miles is it to thy true love?
  Come tell me without any guile : "
"By the faith of my body," then said the young man,
  "It is but five little mile."

Then Robin he hasted over the plain,
  He did neither stint nor lin,
Until he came unto the church,
  Where Allin should keep his wedding.

"What dost thou do here?" the bishop he said,
  "I prithee now tell to me : "
"I am a bold harper," quoth Robin Hood,
  "And the best in the north country."

"O welcome, O welcome," the bishop he said,
  "That musick best pleaseth me ; "
"You shall have no musick," quoth Robin Hood,
  "Till the bride and the bridegroom I see."

With that came in a wealthy knight,
  Which was both grave and old,
And after him a finikin lass,
  Did shine like the glistering gold.

"This is not a fit match," quoth bold Robin Hood,
  "That you do seem to make here ;
For since we are come unto the church,
  The bride shall chuse her own dear."

Then Robin Hood put his horn to his mouth,
  And blew blasts two or three ;
When four and twenty bowmen bold
  Came leaping over the lea.

And when they came into the church-yard,
  Marching all on a row,
The first man was Allin a Dale,
  To give bold Robin his bow.

" This is thy true love," Robin he said,
  " Young Allin, as I hear say;
And you shall be married at this same time,
  Before we depart away."

" That shall not be," the bishop he said,
  " For thy word shall not stand;
They shall be three times askt in the church,
  As the law is of our land."

Robin Hood pulld off the bishop's coat,
  And put it upon Little John;
" By the faith of my body," then Robin said,
  " This cloath doth make thee a man."

When Little John went into the quire,
  The people began for to laugh;
He askt them seven times in the church,
  Lest three times should not be enough.

" Who gives me this maid ? " then said Little John;
  Quoth Robin, " That do I,
And he that takes her from Allin a Dale
  Full dearly he shall her buy."

And thus having ended this merry wedding,
  The bride lookt as fresh as a queen,
And so they returned to the merry greenwood,
  Amongst the leaves so green.

VIII

Robin Hood and the King

THE SEVENTH FYTTE OF A GEST OF ROBIN HOOD

The kynge came to Notynghame,
  With knyghtes in grete araye,
For to take that gentyll knyght
  And Robyn Hode, and yf he may.

He asked men of that countrë,
  After Robyn Hode,
And after that gentyll knyght,
  That was so bolde and stout.

Whan they had tolde hym the case
  Our kynge understode ther tale,
And seased in his honde
  The knyghtës londës all.

All the passe of Lancasshyre
  He went both ferre and nere,
Tyll he came to Plomton Parke;
  He faylyd many of his dere.

There our kynge was wont to se
  Herdës many one,
He coud unneth fynde one dere,
  That bare ony good horne.

The kynge was wonder wroth with all,
  And swore by the Trynytë,
"I wolde I had Robyn Hode,
  With eyen I myght hym se.

"And he that wolde smyte of the knyghtës hede,
　And brynge it to me,
He shall have the knyghtës londes,
　Syr Rycharde at the Le.

"I gyve it hym with my charter,
　And sele it with my honde,
To have and holde for ever more,
　In all mery Englonde."

Than bespake a fayre olde knyght,
　That was treue in his fay:
"A, my leegë lorde the kynge,
　One worde I shall you say.

"There is no man in this countrë
　May have the knyghtës londes,
Whyle Robyn Hode may ryde or gone,
　And bere a bowe in his hondes,

"That he ne shall lese his hede,
　That is the best ball in his hode:
Give it no man, my lorde the kynge,
　That ye wyll any good."

Half a yere dwelled our comly kynge
　In Notyngham, and well more;
Coude he not here of Robyn Hode,
　In what countrë that he were.

But alway went good Robyn
　By halke and eke by hyll,
And alway slewe the kyngës dere,
　And welt them at his wyll.

Than bespake a proude fostere,
  That stode by our kyngës kne:
"Yf ye wyll see good Robyn,
  Ye must do after me.

"Take fyve of the best knyghtes
  That be in your lede,
And walke downe by yon abbay,
  And gete you monkës wede.

"And I wyll be your ledes-man,
  And lede you the way,
And or ye come to Notyngham,
  Myn hede then dare I lay,

"That ye shall mete with good Robyn,
  On lyve yf that he be;
Or ye come to Notyngham,
  With eyen ye shall hym se."

Full hastely our kynge was dyght,
  So were his knyghtyës fyve,
Everych of them in monkës wede,
  And hasted them thyder blyve.

Our kynge was grete above his cole,
  A brode hat on his crowne,
Ryght as he were abbot-lyke,
  They rode up into the towne.

Styf botes our kynge had on,
  Forsoth as I you say;
He rode syngynge to grene wode,
  The covent was clothed in graye.

His male-hors and his grete somers
    Folowed our kynge behynde,
Tyll they came to grene wode,
    A myle under the lynde.

There they met with good Robyn,
    Stondynge on the waye,
And so dyde many a bolde archere,
    For soth as I you say.

Robyn toke the kyngës hors,
    Hastely in that stede,
And sayd, "Syr abbot, by your leve,
    A whyle ye must abyde.

"We be yemen of this foreste,
    Under the grene-wode tre;
We lyve by our kyngës dere,
    Other shift have not wee.

"And ye have chyrches and rentës both,
    And gold full grete plentë;
Gyve us some of your spendynge,
    For saynt charytë."

Than bespake our cumly kynge,
    Anone than sayd he;
"I brought no more to grene wode
    But forty pounde with me.

"I have layne at Notyngham,
    This fourtynyght with our kynge,
And spent I have full moche good
    On many a grete lordynge.

"And I have but forty pounde,
  No more than have I me:
But if I had an hondred pounde,
  I would give it to thee."

Robyn toke the forty pounde,
  And departed it in two partye;
Halfendell he gave his mery men,
  And bad them mery to be.

Full curteysly Robyn gan say;
  "Syr, have this for your spendyng;
We shall mete another day."
  "Gramercy," than sayd our kynge.

"But well the greteth Edwarde, our kynge,
  And sent to the his seale,
And byddeth the com to Notyngham,
  Both to mete and mele."

He toke out the brode targe,
  And sone he lete hym se;
Robyn coud his courteysy,
  And set hym on his kne.

"I love no man in all the worlde
  So well as I do my kynge;
Welcome is my lordës seale;
  And, monke, for thy tydynge,

"Syr abbot, for thy tydynges,
  To day thou shalt dyne with me,
For the love of my kynge,
  Under my trystell-tre."

Forth he lad our comly kynge,
  Full fayre by the honde;
Many a dere there was slayne,
  And full fast dyghtande.

Robyn toke a full grete horne,
  And loude he gan blowe;
Seven score of wyght yonge men
  Came redy on a rowe.

All they kneled on theyr kne,
  Full fayre before Robyn:
The kynge sayd hym selfe untyll,
  And swore by Saynt Austyn,

"Here is a wonder semely sight;
  Me thynketh, by Goddës pyne,
His men are more at his byddynge
  Then my men be at myn."

Full hastely was theyr dyner idyght,
  And therto gan they gone;
They served our kynge with all theyr myght,
  Both Robyn and Lytell Johan.

Anone before our kynge was set
  The fattë venyson,
The good whyte brede, the good rede wyne,
  And therto the fyne ale and browne.

"Make good chere," said Robyn,
  "Abbot, for charytë;
And for this ylkë tydynge,
  Blyssed mote thou be.

"Now shalte thou se what lyfe we lede,
    Or thou hens wende;
Than thou may enfourme our kynge,
    Whan ye togyder lende."

Up they sterte all in hast,
    Theyr bowes were smartly bent;
Our kynge was never so sore agast,
    He wende to have be shente.

Two yerdes there were up set,
    Thereto gan they gange;
By fyfty pase, our kynge sayd,
    The merkës were to longe.

On every syde a rose-garlonde,
    They shot under the lyne:
"Who so fayleth of the rose-garlonde," sayd Robyn,
"His takyll he shall tyne,

"And yelde it to his mayster,
    Be it never so fyne;
For no man wyll I spare,
    So drynke I ale or wyne;

"And bere a buffet on his hede,
    I-wys ryght all bare:"
And all that fell in Robyns lote,
    He smote them wonder sare.

Twyse Robyn shot aboute,
    And ever he cleved the wande,
And so dyde good Gylberte
    With the whytë hande.

Lytell Johan and good Scathelocke,
 For nothynge wolde they spare;
When they fayled of the garlonde,
 Robyn smote them full sare.

At the last shot that Robyn shot,
 For all his frendës fare,
Yet he fayled of the garlonde
 Thre fyngers and mare.

Than bespake good Gylberte,
 And thus he gan say;
"Mayster," he sayd, "your takyll is lost,
 Stande forth and take your pay."

"If it be so," sayd Robyn,
 "That may no better be,
Syr abbot, I delyver the myn arowe,
 I pray the, syr, serve thou me."

"It falleth not for myn ordre," sayd our kynge,
 "Robyn, by thy leve,
For to smyte no good yeman,
 For doute I sholde hym greve."

"Smyte on boldely," sayd Robyn,
 "I give the largë leve:"
Anone our kynge, with that worde,
 He folde up his sleve,

And sych a buffet he gave Robyn,
 To grounde he yede full nere:
"I make myn avowe to God," sayd Robyn,
 "Thou arte a stalworthe frere.

"There is pith in thyn arme," sayd Robyn,
  "I trowe thou canst well shete;"
Thus our kynge and Robyn Hode
  Togeder gan they mete.

Robyn behelde our comly kynge
  Wystly in the face,
So dyde Syr Rycharde at the Le,
  And kneled downe in that place.

And so dyde all the wylde outlawes,
  Whan they se them knele:
"My lorde the kynge of Englonde,
  Now I knowe you well."

"Mercy then, Robyn," sayd our kynge,
  "Under your trystyll-tre,
Of thy goodnesse and thy grace,
  For my men and me!"

"Yes, for God," sayd Robyn,
  "And also God me save,
I aske mercy, my lorde the kynge,
  And for my men I crave."

"Yes, for God," than sayd our kynge,
  "And therto sent I me,
With that thou leve the grene wode,
  And all thy company;

"And come home, syr, to my courte,
  And there dwell with me."
"I make myn avowe to God," sayd Robyn,
  "And ryght so shall it be.

"I wyll come to your courte,
  Your servyse for to se,
And brynge with me of my men
  Seven score and thre.

"But me lyke well your servyse,
  I wyll come agayne full soone,
And shote at the donnë dere,
  As I am wonte to done."

IX

Robin Hood's Death and Burial

When Robin Hood and Little John,
  Down a down, a down, a down,
  Went o'er yon bank of broom,
Said Robin Hood bold to Little John,
  "We have shot for many a pound:"
  Hey down, a down, a down.

"But I am not able to shoot one shot more,
  My broad arrows will not flee;
But I have a cousin lives down below,
  Please God, she will bleed me."

Now Robin is to fair Kirkley gone,
  As fast as he can win;
But before he came there, as we do hear,
  He was taken very ill.

And when that he came to fair Kirkley-hall,
  He knocked all at the ring,
But none was so ready as his cousin herself
  For to let bold Robin in.

"Will you please to sit down, cousin Robin," she said,
  "And drink some beer with me?"
"No, I will neither eat nor drink,
  Till I am blooded by thee."

"Well, I have a room, cousin Robin," she said,
  "Which you did never see,
And if you please to walk therein,
  You blooded by me shall be."

She took him by the lily-white hand,
  And led him to a private room,
And there she blooded bold Robin Hood,
  While one drop of blood would run down.

She blooded him in a vein of the arm,
  And locked him up in the room;
Then did he bleed all the livelong day,
  Until the next day at noon.

He then bethought him of a casement there,
  Thinking for to get down;
He was so weak he could not leap,
  He could not get him down.

He then bethought him of his bugle-horn,
  Which hung low down to his knee;
He set his horn unto his mouth,
  And blew out weak blasts three.

Then Little John, when hearing him,
  As he sat under a tree,
"I fear my master is now near dead,
  He blows so wearily."

Robin Hood's Death and Burial

Then Little John to fair Kirkley is gone,
    As fast as he can dree;
But when he came to Kirkley-hall,
    He broke locks two or three:

Until he came bold Robin to,
    Then he fell on his knee:
"A boon, a boon," cries Little John,
    "Master, I beg of thee."

"What is that boon," quoth Robin Hood,
    "Little John, thou begs of me?"
"It is to burn fair Kirkley-hall,
    And all their nunnery."

"Now nay, now nay," quoth Robin Hood,
    "That boon I'll not grant thee;
I never hurt woman in all my life,
    Nor man in woman's company.

"I never hurt fair maid in all my time,
    Nor at my end shall it be;
But give me my bent bow in my hand,
    And a broad arrow I'll let flee;
And where this arrow is taken up,
    There shall my grave digg'd be.

"Lay me a green sod under my head,
    And another at my feet;
And lay my bent bow by my side,
    Which was my music sweet;
And make my grave of gravel and green,
    Which is most right and meet.

"Let me have length and breadth enough,
   With under my head a green sod;
That they may say, when I am dead,
   Here lies bold Robin Hood."

These words they readily promised him,
   Which did bold Robin please;
And there they buried bold Robin Hood,
   Near to the fair Kirklèys.

X

The Douglas Tragedy

"Rise up, rise up, now, Lord Douglas," she says,
   "And put on your armour so bright;
Let it never be said that a daughter of thine
   Was married to a lord under night.

"Rise up, rise up, my seven bold sons,
   And put on your armour so bright,
And take better care of your youngest sister,
   For your eldest 's awa the last night."

He 's mounted her on a milk-white steed,
   And himself on a dapple gray,
With a bugelet horn hung down by his side,
   And lightly they rode away.

Lord William lookit o'er his left shoulder,
   To see what he could see,
And there he spy'd her seven brethren bold,
   Come riding over the lee.

"Light down, light down, Lady Margret," he said,
  "And hold my steed in your hand,
Until that against your seven brethren bold,
  And your father, I mak a stand."

She held his steed in her milk-white hand,
  And never shed one tear,
Until that she saw her seven brethren fa',
  And her father hard fighting, who lov'd her so dear.

"O hold your hand, Lord William!" she said,
  "For your strokes they are wondrous sair;
True lovers I can get many a ane,
  But a father I can never get mair."

O she 's ta'en out her handkerchief,
  It was o' the holland sae fine,
And aye she dighted her father's bloody wounds,
  That were redder than the wine.

"O chuse, O chuse, Lady Margret," he said,
  "O whether will ye gang or bide?"
"I 'll gang, I 'll gang, Lord William," she said,
  "For ye have left me nae other guide."

He 's lifted her on a milk-white steed,
  And himself on a dapple gray,
With a bugelet horn hung down by his side,
  And slowly they baith rade away.

O they rade on, and on they rade,
  And a' by the light of the moon,
Until they came to yon wan water,
  And there they lighted down.

They lighted down to tak' a drink
  Of the spring that ran sae clear,
And down the stream ran his gude heart's blood,
  And sair she gan to fear.

"Hold up, hold up, Lord William," she says,
  "For I fear that you are slain."
"'T is naething but the shadow of my scarlet cloak,
  That shines in the water sae plain."

O they rade on, and on they rade,
  And a' by the light of the moon,
Until they cam' to his mother's ha' door,
  And there they lighted down.

"Get up, get up, lady mother," he says,
  "Get up, and let me in!
Get up, get up, lady mother," he says,
  "For this night my fair lady I 've win.

"O mak my bed, lady mother," he says,
  "O mak it braid and deep,
And lay Lady Margret close at my back,
  And the sounder I will sleep."

Lord William was dead lang ere midnight,
  Lady Margret lang ere day,
And all true lovers that go thegither,
  May they have mair luck than they!

Lord William was buried in St. Mary's kirk,
  Lady Margret in Mary's quire;
Out o' the lady's grave grew a bonny red rose,
  And out o' the knight's a briar.

And they twa met, and they twa plat,
    And fain they wad be near;
And a' the warld might ken right weel
    They were twa lovers dear.

But by and rade the Black Douglas,
    And wow but he was rough!
For he pull'd up the bonny briar,
    And flang 't in St. Mary's Loch.

XI

Lord Randal

"O where hae ye been, Lord Randal, my son?
O where hae ye been, my handsome young man?"
"I hae been to the wild wood; mother, make my bed soon,
For I 'm weary wi hunting, and fain wald lie down."

"Where gat ye your dinner, Lord Randal, my son?
Where gat ye your dinner, my handsome young man?"
"I din'd wi my true-love; mother, make my bed soon,
For I 'm weary wi hunting, and fain wald lie down."

"What gat ye to your dinner, Lord Randal, my son?
What gat ye to your dinner, my handsome young man?"
"I gat eels boiled in broo; mother, make my bed soon,
For I 'm weary wi hunting, and fain wald lie down."

"What became of your bloodhounds, Lord Randal, my son?
What became of your bloodhounds, my handsome young man?"

"O they swelld and they died; mother, make my bed
    soon,
For I'm weary wi hunting, and fain wald lie down."

"O I fear ye are poisond, Lord Randal, my son!
O I fear ye are poisond, my handsome young man!"
"O yes! I am poisond; mother, make my bed soon,
For I'm sick at the heart, and I fain wald lie down."

XII

Bonnie George Campbell

High upon Highlands,
    and low upon Tay,
Bonnie George Campbell
    rade out on a day.

Saddled and bridled
    and gallant rade he;
Hame cam his guid horse,
    but never cam he.

Out cam his auld mither
    greeting fu' sair,
And out cam his bonnie bride
    riving her hair.

Saddled and bridled
    and booted rade he;
Toom hame cam the saddle,
    but never cam he.

"My meadow lies green,
   and my corn is unshorn,
My barn is to build,
   and my babe is unborn."

Saddled and bridled
   and booted rade he;
Toom hame cam the saddle,
   but never cam he.

XIII

Bessie Bell and Mary Gray

O Bessie Bell and Mary Gray,
   They war twa bonnie lasses!
They bigget a bower on yon burn-brae,
   And theekit it o'er wi rashes.

They theekit it o'er wi rashes green,
   They theekit it o'er wi heather;
But the pest cam frae the burrows-town,
   And slew them baith thegither.

They thought to lie in Methven kirk-yard
   Amang their noble kin;
But they maun lye in Stronach haugh,
   To biek forenent the sin.

And Bessie Bell and Mary Gray,
   They war twa bonnie lasses;
They biggit a bower on yon burn-brae,
   And theekit it o'er wi rashes.

XIV

The Twa Corbies

As I was walking all alane,
I heard twa corbies making a maen;
The tane into the t'ither did say,
"Whaur shall we gang and dine the day?"

"O doun beside yon auld fail dyke,
I wot there lies a new-slain knight;
Nae living kens that he lies there,
But his hawk, his hound, and his lady fair.

"His hound is to the hunting gane,
His hawk to fetch the wildfowl hame,
His lady's ta'en another mate,
Sae we may mak' our dinner sweet.

"O we'll sit on his white hause bane,
And I'll pyke out his bonny blue e'en,
Wi' ae lock o' his gowden hair
We'll theek our nest when it blaws bare.

"Mony a ane for him makes maen,
But nane shall ken whaur he is gane;
Over his banes when they are bare,
The wind shall blaw for evermair."

XV

Helen of Kirconnell

I wad I were where Helen lies;
Night and day on me she cries;
O that I were where Helen lies
    On fair Kirconnell lea!

Curst be the heart that thought the thought,
And curst the hand that fired the shot,
When in my arms burd Helen dropt,
    And died to succor me!

O think na ye my heart was sair
When my love dropt down and spak nae mair!
I laid her down wi' meikle care
    On fair Kirconnell lea.

As I went down the water-side,
Nane but my foe to be my guide,
Nane but my foe to be my guide,
    On fair Kirconnell lea;

I lighted down, my sword did draw,
I hackèd him in pieces sma',
I hackèd him in pieces sma',
    For her sake that died for me.

O Helen fair, beyond compare!
I 'll make a garland of thy hair
Shall bind my heart for evermair
    Until the day I dee.

O that I were where Helen lies!
Night and day on me she cries;
Out of my bed she bids me rise,
    Says, "Haste and come to me!"

O Helen fair! O Helen chaste!
If I were with thee, I were blest,
Where thou lies low and takes thy rest
    On fair Kirconnell lea.

I wad my grave were growing green,
A winding-sheet drawn o'er my een,
And I in Helen's arms lying,
    On fair Kirconnell lea.

I wad I were where Helen lies;
Night and day on me she cries;
And I am weary of the skies,
    For her sake that died for me.

XVI

The Wife of Usher's Well

There lived a wife at Usher's Well,
    And a wealthy wife was she;
She had three stout and stalwart sons,
    And sent them o'er the sea.

They hadna been a week from her,
    A week but barely ane,
When word came to the carline wife
    That her three sons were gane.

They hadna been a week from her,
  A week but barely three,
When word came to the carlin wife
  That her sons she 'd never see.

"I wish the wind may never cease,
  Nor fashes in the flood,
Till my three sons come hame to me,
  In earthly flesh and blood."

It fell about the Martinmass,
  When nights are lang and mirk,
The carlin wife's three sons came hame,
  And their hats were o' the birk.

It neither grew in syke nor ditch,
  Nor yet in ony sheugh;
But at the gates o' Paradise,
  That birk grew fair eneugh.

. . . .

"Blow up the fire, my maidens!
  Bring water from the well!
For a' my house shall feast this night,
  Since my three sons are well."

And she has made to them a bed,
  She 's made it large and wide,
And she 's ta'en her mantle her about,
  Sat down at the bed-side.

. . . .

Up then crew the red, red cock,
  And up and crew the gray;
The eldest to the youngest said,
  "'T is time we were away."

The cock he hadna craw'd but once,
    And clapped his wings at a',
When the youngest to the eldest said,
    "Brother, we must awa.

"The cock doth craw, the day doth daw,
    The channerin worm doth chide;
Gin we be mist out o' our place,
    A sair pain we maun bide.

"Fare ye weel, my mother dear!
    Fareweel to barn and byre!
And fare ye weel, the bonny lass
    That kindles my mother's fire!"

XVII

The Demon Lover

"O, where hae ye been, my lang-lost love,
    This lang seven years an' more?"
"O, I'm come to seek my former vows
    Ye granted me before."

"O, haud your tongue o' your former vows,
    For they'll breed bitter strife;
O, haud your tongue o' your former vows,
    For I am become a wife."

He turned him right an' round about,
    And the tear blinded his e'e;
"I wad never hae trodden on Irish ground
    If it hadna been for thee.

"I might hae had a king's daughter
  Far, far beyond the sea,
I might hae had a king's daughter,
  Had it nae been for love o' thee."

"If ye might hae had a king's daughter,
  Yoursel' ye hae to blame;
Ye might hae taken the king's daughter,
  For ye kenn'd that I was nane."

"O fause be the vows o' womankind,
  But fair is their fause bodie;
I wa'd never hae trodden on Irish ground
  Had it nae been for love o' thee."

"If I was to leave my husband dear,
  And my twa babes also,
O where is it ye would tak' me to,
  If I with thee should go?"

"I hae seven ships upon the sea,
  The eighth brouct me to land,
Wi' four-and-twenty bold mariners,
  And music of ilka hand."

She has taken up her twa little babes,
  Kiss'd them baith cheek and chin;
"O fare ye weel, my ain twa babes,
  For I 'll never see you again."

She set her foot upon the ship,
  No mariners could she behold;
But the sails were o' the taffetie,
  And the masts o' the beaten gold.

"O how do you love the ship?" he said,
  "O how do you love the sea?
And how do you love the bold mariners
  That wait upon thee and me?"

"O I do love the ship," she said,
  "And I do love the sea;
But wae to the dim mariners
  That naewhere I can see!"

They hadna sailed a league, a league,
  A league but barely three,
When dismal grew his countenance,
  And drumly grew his e'e.

The masts that were like the beaten gold,
  Bent not on the heaving seas;
The sails that were o' the taffetie
  Fill'd not in the east land breeze.

They hadna sailed a league, a league,
  A league but barely three,
Until she espied his cloven hoof,
  And she wept right bitterlie.

"O haud your tongue o' your weeping," he says:
  "O' your weeping now let me be;
I will show you how the lilies grow
  On the banks of Italy."

"O what hills are yon, yon pleasant hills,
  That the sun shines sweetly on?"
"O yon are the hills o' heaven," he said,
  "Where you will never win."

The Demon Lover

"O what'n a mountain 's yon," she said,
 "Sae dreary wi' frost an' snow?"
"O yon is the mountain o' hell," he cried,
 "Where you and I maun go!"

And aye when she turn'd her round about,
 Aye taller he seemed for to be;
Until that the tops o' that gallant ship
 Nae taller were than he.

The clouds grew dark, and the wind grew loud,
 And the levin fill'd her e'e;
And waesome wail'd the snaw-white sprites
 Upon the gurlie sea.

He strack the tapmast wi' his hand,
 The foremast wi' his knee;
And he brak that gallant ship in twain,
 And sank her i' the sea.

BOOK SECOND — POEMS OF ENGLAND: HISTORICAL AND PATRIOTIC

XVIII

God Save the King

God save our gracious King!
Long live our noble King!
  God save the King!
Send him victorious,
Happy and glorious,
Long to reign over us!
  God save the King!

O Lord our God, arise!
Scatter his enemies,
  And make them fall;
Confound their politics,
Frustrate their knavish tricks:
On Thee our hopes we fix —
  God save us all!

Thy choicest gifts in store
On him be pleased to pour;
  Long may he reign!

>   May he defend our laws,
>   And ever give us cause
>   To sing with heart and voice,
>   God save the King!

XIX

England

1399

This royal throne of kings, this scepter'd isle,
This earth of Majesty, this seat of Mars,
This other Eden, demi-paradise,
This fortress built by Nature for herself
Against infection and the hand of war,
This happy breed of men, this little world,
This precious stone set in the silver sea,
Which serves it in the office of a wall,
Or as a moat defensive to a house,
Against the envy of less happier lands,
This blessed plot, this earth, this realm, this England,
This nurse, this teeming womb of royal kings,
Fear'd by their breed and famous by their birth,
Renowned for their deeds as far from home,
For Christian service and true chivalry,
As is the sepulchre in stubborn Jewry
Of the world's ransom, blessed Mary's Son;
This land of such dear souls, this dear dear land,
Dear for her reputation through the world,
Is now leased out, I die pronouncing it,
Like to a tenement or pelting farm:
England, bound in with the triumphant sea,

Whose rocky shore beats back the envious siege
Of watery Neptune, is now bound in with shame,
With inky blots and rotten parchment bonds:
That England, that was wont to conquer others,
Hath made a shameful conquest of itself.
Ah, would the scandal vanish with my life,
How happy then were my ensuing death!

Shakespeare

XX

Henry the Fifth's Address to his Soldiers before Harfleur

1415

Once more unto the breach, dear friends, once more;
Or close the wall up with our English dead.
In peace there's nothing so becomes a man
As modest stillness and humility:
But when the blast of war blows in our ears,
Then imitate the action of the tiger;
Stiffen the sinews, summon up the blood,
Disguise fair nature with hard-favour'd rage;
Then lend the eye a terrible aspèct;
Let it pry through the portage of the head
Like the brass cannon; let the brow o'erwhelm it
As fearfully as doth a galled rock
O'erhang and jutty his confounded base,
Swill'd with the wild and wasteful ocean.
Now set the teeth and stretch the nostril wide,
Hold hard the breath and bend up every spirit
To his full height.   On, on, you noblest English,

Whose blood is fet from fathers of war-proof!
Fathers that, like so many Alexanders,
Have in these parts from morn till even fought
And sheathed their swords for lack of argument:
Dishonour not your mothers; now attest
That those whom you call'd fathers did beget you.
Be copy now to men of grosser blood,
And teach them how to war.   And you, good yeomen,
Whose limbs were made in England, show us here
The mettle of your pasture; let us swear
That you are worth your breeding; which I doubt not;
For there is none of you so mean and base,
That hath not noble lustre in your eyes.
I see you stand like greyhounds in the slips,
Straining upon the start.   The game's afoot:
Follow your spirit, and upon this charge
Cry "God for Harry, England, and St. George!"

Shakespeare

XXI

King Henry the Fifth before Agincourt

1415

. . . He which hath no stomach to this fight,
Let him depart; his passport shall be made
And crowns for convoy put into his purse:
We would not die in that man's company
That fears his fellowship to die with us.
This day is call'd the feast of Crispian:
He that outlives this day, and comes safe home,
Will stand a tip-toe when this day is named,

King Henry the Fifth before Agincourt

And rouse him at the name of Crispian.
He that shall live this day, and see old age,
Will yearly on the vigil feast his neighbours,
And say " To-morrow is Saint Crispian : "
Then will he strip his sleeve and show his scars,
And say " These wounds I had on Crispin's day."
Old men forget ; yet all shall be forgot,
But he 'll remember with advantages
What feats he did that day : then shall our names,
Familiar in his mouth as household words,
Harry the king, Bedford and Exeter,
Warwick and Talbot, Salisbury and Gloucester,
Be in their flowing cups freshly remember'd.
This story shall the good man teach his son ;
And Crispin Crispian shall ne'er go by,
From this day to the ending of the world,
But we in it shall be rememberèd ;
We few, we happy few, we band of brothers ;
For he to-day that sheds his blood with me
Shall be my brother ; be he ne'er so vile,
This day shall gentle his condition :
And gentlemen in England now a-bed
Shall think themselves accursed they were not here,
And hold their manhoods cheap whiles any speaks
That fought with us upon Saint Crispin's day.

Shakespeare

XXII

To the Cambrio-Britons and their Harp, his Ballad of Agincourt

1415

Fair stood the wind for France,
When we our sails advance,
Nor now to prove our chance
    Longer will tarry;
But putting to the main,
At Kaux, the mouth of Seine,
With all his martial train,
    Landed King Harry.

And taking many a fort,
Furnished in warlike sort,
Marchèd towards Agincourt
    In happy hour —
Skirmishing day by day
With those that stopped his way
Where the French gen'ral lay
    With all his power,

Which in his height of pride,
King Henry to deride,
His ransom to provide
    To the king sending;
Which he neglects the while,
As from a nation vile,
Yet, with an angry smile,
    Their fall portending.

The Ballad of Agincourt

And turning to his men,
Quoth our brave Henry then:
"Though they to one be ten,
    Be not amazed.
Yet have we well begun —
Battles so bravely won
Have ever to the sun
    By fame been raised.

"And for myself," quoth he,
"This my full rest shall be;
England ne'er mourn for me,
    Nor more esteem me.
Victor I will remain,
Or on this earth lie slain;
Never shall she sustain
    Loss to redeem me.

"Poitiers and Cressy tell,
When most their pride did swell,
Under our swords they fell;
    No less our skill is
Than when our grandsire great,
Claiming the regal seat,
By many a warlike feat
    Lopped the French lilies."

The Duke of York so dread
The eager vaward led;
With the main Henry sped,
    Amongst his henchmen.
Excester had the rear —
A braver man not there:
O Lord! how hot they were
    On the false Frenchmen!

They now to fight are gone;
Armor on armor shone,
Drum now to drum did groan —
    To hear was wonder;
That with cries they make
The very earth did shake;
Trumpet to trumpet spake,
    Thunder to thunder.

Well it thine age became,
O noble Erpingham!
Which did the signal aim
    To our hid forces;
When, from a meadow by,
Like a storm suddenly,
The English archery
    Stuck the French horses,

With Spanish yew so strong,
Arrows a cloth-yard long,
That like to serpents stung,
    Piercing the weather;
None from his fellow starts,
But playing manly parts,
And like true English hearts,
    Stuck close together.

When down their bows they threw,
And forth their bilbows drew,
And on the French they flew,
    Not one was tardy:
Arms were from shoulders sent;
Scalps to the teeth were rent;
Down the French peasants went;
    Our men were hardy.

This while our noble king,
His broadsword brandishing,
Down the French host did ding,
    As to o'erwhelm it;
And many a deep wound lent,
His arms with blood besprent,
And many a cruel dent
    Bruised his helmet.

Glo'ster, that duke so good,
Next of the royal blood,
For famous England stood,
    With his brave brother,
Clarence, — in steel so bright,
Though but a maiden knight, —
Yet in that furious fight
    Scarce such another.

Warwick in blood did wade,
Oxford the foe invade,
And cruel slaughter made,
    Still as they ran up;
Suffolk his axe did ply;
Beaumont and Willoughby
Bare them right doughtily,
    Ferrers and Fanhope.

Upon Saint Crispin's day
Fought was this noble fray,
Which fame did not delay
    To England to carry;
Oh, when shall Englishmen
With such acts fill a pen,
Or England breed again
    Such a King Harry!

Michael Drayton

XXIII

The "Revenge"

A Ballad of the Fleet, 1591

At Florès in the Azorès, Sir Richard Grenville lay,
And a pinnace, like a fluttered bird, came flying from far away:
"Spanish ships-of-war at sea! we have sighted fifty-three!"
Then sware Lord Thomas Howard: "'Fore God I am no coward;
But I cannot meet them here, for my ships are out of gear,
And the half my men are sick. I must fly, but follow quick.
We are six ships of the line; can we fight with fifty-three?"

Then spake Sir Richard Grenville: "I know you are no coward;
You fly them for a moment to fight with them again.
But I've ninety men and more that are lying sick ashore.
I should count myself the coward if I left them, my Lord Howard,
To these Inquisition dogs and the devildoms of Spain."

So Lord Howard passed away with five ships of war that day,
Till he melted like a cloud in the silent summer heaven;
But Sir Richard bore in hand all his sick men from the land
Very carefully and slow,
Men of Bideford in Devon,
And we laid them on the ballast down below;

For we brought them all aboard,
And they blest him in their pain, that they were not left to Spain,
To the thumbscrew and the stake, for the glory of the Lord.

He had only a hundred seamen to work the ship and to fight,
And he sailed away from Florès till the Spaniard came in sight,
With his huge sea-castles heaving upon the weather bow.
"Shall we fight or shall we fly?
Good Sir Richard, tell us now,
For to fight is but to die!
There'll be little of us left by the time this sun be set."
And Sir Richard said again: "We be all good Englishmen.
Let us bang these dogs of Seville, the children of the devil,
For I never turned my back upon Don or devil yet."

Sir Richard spoke and he laughed, and we roared a hurrah, and so
The little *Revenge* ran on sheer into the heart of the foe,
With her hundred fighters on deck, and her ninety sick below;
For half of their fleet to the right and half to the left were seen,
And the little *Revenge* ran on through the long sea-lane between.

Thousands of their soldiers looked down from their decks and laughed,
Thousands of their seamen made mock at the mad little craft

Running on and on, till delayed
By their mountain-like *San Philip* that, of fifteen hundred tons,
And up-shadowing high above us with her yawning tiers of guns,
Took the breath from our sails, and we stayed.

And while now the great *San Philip* hung above us like a cloud,
Whence the thunderbolt will fall
Long and loud,
Four galleons drew away
From the Spanish fleet that day,
And two upon the larboard and two upon the starboard lay,
And the battle-thunder broke from them all.

But anon the great *San Philip*, she bethought herself and went,
Having that within her womb that had left her ill-content;
And the rest they came aboard us, and they fought us hand to hand,
For a dozen times they came with their pikes and musqueteers,
And a dozen times we shook 'em off as a dog that shakes his ears,
When he leaps from the water to the land.

And the sun went down, and the stars came out far over the summer sea,
But never a moment ceased the fight of the one and the fifty-three.

Ship after ship, the whole night long, their high-built galleons came,
Ship after ship, the whole night long, with her battle-thunder and flame;
Ship after ship, the whole night long, drew back with her dead and her shame,
For some were sunk and many were shattered, and so could fight us no more —
God of battles, was ever a battle like this in the world before?

For he said "Fight on! fight on!"
Tho' his vessel was all but a wreck;
And it chanced that, when half of the summer night was gone,
With a grisly wound to be drest, he had left the deck,
But a bullet struck him that was dressing it suddenly dead,
And himself, he was wounded again in the side and the head,
And he said, "Fight on! fight on!"

And the night went down, and the sun smiled out far over the summer sea,
And the Spanish fleet with broken sides lay round us all in a ring;
But they dared not touch us again, for they feared that we still could sting,
So they watched what the end would be.
And we had not fought them in vain,
But in perilous plight were we,
Seeing forty of our poor hundred were slain,

And half of the rest of us maim'd for life
In the crash of the cannonades and the desperate strife;
And the sick men down in the hold were most of them stark and cold,
And the pikes were all broken or bent, and the powder was all of it spent;
And the masts and the rigging were lying over the side;
But Sir Richard cried in his English pride,
"We have fought such a fight, for a day and a night,
As may never be fought again!
We have won great glory, my men!
And a day less or more
At sea or ashore,
We die — does it matter when?
Sink me the ship, Master Gunner — sink her, split her in twain!
Fall into the hands of God, not into the hands of Spain!"

And the gunner said, "Ay, ay," but the seamen made reply:
"We have children, we have wives,
And the Lord hath spared our lives.
We will make the Spaniard promise, if we yield, to let us go;
We shall live to fight again and to strike another blow."
And the lion there lay dying, and they yielded to the foe.

And the stately Spanish men to their flagship bore him then,
Where they laid him by the mast, old Sir Richard caught at last,
And they praised him to his face with their courtly foreign grace;

But he rose upon their decks, and he cried:
"I have fought for Queen and Faith like a valiant man and
    true;
I have only done my duty as a man is bound to do:
With a joyful spirit I, Sir Richard Grenville, die!"
And he fell upon their decks, and he died.

And they stared at the dead that had been so valiant and
    true,
And had holden the power and glory of Spain so cheap
That he dared her with one little ship and his English few;
Was he devil or man? He was devil for aught they knew,
But they sank his body with honor down into the deep,
And they manned the *Revenge* with a swarthier, alien crew,
And away she sail'd with her loss and long'd for her own;
When a wind from the lands they had ruin'd awoke from
    sleep,
And the water began to heave and the weather to moan,
And or ever that evening ended, a great gale blew,
And a wave like the wave that is raised by an earthquake
    grew,
Till it smote on their hulls and their sails and their masts
    and their flags,
And the whole sea plunged and fell on the shot-shatter'd
    navy of Spain,
And the little *Revenge* herself went down by the island
    crags
To be lost evermore in the main.

Alfred Tennyson

XXIV

Give a Rouse

1642–1649

King Charles, and who 'll do him right now?
King Charles, and who 's ripe for fight now?
Give a rouse : here 's, in hell's despite now,
King Charles!

Who gave me the goods that went since?
Who raised me the house that sank once?
Who helped me to gold I spent since?
Who found me in wine you drank once?

Chorus

> King Charles, and who 'll do him right now?
> King Charles, and who 's ripe for fight now?
> Give a rouse : here 's, in hell's despite now,
> King Charles!

To whom used my boy George quaff else,
By the old fool's side that begot him?
For whom did he cheer and laugh else,
While Noll's damned troopers shot him?

Chorus

> King Charles, and who 'll do him right now?
> King Charles, and who 's ripe for fight now?
> Give a rouse : here 's, in hell's despite now,
> King Charles!

Robert Browning

XXV

The Sally from Coventry

" Passion o' me ! " cried Sir Richard Tyrone,
Spurning the sparks from the broad paving-stone,
" Better turn nurse and rock children to sleep,
Than yield to a rebel old Coventry Keep.
No, by my halidom, no one shall say,
Sir Richard Tyrone gave a city away."

Passion o' me ! how he pulled at his beard,
Fretting and chafing if any one sneered,
Clapping his breastplate and shaking his fist,
Giving his grizzly moustachios a twist,
Running the protocol through with his steel, [a document]
Grinding the letter to mud with his heel.

Then he roared out for a pottle of sack, [measure of bag or vat]
Clapped the old trumpeter twice on the back,
Leaped on his bay with a dash and a swing,
Bade all the bells in the city to ring,
And when the red flag from the steeple went down,
Open they flung every gate in the town.

To boot ! and to horse ! and away like a flood,
A fire in their eyes, and a sting in their blood ;
Hurrying out with a flash and a flare,
A roar of hot guns, a loud trumpeter's blare,
And first, sitting proud as a king on his throne,
At the head of them all dashed Sir Richard Tyrone.

Crimson and yellow, and purple and dun, [dull brown]
Fluttering scarf, flowing bright in the sun,

Steel like a mirror on brow and on breast,
Scarlet and white on their feather and crest,
Banner that blew in a torrent of red,
Borne by Sir Richard, who rode at their head.

The "trumpet" went down — with a gash on his poll,
Struck by the parters of body and soul.
Forty saddles were empty; the horses ran red
With foul Puritan blood from the slashes that bled.
Curses and cries and a gnashing of teeth,
A grapple and stab on the slippery heath,
And Sir Richard leaped up on the fool that went down,
Proud as a conqueror donning his crown.

They broke them a way through a flooding of fire,
Trampling the best blood of London to mire,
When suddenly rising a smoke and a blaze,
Made all "the dragon's sons" stare in amaze:
"O ho!" quoth Sir Richard, "my city grows hot,
I've left it rent paid to the villanous Scot."

Walter Thornbury

XXVI

The Battle of Naseby

BY OBADIAH BIND-THEIR-KINGS-IN-CHAINS-AND-THEIR-
NOBLES-WITH-LINKS-OF-IRON, Sergeant in Ireton's Regiment

1645

Oh! wherefore come ye forth in triumph from the north,
  With your hands, and your feet, and your raiment all red?
And wherefore doth your rout send forth a joyous shout?
  And whence be the grapes of the wine-press which ye tread?

Oh! evil was the root, and bitter was the fruit,
    And crimson was the juice of the vintage that we trod;
For we trampled on the throng of the haughty and the strong,
    Who sate in the high places and slew the saints of God.
It was about the noon of a glorious day of June,
    That we saw their banners dance and their cuirasses shine,
And the Man of Blood was there, with his long essenced hair,
    And Astley, and Sir Marmaduke, and Rupert of the Rhine.

Like a servant of the Lord, with his Bible and his sword,
    The general rode along us to form us to the fight;
When a murmuring sound broke out, and swelled into a shout
    Among the godless horsemen upon the tyrant's right.
And hark! like the roar of the billows on the shore,
    The cry of battle rises along their charging line:
For God! for the Cause! for the Church! for the Laws!
    For Charles, King of England, and Rupert of the Rhine!
The furious German comes, with his clarions and his drums,
    His bravoes of Alsatia and pages of Whitehall;
They are bursting on our flanks! Grasp your pikes! Close your ranks!
    For Rupert never comes but to conquer or to fall.

They are here — they rush on — we are broken — we are gone —
    Our left is borne before them like stubble on the blast.
O Lord, put forth thy might! O Lord, defend the right!
    Stand back to back, in God's name! and fight it to the last!

Stout Skippon hath a wound — the centre hath given ground.
  Hark! hark! what means the trampling of horsemen on our rear?
Whose banner do I see, boys? 'T is he! thank God! 't is he, boys!
  Bear up another minute! Brave Oliver is here!
Their heads all stooping low, their points all in a row:
  Like a whirlwind on the trees, like a deluge on the dikes,
Our cuirassiers have burst on the ranks of the Accurst,
  And at a shock have scattered the forest of his pikes.

Fast, fast, the gallants ride, in some safe nook to hide
  Their coward heads, predestined to rot on Temple Bar;
And he — he turns! he flies! shame on those cruel eyes
  That bore to look on torture, and dare not look on war!
Ho, comrades! scour the plain; and ere ye strip the slain,
  First give another stab to make your search secure;
Then shake from sleeves and pockets their broad-pieces and lockets,
  The tokens of the wanton, the plunder of the poor.
Fools! your doublets shone with gold, and your hearts were gay and bold,
  When you kissed your lily hands to your lemans to-day;
And to-morrow shall the fox from her chambers in the rocks
  Lead forth her tawny cubs to howl above the prey.

Where be your tongues that late mocked at heaven, and hell, and fate?
  And the fingers that once were so busy with your blades?
Your perfumed satin clothes, your catches and your oaths?
  Your stage plays and your sonnets, your diamonds and your spades?

Down! down! for ever down, with the mitre and the crown!
  With the Belial of the court, and the Mammon of the
    Pope!
There is woe in Oxford halls, there is wail in Durham's
    stalls;
  The Jesuit smites his bosom, the bishop rends his cope.
And she of the seven hills shall mourn her children's ills,
  And tremble when she thinks on the edge of England's
    sword;
And the kings of earth in fear shall shudder when they hear
  What the hand of God hath wrought for the Houses and
    the Word!
                                                Lord Macaulay

XXVII

The Three Troopers

[DURING THE PROTECTORATE, 1653–1658]

Into the Devil tavern
    Three booted troopers strode,
From spur to feather spotted and splashed
    With the mud of a winter road.
In each of their cups they dropped a crust,
    And stared at the guests with a frown;
Then drew their swords, and roared for a toast,
    "God send this Crum-well-down!"

A blue smoke rose from their pistol locks,
    Their sword blades were still wet;
There were long red smears on their jerkins of buff,
    As they the table overset.

Then into their cups they stirred the crusts,
    And cursed old London town;
They waved their swords, and drank with a stamp,
    "God send this Crum-well-down!"

The 'prentice dropped his can of beer,
    The host turned pale as a clout;
The ruby nose of the toping squires
    Grew white at the wild men's shout.
Then into their cups they flung their crusts,
    And shewed their teeth with a frown;
They flashed their swords as they gave the toast,
    "God send this Crum-well-down!"

The gambler dropped his dog's-ear'd cards,
    The waiting-women screamed,
As the light of the fire, like stains of blood,
    On the wild men's sabres gleamed.
Then into their cups they splashed their crusts,
    And cursed the fool of a town,
And leapt on the table, and roared a toast,
    "God send this Crum-well-down!"

Till on a sudden fire-bells rang,
    And the troopers sprang to horse
The eldest muttered between his teeth,
    Hot curses — deep and coarse.
In their stirrup cups they flung the crusts,
    And cried as they spurred through the town,
With their keen swords drawn and their pistols cocked,
    "God send this Crum-well-down!"

Away they dashed through Temple Bar,
    Their red cloaks flowing free,
Their scabbards clashed, each back-piece shone —
    None like to touch the three.
The silver cups that held the crusts
    They flung to the startled town,
Shouting again, with a blaze of swords,
    "God send this Crum-well-down!"

Walter Thornbury

XXVIII

The British Grenadiers

c. 1690

Some talk of Alexander, and some of Hercules;
Of Hector and Lysander, and such great names as these;
But of all the world's brave heroes, there's none that can compare,
With a tow, row, row, row, row, row, to the British Grenadier.

Those heroes of antiquity ne'er saw a cannon ball,
Or knew the force of powder to slay their foes withal;
But our brave boys do know it, and banish all their fears,
Sing tow, row, row, row, row, row, for the British Grenadiers.

Whene'er we are commanded to storm the palisades,
Our leaders march with fusees, and we with hand grenades;
We throw them from the glacis, about the enemies' ears,
Sing tow, row, row, row, row, row, for the British Grenadiers.

And when the siege is over, we to the town repair,
The townsmen cry Hurra, boys, here comes a Grenadier,
Here come the Grenadiers, my boys, who know no doubts
  or fears,
Then sing tow, row, row, row, row, row, for the British
  Grenadiers.

Then let us fill a bumper and drink a health to those
Who carry caps and pouches, and wear the louped clothes;
May they and their commanders live happy all their years,
With a tow, row, row, row, row, row, for the British
  Grenadiers.   *Anonymous*

XXIX

Rule, Britannia

1740

When Britain first, at Heaven's command,
    Arose from out the azure main,
This was the charter of the land,
    And guardian angels sung this strain:
      "Rule, Britannia, rule the waves,
      Britons never will be slaves.

"The nations not so blessed as thee
    Must in their turn to tyrants fall;
While thou shalt flourish great and free,
    The dread and envy of them all.
      Rule, Britannia, rule the waves,
      Britons never will be slaves.

" Still more majestic shalt thou rise,
More dreadful from each foreign stroke;
As the loud blast that tears the skies
    Serves but to root thy native oak.
    Rule, Britannia, rule the waves,
    Britons never will be slaves.

" Thee haughty tyrants ne'er shall tame:
    All their attempts to bend thee down
Will but arouse thy generous flame,
    But work their woe and thy renown.
    Rule, Britannia, rule the waves,
    Britons never will be slaves.

" To thee belongs the rural reign;
    Thy cities shall with commerce shine:
All thine shall be the subject main, —
    And every shore it circles, thine.
    Rule, Britannia, rule the waves,
    Britons never will be slaves.

" The Muses, still with freedom found,
    Shall to thy happy coast repair:
Blessed isle! with matchless beauty crowned,
    And manly hearts to guard the fair.
    Rule, Britannia, rule the waves,
    Britons never will be slaves."

James Thomson

XXX

Ode, Written in the Year 1746

How sleep the brave who sink to rest,
By all their country's wishes blest!
When Spring, with dewy fingers cold,
Returns to deck their hallowed mould,
She there shall dress a sweeter sod
Than Fancy's feet have ever trod.

By fairy hands their knell is rung,
By forms unseen their dirge is sung:
There Honor comes, a pilgrim gray,
To bless the turf that wraps their clay;
And Freedom shall awhile repair,
To dwell a weeping hermit there!

William Collins

XXXI

Battle of the Baltic

1801

Of Nelson and the North
  Sing the glorious day's renown,
When to battle fierce came forth
  All the might of Denmark's crown,
And her arms along the deep proudly shone;
  By each gun the lighted brand
  In a bold, determined hand,
  And the Prince of all the land
Led them on.

Like leviathans afloat
   Lay their bulwarks on the brine;
While the sign of battle flew
   On the lofty British line —
It was ten of April morn by the chime;
   As they drifted on their path
   There was silence deep as death,
   And the boldest held his breath
For a time.

But the might of England flushed
   To anticipate the scene;
And her van the fleeter rushed
   O'er the deadly space between. —
"Hearts of oak!" our captain cried, when each gun
   From its adamantine lips
   Spread a death-shade round the ships,
   Like the hurricane eclipse
Of the sun.

Again! again! again!
   And the havoc did not slack,
Till a feeble cheer the Dane
   To our cheering sent us back;
Their shots along the deep slowly boom: —
   Then ceased — and all is wail,
   As they strike the shattered sail,
   Or in conflagration pale,
Light the gloom.

Out spoke the victor then,
   As he hailed them o'er the wave:
"Ye are brothers! ye are men!
   And we conquer but to save; —

So peace instead of death let us bring:
   But yield, proud foe, thy fleet,
   With the crews, at England's feet,
   And make submission meet
To our King."

Then Denmark blessed our chief,
   That he gave her wounds repose;
   And the sounds of joy and grief
   From her people wildly rose,
As death withdrew his shades from the day:
   While the sun looked smiling bright
   O'er a wide and woeful sight,
   Where the fires of funeral light
Died away.

Now joy, old England, raise!
   For the tidings of thy might,
By the festal cities' blaze,
   Whilst the wine-cup shines in light;
And yet, amidst that joy and uproar,
   Let us think of them that sleep
   Full many a fathom deep,
   By thy wild and stormy steep,
Elsinore!

Brave hearts! to Britain's pride
   Once so faithful and so true,
On the deck of fame that died,
   With the gallant, good Riou:—
Soft sigh the winds of heaven o'er their grave!
   While the billow mournful rolls,
   And the mermaid's song condoles,
   Singing glory to the souls
Of the brave!   *Thomas Campbell*

XXXII

Ye Mariners of England

1805

Ye mariners of England,
That guard our native seas,
Whose flag has braved, a thousand years,
The battle and the breeze,
Your glorious standard launch again,
To match another foe!
And sweep through the deep
While the stormy winds do blow —
While the battle rages loud and long,
And the stormy winds do blow.

The spirits of your fathers
Shall start from every wave!
For the deck it was their field of fame,
And ocean was their grave.
Where Blake and mighty Nelson fell
Your manly hearts shall glow,
As ye sweep through the deep
While the stormy winds do blow —
While the battle rages loud and long,
And the stormy winds do blow.

Britannia needs no bulwarks,
No towers along the steep;
Her march is o'er the mountain-wave,
Her home is on the deep.
With thunders from her native oak

She quells the floods below,
As they roar on the shore
When the stormy winds do blow —
When the battle rages loud and long,
And the stormy winds do blow.

The meteor flag of England
Shall yet terrific burn,
Till danger's troubled night depart,
And the star of peace return.
Then, then, ye ocean-warriors!
Our song and feast shall flow
To the fame of your name,
When the storm has ceased to blow —
When the fiery fight is heard no more,
And the storm has ceased to blow.

Thomas Campbell

XXXIII

Character of the Happy Warrior

Who is the happy Warrior? Who is he
That every man in arms should wish to be?
 — It is the generous spirit, who, when brought
Among the tasks of real life, hath wrought
Upon the plan that pleased his childish thought:
Whose high endeavors are an inward light
That makes the path before him always bright:
Who, with a natural instinct to discern
What knowledge can perform, is diligent to learn;
Abides by this resolve, and stops not there,
But makes his moral being his prime care;

Character of the Happy Warrior

Who, doomed to go in company with Pain
And Fear and Bloodshed, miserable train!
Turns his necessity to glorious gain;
In face of these doth exercise a power
Which is our human nature's highest dower;
Controls them and subdues, transmutes, bereaves
Of their bad influence, and their good receives:
By objects which might force the soul to abate
Her feeling rendered more compassionate;
Is placable — because occasions rise
So often that demand such sacrifice;
More skilful in self-knowledge, even more pure,
As tempted more; more able to endure,
As more exposed to suffering and distress;
Thence, also, more alive to tenderness.
— 'T is he whose law is reason; who depends
Upon that law as on the best of friends;
Whence, in a state where men are tempted still
To evil for a guard against worse ill,
And what in quality or act is best
Doth seldom on a right foundation rest,
He fixes good on good alone, and owes
To virtue every triumph that he knows:
— Who, if he rise to station of command,
Rises by open means; and there will stand
On honorable terms, or else retire,
And in himself possess his own desire;
Who comprehends his trust, and to the same
Keeps faithful with a singleness of aim,
And therefore does not stoop, nor lie in wait
For wealth, or honors, or for worldly state;
Whom they must follow; on whose head must fall,
Like showers of manna, if they come at all:

Whose powers shed round him in the common strife,
Or mild concerns of ordinary life,
A constant influence, a peculiar grace;
But who, if he be called upon to face
Some awful moment to which Heaven has joined
Great issues, good or bad for human-kind,
Is happy as a lover; and attired
With sudden brightness, like a man inspired;
And, through the heat of conflict, keeps the law
In calmness made, and sees what he foresaw;
Or, if an unexpected call succeed,
Come when it will, is equal to the need:
  — He who, though thus endued, as with a sense
And faculty for storm and turbulence,
Is yet a Soul whose master-bias leans
To homefelt pleasures and to gentle scenes;
Sweet images! which, wheresoe'er he be,
Are at his heart; and such fidelity
It is his darling passion to approve;
More brave for this, that he hath much to love.
  — 'T is, finally, the man, who, lifted high,
Conspicuous object in a Nation's eye,
Or left unthought-of in obscurity, —
Who, with a toward or untoward lot,
Prosperous or adverse, to his wish or not,
Plays, in the many games of life, that one
Where what he most doth value must be won:
Whom neither shape of danger can dismay,
Nor thought of tender happiness betray:
Who, not content that former worth stand fast,
Looks forward, persevering to the last,
From well to better, daily self-surpassed:
Who, — whether praise of him must walk the earth

Forever, and to noble deeds give birth,
Or he must go to dust without his fame,
And leave a dead, unprofitable name, —
Finds comfort in himself and in his cause;
And, while the mortal mist is gathering, draws
His breath in confidence of Heaven's applause: —
This is the happy warrior; this is he
Whom every man in arms should wish to be.

William Wordsworth

XXXIV

The Burial of Sir John Moore at Corunna

1809

Not a drum was heard, not a funeral note,
   As his corse to the rampart we hurried;
Not a soldier discharged his farewell shot
   O'er the grave where our hero we buried.

We buried him darkly at dead of night,
   The sod with our bayonets turning;
By the struggling moonbeam's misty light,
   And the lantern dimly burning.

No useless coffin enclosed his breast,
   Not in sheet nor in shroud we wound him;
But he lay like a warrior taking his rest,
   With his martial cloak around him.

Few and short were the prayers we said,
   And we spoke not a word of sorrow;
But we steadfastly gazed on the face that was dead,
   And we bitterly thought of the morrow.

We thought, as we hollowed his narrow bed,
    And smoothed down his lonely pillow,
That the foe and the stranger would tread o'er his head,
    And we far away on the billow!

Lightly they'll talk of the spirit that's gone,
    And o'er his cold ashes upbraid him;
But little he'll reck if they let him sleep on,
    In the grave where a Briton has laid him.

But half of our heavy task was done,
    When the clock struck the hour for retiring;
And we heard the distant and random gun
    That the foe was sullenly firing.

Slowly and sadly we laid him down,
    From the field of his fame fresh and gory;
We carved not a line, and we raised not a stone —
    But we left him alone in his glory!

Charles Wolfe

XXXV

The Field of Waterloo

1815

Stop! for thy tread is on an Empire's dust!
An Earthquake's spoil is sepulchred below!
Is the spot marked with no colossal bust?
Nor column trophied for triumphal show?
None; but the moral's truth tells simpler so,
As the ground was before, thus let it be;
How that red rain hath made the harvest grow!

The Field of Waterloo

And is this all the world has gained by thee,
Thou first and last of fields! king-making Victory?

. . . .

There was a sound of revelry by night,
And Belgium's capital had gathered then
Her Beauty and her Chivalry, and bright
The lamps shone o'er fair women and brave men.
A thousand hearts beat happily; and when
Music arose with its voluptuous swell,
Soft eyes looked love to eyes which spake again,
And all went merry as a marriage bell;
But hush! hark! a deep sound strikes like a rising knell!

Did ye not hear it? — No; 't was but the wind,
Or the car rattling o'er the stony street;
On with the dance! let joy be unconfined;
No sleep till morn, when Youth and Pleasure meet
To chase the glowing Hours with flying feet.
But hark! — that heavy sound breaks in once more,
As if the clouds its echo would repeat;
And nearer, clearer, deadlier than before;
Arm! arm! it is — it is — the cannon's opening roar!

Within a windowed niche of that high hall
Sate Brunswick's fated chieftain; he did hear
That sound the first amidst the festival,
And caught its tone with Death's prophetic ear;
And when they smiled because he deemed it near,
His heart more truly knew that peal too well
Which stretched his father on a bloody bier,
And roused the vengeance blood alone could quell:
He rushed into the field, and, foremost fighting, fell.

Ah! then and there was hurrying to and fro,
And gathering tears, and tremblings of distress,
And cheeks all pale, which, but an hour ago,
Blushed at the praise of their own loveliness.
And there were sudden partings, such as press
The life from out young hearts, and choking sighs
Which ne'er might be repeated; who would guess
If ever more should meet those mutual eyes,
Since upon night so sweet such awful morn could rise!

And there was mounting in hot haste; the steed,
The mustering squadron, and the clattering car,
Went pouring forward with impetuous speed,
And swiftly forming in the ranks of war;
And the deep thunder, peal on peal afar;
And near, the beat of the alarming drum
Roused up the soldier ere the morning star;
While thronged the citizens with terror dumb,
Or whispering, with white lips — "The foe! they come! they come!"

And wild and high the "Cameron's gathering" rose!
The war-note of Lochiel, which Albyn's hills
Have heard, and heard, too, have her Saxon foes —
How in the noon of night that pibroch thrills,
Savage and shrill! but with the breath which fills
Their mountain-pipe, so fill the mountaineers
With the fierce native daring which instils
The stirring memory of a thousand years;
And Evan's, Donald's fame rings in each clansman's ears.

And Ardennes waves above them her green leaves,
Dewy with nature's tear-drops, as they pass,
Grieving, if aught inanimate e'er grieves,
Over the unreturning brave — alas!

Ere evening to be trodden like the grass
Which now beneath them, but above shall grow
In its next verdure, when this fiery mass
Of living valor rolling on the foe,
And burning with high hope, shall moulder cold and low.

Last noon beheld them full of lusty life,
Last eve in Beauty's circle proudly gay;
The midnight brought the signal-sound of strife,
The morn the marshaling in arms, — the day
Battle's magnificently-stern array!
The thunder-clouds close o'er it, which, when rent,
The earth is covered thick with other clay,
Which her own clay shall cover, heaped and pent,
Rider and horse, — friend, foe, — in one red burial blent!

Lord Byron

XXXVI

The Lost Leader

Just for a handful of silver he left us,
    Just for a riband to stick in his coat —
Found the one gift of which fortune bereft us,
    Lost all the others she lets us devote;
They, with the gold to give, doled him out silver,
    So much was theirs who so little allowed:
How all our copper had gone for his service!
    Rags — were they purple, his heart had been proud!
We that had loved him so, followed him, honored him,
    Lived in his mild and magnificent eye,
Learned his great language, caught his clear accents,
    Made him our pattern to live and to die!

Shakespeare was of us, Milton was for us,
  Burns, Shelley, were with us, — they watch from their
    graves!
He alone breaks from the van and the freemen,
  — He alone sinks to the rear and the slaves!

We shall march prospering, — not thro' his presence;
  Songs may inspirit us, — not from his lyre;
Deeds will be done, — while he boasts his quiescence,
  Still bidding crouch whom the rest bade aspire:
Blot out his name, then, record one lost soul more,
  One task more declined, one more footpath untrod,
One more devil's-triumph and sorrow for angels,
  One wrong more to man, one more insult to God!
Life's night begins: let him never come back to us!
  There would be doubt, hesitation and pain,
Forced praise on our part — the glimmer of twilight,
  Never glad confident morning again!
Best fight on well, for we taught him — strike gallantly
  Menace our heart ere we master his own;
Then let him receive the new knowledge and wait us,
  Pardoned in heaven, the first by the throne!

Robert Browning

XXXVII

Memorial Verses on the Death of Wordsworth

1850

Goethe in Weimar sleeps, and Greece,
Long since, saw Byron's struggle cease.
But one such death remained to come —
The last poetic voice is dumb,
We stand to-day by Wordsworth's tomb.

When Byron's eyes were shut in death,
We bowed our head and held our breath.
He taught us little; but our soul
Had *felt* him like the thunder's roll.
With shivering heart the strife we saw
Of passion with eternal law;
And yet with reverential awe
We watched the fount of fiery life
Which served for that Titanic strife.

When Goethe's death was told, we said:
Sunk, then, is Europe's sagest head.
Physician of the iron age,
Goethe has done his pilgrimage.
He took the suffering human race,
He read each wound, each weakness clear;
And struck his finger on the place,
And said: *Thou ailest here, and here!*
He looked on Europe's dying hour
Of fitful dream and feverish power;
His eye plunged down the weltering strife,
The turmoil of expiring life —
He said: *The end is everywhere,*
Art still has truth, take refuge there!
And he was happy, if to know
Causes of things, and far below
His feet to see the lurid flow
Of terror, and insane distress,
And headlong fate, be happiness.

And Wordsworth! — Ah, pale ghosts, rejoice!
For never has such soothing voice
Been to your shadowy world conveyed,
Since erst, at morn, some wandering shade

Heard the clear song of Orpheus come
Through Hades, and the mournful gloom.
Wordsworth has gone from us — and ye,
Ah, may ye feel his voice as we!
He too upon a wintry clime
Had fallen — on this iron time
Of doubts, disputes, distractions, fears.
He found us when the age had bound
Our souls in its benumbing round;
He spoke, and loosed our heart in tears.
He laid us as we lay at birth
On the cool flowery lap of earth,
Smiles broke from us and we had ease;
The hills were round us, and the breeze
Went o'er the sun-lit fields again;
Our foreheads felt the wind and rain.
Our youth returned; for there was shed
On spirits that had long been dead,
Spirits dried up and closely furled,
The freshness of the early world.
Ah! since dark days still bring to light
Man's prudence and man's fiery might,
Time may restore us in his course
Goethe's sage mind and Byron's force;
But where will Europe's latter hour
Again find Wordsworth's healing power?
Others will teach us how to dare,
And against fear our breast to steel;
Others will strengthen us to bear —
But who, ah! who, will make us feel?
The cloud of mortal destiny,
Others will front it fearlessly —
But who, like him, will put it by?

Keep fresh the grass upon his grave
O Rotha, with thy living wave!
Sing him thy best! for few or none
Hears thy voice right, now he is gone.

Matthew Arnold

XXXVIII

Ode on the Death of the Duke of Wellington

1852

Bury the Great Duke
   With an empire's lamentation,
Let us bury the Great Duke
   To the noise of the mourning of a mighty nation,
Mourning when their leaders fall,
Warriors carry the warrior's pall,
And sorrow darkens hamlet and hall.

Where shall we lay the man whom we deplore?
Here, in streaming London's central roar.
Let the sound of those he wrought for,
And the feet of those he fought for,
Echo round his bones for evermore.

Lead out the pageant: sad and slow,
As fits an universal woe,
Let the long long procession go,
And let the sorrowing crowd about it grow,
And let the mournful martial music blow;
The last great Englishman is low.

Mourn, for to us he seems the last,
Remembering all his greatness in the Past.

No more in soldier fashion will he greet
With lifted hand the gazer in the street.
O friends, our chief state-oracle is mute:
Mourn for the man of long-enduring blood,
The statesman-warrior, moderate, resolute,
Whole in himself, a common good.
Mourn for the man of amplest influence,
Yet clearest of ambitious crime,
Our greatest yet with least pretence,
Great in council and great in war,
Foremost captain of his time,
Rich in saving common-sense,
And, as the greatest only are,
In his simplicity sublime.
O good gray head which all men knew,
O voice from which their omens all men drew,
O iron nerve to true occasion true,
O fall'n at length that tower of strength
Which stood four-square to all the winds that blew!
Such was he whom we deplore.
The long self-sacrifice of life is o'er.
The great World-victor's victor will be seen no more

All is over and done:
Render thanks to the Giver,
England, for thy son.
Let the bell be toll'd.
Render thanks to the Giver,
And render him to the mould.
Under the cross of gold
That shines over city and river,
There he shall rest forever
Among the wise and the bold.

Let the bell be toll'd:
And a reverent people behold
The towering car, the sable steeds:
Bright let it be with his blazon'd deeds,
Dark in its funeral fold.
Let the bell be toll'd:
And a deeper knell in the heart be knoll'd;
And the sound of the sorrowing anthem roll'd
Thro' the dome of the golden cross;
And the volleying cannon thunder his loss;
He knew their voices of old.
For many a time in many a clime
His captain's-ear has heard them boom
Bellowing victory, bellowing doom:
When he with those deep voices wrought,
Guarding realms and kings from shame;
With those deep voices our dead captain taught
The tyrant, and asserts his claim
In that dread sound to the great name,
Which he has worn so pure of blame,
In praise and in dispraise the same,
A man of well-attemper'd frame.
O civic muse, to such a name,
To such a name for ages long,
To such a name,
Preserve a broad approach of fame,
And ever-echoing avenues of song.

Who is he that cometh, like an honor'd guest,
With banner and with music, with soldier and with priest,
With a nation weeping, and breaking on my rest?
Mighty Seaman, this is he
Was great by land as thou by sea.

Thine island loves thee well, thou famous man,
The greatest sailor since our world began.
Now, to the roll of muffled drums,
To thee the greatest soldier comes;
For this is he
Was great by land as thou by sea;
His foes were thine; he kept us free;
O give him welcome, this is he
Worthy of our gorgeous rites,
And worthy to be laid by thee;
For this is England's greatest son,
He that gain'd a hundred fights,
Nor ever lost an English gun;
This is he that far away
Against the myriads of Assaye
Clash'd with his fiery few and won;
And underneath another sun,
Warring on a later day,
Round affrighted Lisbon drew
The treble works, the vast designs
Of his labor'd rampart-lines,
Where he greatly stood at bay,
Whence he issued forth anew,
And ever great and greater grew,
Beating from the wasted vines
Back to France her banded swarms,
Back to France with countless blows,
Till o'er the hills her eagles flew
Beyond the Pyrenean pines,
Follow'd up in valley and glen
With blare of bugle, clamor of men,
Roll of cannon and clash of arms,
And England pouring on her foes.

Such a war had such a close.
Again their ravening eagle rose
In anger, wheel'd on Europe-shadowing wings,
And barking for the thrones of kings;
Till one that sought but Duty's iron crown
On that loud sabbath shook the spoiler down;
A day of onsets of despair!
Dash'd on every rocky square
Their surging charges foam'd themselves away;
Last, the Prussian trumpet blew:
Thro' the long-tormented air
Heaven flash'd a sudden jubilant ray,
And down we swept and charged and overthrew.
So great a soldier taught us there,
What long-enduring hearts could do
In that world-earthquake, Waterloo!
Mighty Seaman, tender and true,
And pure as he from taint of craven guile,
O savior of the silver-coasted isle,
O shaker of the Baltic and the Nile,
If aught of things that here befall
Touch a spirit among things divine,
If love of country move thee there at all,
Be glad, because his bones are laid by thine!
And thro' the centuries let a people's voice
In full acclaim,
A people's voice,
The proof and echo of all human fame,
A people's voice, when they rejoice
At civic revel and pomp and game,
Attest their great commander's claim
With honor, honor, honor, honor to him,
Eternal honor to his name.

A people's voice ! we are a people yet.
Tho' all men else their nobler dreams forget
Confused by brainless mobs and lawless Powers;
Thank Him who isled us here, and roughly set
His Briton in blown seas and storming showers,
We have a voice, with which to pay the debt
Of boundless love and reverence and regret
To those great men who fought, and kept it ours.
And keep it ours, O God, from brute control;
O Statesmen, guard us, guard the eye, the soul
Of Europe, keep our noble England whole,
And save the one true seed of freedom sown
Betwixt a people and their ancient throne,
That sober freedom out of which there springs
Our loyal passion for our temperate kings;
For, saving that, ye help to save mankind
Till public wrong be crumbled into dust,
And drill the raw world for the march of mind,
Till crowds at length be sane and crowns be just.
But wink no more in slothful overtrust.
Remember him who led your hosts;
He bade you guard the sacred coasts.
Your cannons moulder on the seaward wall;
His voice is silent in your council-hall
Forever; and whatever tempests lower
Forever silent; even if they broke
In thunder, silent; yet remember all
He spoke among you, and the Man who spoke;
Who never sold the truth to serve the hour,
Nor palter'd with Eternal God for power;
Who let the turbid streams of rumor flow
Thro' either babbling world of high and low;
Whose life was work, whose language rife

Ode on the Death of the Duke of Wellington

With rugged maxims hewn from life;
Who never spoke against a foe;
Whose eighty winters freeze with one rebuke
All great self-seekers trampling on the right:
Truth-teller was our England's Alfred named;
Truth-lover was our English Duke;
Whatever record leap to light
He never shall be shamed.

Lo, the leader in these glorious wars
Now to glorious burial slowly borne,
Follow'd by the brave of other lands,
He, on whom from both her open hands
Lavish Honor shower'd all her stars,
And affluent Fortune emptied all her horn.
Yea, let all good things await
Him who cares not to be great,
But as he saves or serves the state.
Not once or twice in our rough island-story,
The path of duty was the way to glory:
He that walks it, only thirsting
For the right, and learns to deaden
Love of self, before his journey closes,
He shall find the stubborn thistle bursting
Into glossy purples, which outredden
All voluptuous garden-roses.
Not once or twice in our fair island-story,
The path of duty was the way to glory:
He, that ever following her commands,
On with toil of heart and knees and hands,
Thro' the long gorge to the far light has won
His path upward, and prevail'd,
Shall find the toppling crags of Duty scaled
Are close upon the shining table-lands

To which our God Himself is moon and sun.
Such was he: his work is done.
But while the races of mankind endure,
Let his great example stand
Colossal, seen of every land,
And keep the soldier firm, the statesman pure;
Till in all lands and thro' all human story
The path of duty be the way to glory:
And let the land whose hearths he saved from shame
For many and many an age proclaim
At civic revel and pomp and game,
And when the long-illumined cities flame,
Their ever-loyal iron leader's fame,
With honor, honor, honor, honor to him,
Eternal honor to his name.

Peace, his triumph will be sung
By some yet unmoulded tongue
Far on in summers that we shall not see:
Peace, it is a day of pain
For one about whose patriarchal knee
Late the little children clung:
O peace, it is a day of pain
For one, upon whose hand and heart and brain
Once the weight and fate of Europe hung.
Ours the pain, be his the gain!
More than is of man's degree
Must be with us, watching here
At this, our great solemnity.
Whom we see not we revere;
We revere, and we refrain
From talk of battles loud and vain,
And brawling memories all too free
For such a wise humility

Ode on the Death of the Duke of Wellington

As befits a solemn fane:
We revere, and while we hear
The tides of Music's golden sea
Setting toward eternity,
Uplifted high in heart and hope are we,
Until we doubt not that for one so true
There must be other nobler work to do
Than when he fought at Waterloo,
And Victor he must ever be.
For tho' the Giant Ages heave the hill
And break the shore, and evermore
Make and break, and work their will;
Tho' world on world in myriad myriads roll
Round us, each with different powers,
And other forms of life than ours,
What know we greater than the soul?
On God and Godlike men we build our trust.
Hush, the Dead March wails in the people's ears:
The dark crowd moves, and there are sobs and tears:
The black earth yawns: the mortal disappears;
Ashes to ashes, dust to dust;
He is gone who seem'd so great. —
Gone; but nothing can bereave him
Of the force he made his own
Being here, and we believe him
Something far advanced in State,
And that he wears a truer crown
Than any wreath that man can weave him.
Speak no more of his renown,
Lay your earthly fancies down,
And in the vast cathedral leave him,
God accept him, Christ receive him.

Alfred Tennyson

XXXIX

The Loss of the "Birkenhead"

1852

Right on our flank the crimson sun went down,
  The deep sea rolled around in dark repose,
When, like the wild shriek from some captured town,
    A cry of women rose.

The stout ship *Birkenhead* lay hard and fast,
  Caught, without hope, upon a hidden rock;
Her timbers thrilled as nerves, when through them passed
    The spirit of that shock.

And ever like base cowards, who leave their ranks
  In danger's hour, before the rush of steel,
Drifted away, disorderly, the planks
    From underneath her keel.

Confusion spread, for, though the coast seemed near,
  Sharks hovered thick along that white sea-brink.
The boats could hold? — not all; and it was clear
    She was about to sink.

"Out with those boats, and let us haste away,"
  Cried one, "ere yet yon sea the bark devours."
The man thus clamoring was, I scarce need say,
    No officer of ours.

We knew our duty better than to care
  For such loose babblers, and made no reply,
Till our good colonel gave the word, and there
    Formed us in line to die.

There rose no murmur from the ranks, no thought,
  By shameful strength, unhonored life to seek;
Our post to quit we were not trained, nor taught
    To trample down the weak.

So we made women with their children go,
  The oars ply back again, and yet again;
Whilst, inch by inch, the drowning ship sank low,
    Still under steadfast men.

What follows, why recall? The brave who died,
  Died without flinching in the bloody surf;
They sleep as well, beneath that purple tide,
    As others, under turf; —

They sleep as well, and, roused from their wild grave,
  Wearing their wounds like stars, shall rise again,
Joint-heirs with Christ, because they bled to save
    His weak ones, not in vain.

If that day's work no clasp or medal mark,
  If each proud heart no cross of bronze may press,
Nor cannon thunder loud from Tower and Park,
    This feel we, none the less:

That those whom God's high grace there saved from ill —
  Those also, left His martyrs in the bay —
Though not by siege, though not in battle, still
    Full well had earned their pay.

Sir Francis Hastings Doyle

XL

The Charge of the Light Brigade

1854

Half a league, half a league,
Half a league onward,
All in the valley of Death
   Rode the six hundred.
"Forward, the Light Brigade!
Charge for the guns!" he said:
Into the valley of Death
   Rode the six hundred.

"Forward, the Light Brigade!"
Was there a man dismay'd?
Not tho' the soldier knew
   Some one had blundered.
Theirs not to make reply,
Theirs not to reason why,
Theirs but to do and die:
Into the valley of Death
   Rode the six hundred.

Cannon to right of them,
Cannon to left of them,
Cannon in front of them
   Volley'd and thunder'd;
Storm'd at with shot and shell,
Boldly they rode and well:
Into the jaws of Death,
Into the mouth of Hell
   Rode the six hundred.

Flash'd all their sabres bare,
Flash'd as they turn'd in air
Sabring the gunners there,
Charging an army, while
　All the world wonder'd:
Plunged in the battery-smoke,
Right through the line they broke;
Cossack and Russian
Reel'd from the sabre-stroke
　Shatter'd and sunder'd.
Then they rode back, but not,
　Not the six hundred.

Cannon to right of them,
Cannon to left of them,
Cannon behind them
　Volley'd and thunder'd;
Storm'd at with shot and shell,
While horse and hero fell,
They that had fought so well
Came through the jaws of Death
Back from the mouth of Hell,
All that was left of them,
　Left of six hundred.

When can their glory fade?
O, the wild charge they made!
　All the world wonder'd.
Honor the charge they made!
Honor the Light Brigade,
　Noble six hundred!

Alfred Tennyson

XLI

Santa Filomena

(A Tribute to Florence Nightingale)

1854

Whene'er a noble deed is wrought,
Whene'er is spoken a noble thought,
   Our hearts, in glad surprise,
   To higher levels rise.

The tidal wave of deeper souls
Into our inmost being rolls,
   And lifts us unawares
   Out of all meaner cares.

Honor to those whose words or deeds
Thus help us in our daily needs,
   And by their overflow
   Raise us from what is low!

Thus thought I, as by night I read
Of the great army of the dead,
   The trenches cold and damp,
   The starved and frozen camp, —

The wounded from the battle-plain,
In dreary hospitals of pain,
   The cheerless corridors,
   The cold and stony floors.

Lo! in that house of misery
A lady with a lamp I see
   Pass through the glimmering gloom,
   And flit from room to room.

And slow, as in a dream of bliss,
The speechless sufferer turns to kiss
   Her shadow, as it falls
   Upon the darkening walls.

As if a door in heaven should be
Opened and then closed suddenly,
   The vision came and went,
   The light shone and was spent.

On England's annals, through the long
Hereafter of her speech and song,
   That light its rays shall cast
   From portals of the past.

A Lady with a Lamp shall stand
In the great history of the land,
   A noble type of good,
   Heroic womanhood.

Nor even shall be wanting here
The palm, the lily, and the spear,
   The symbols that of yore
   Saint Filomena bore.

Henry W. Longfellow

XLII

The Song of the Camp

1855

"Give us a song!" the soldiers cried,
   The outer trenches guarding,
When the heated guns of the camps allied
   Grew weary of bombarding.

The dark Redan, in silent scoff,
    Lay, grim and threatening, under;
And the tawny mound of the Malakoff
    No longer belched its thunder.

There was a pause. A guardsman said:
    "We storm the forts to-morrow;
Sing while we may, another day
    Will bring enough of sorrow."

They lay along the battery's side,
    Below the smoking cannon, —
Brave hearts from Severn and from Clyde
    And from the banks of Shannon.

They sang of love, and not of fame;
    Forgot was Britain's glory;
Each heart recalled a different name,
    But all sang *Annie Laurie*.

Voice after voice caught up the song,
    Until its tender passion
Rose like an anthem, rich and strong,
    Their battle-eve confession.

Dear girl, her name he dared not speak,
    But, as the song grew louder,
Something upon the soldier's cheek
    Washed off the stains of powder.

Beyond the darkening ocean burned
    The bloody sunset's embers,
While the Crimean valleys learned
    How English love remembers.

And once again a fire of hell
  Rained on the Russian quarters,
With scream of shot, and burst of shell,
  And bellowing of the mortars!

And Irish Nora's eyes are dim
  For a singer, dumb and gory;
And English Mary mourns for him
  Who sang of *Annie Laurie*.

Sleep, soldiers! still in honored rest
  Your truth and valor wearing;
The bravest are the tenderest, —
  The loving are the daring.

Bayard Taylor

XLIII

The Relief of Lucknow

1857

Oh, that last day in Lucknow fort!
  We knew that it was the last;
That the enemy's mines crept surely in,
  And the end was coming fast.

To yield to that foe meant worse than death;
  And the men and we all worked on;
It was one day more of smoke and roar,
  And then it would all be done.

There was one of us, a corporal's wife,
  A fair, young, gentle thing,
Wasted with fever in the siege,
  And her mind was wandering.

She lay on the ground, in her Scottish plaid,
   And I took her head on my knee;
"When my father comes hame frae the pleugh,"
    she said,
   "Oh! then please wauken me."

She slept like a child on her father's floor,
   In the flecking of wood-bine shade,
When the house-dog sprawls by the open door,
   And the mother's wheel is stayed.

It was smoke and roar and powder-stench,
   And hopeless waiting for death;
And the soldier's wife, like a full-tired child,
   Seemed scarce to draw her breath.

I sank to sleep; and I had my dream
   Of an English village-lane,
And wall and garden; but one wild scream
   Brought me back to the roar again.

There Jessie Brown stood listening
   Till a sudden gladness broke
All over her face; and she caught my hand
   And drew me near and spoke:

"The Hielanders! Oh! dinna ye hear
   The slogan far awa?
The McGregor's? Oh! I ken it weel;
   It's the grandest o' them a'!

"God bless thae bonny Hielanders!
   We're saved! we're saved!" she cried;
And fell on her knees; and thanks to God
   Flowed forth like a full flood-tide.

The Relief of Lucknow

Along the battery line her cry
    Had fallen among the men,
And they started back; — they were there to die;
    But was life so near them, then?

They listened for life; the rattling fire
    Far off, and the far-off roar,
Were all; and the colonel shook his head,
    And they turned to their guns once more.

Then Jessie said, "That slogan's done;
    But can ye hear them noo,
The Campbells are comin'?   It's no a dream;
    Our succors hae broken through."

We heard the roar and the rattle afar,
    But the pipes we could not hear;
So the men plied their work of hopeless war,
    And knew that the end was near.

It was not long ere it made its way,
    A thrilling, ceaseless sound:
It was no noise from the strife afar,
    Or the sappers under ground.

It *was* the pipers of the Highlanders!
    And now they played *Auld Lang Syne*.
It came to our men like the voice of God,
    And they shouted along the line.

And they wept, and shook one another's hands,
    And the women sobbed in a crowd;
And every one knelt down where he stood,
    And we all thanked God aloud.

That happy day, when we welcomed them,
    Our men put Jessie first;
And the general gave her his hand, and cheers
    Like a storm from the soldiers burst.

And the pipers' ribbons and tartan streamed,
    Marching round and round our line;
And our joyful cheers were broken with tears,
    As the pipes played *Auld Lang Syne*.

Robert Trail Spence Lowell

XLIV

The March of the Workers

1885

What is this, the sound and rumor? What is this that all men hear,
Like the wind in hollow valleys when the storm is drawing near,
Like the rolling on of ocean in the eventide of fear?
    'T is the people marching on.

Whither go they, and whence come they? What are these of whom ye tell?
In what country are they dwelling 'twixt the gates of heaven and hell?
Are they mine or thine for money? Will they serve a master well?
    Still the rumor's marching on.
    Hark the rolling of the thunder!
    Lo, the sun! and lo, thereunder,
    Riseth wrath, and hope, and wonder,
    And the host comes marching on.

Forth they come from grief and torment; on they wend
toward health and mirth,
All the wide world is their dwelling, every corner of the
earth.
Buy them, sell them for thy service! Try the bargain
what 't is worth
    For the days are marching on.

These are they who build thy houses, weave thy raiment,
win thy wheat,
Smooth the rugged, fill the barren, turn the bitter into
sweet.
All for thee this day — and ever. What reward for them
is meet?
    Till the host comes marching on.
    Hark the rolling of the thunder!
    Lo, the sun! and lo, thereunder,
    Riseth wrath, and hope, and wonder,
    And the host comes marching on.

Many a hundred years passed over have they labored deaf
and blind;
Never tidings reached their sorrow, never hope their toil
might find.
Now at last they 've heard and hear it, and the cry comes
down the wind,
    And their feet are marching on.

O ye rich men hear and tremble! for with words the sound
is rife:
"Once for you and death we labored; changed hencefor-
ward is the strife.
We are men, and we shall battle for the world of men and life;

                And our host is marching on."
            Hark the rolling of the thunder!
            Lo, the sun! and lo, thereunder,
            Riseth wrath, and hope, and wonder,
                And the host comes marching on.

"Is it war, then? Will ye perish as the dry wood in the fire?
Is it peace? Then be ye of us, let your hope be our desire.
Come and live! for life awaketh, and the world shall never
    tire;
                And hope is marching on."

"On we march then, we the workers, and the rumor that
    ye hear
Is the blended sound of battle and deliv'rance drawing near;
For the hope of every creature is the banner that we bear,
                And the world is marching on."
            Hark the rolling of the thunder!
            Lo, the sun! and lo, thereunder,
            Riseth wrath, and hope, and wonder,
                And the host comes marching on.

William Morris

XLV

Recessional

1897

God of our fathers, known of old —
    Lord of our far-flung battle-line —
Beneath Whose awful Hand we hold
    Dominion over palm and pine —
Lord God of Hosts, be with us yet,
Lest we forget — lest we forget!

Recessional

The tumult and the shouting dies —
  The captains and the kings depart —
Still stands Thine ancient Sacrifice,
  An humble and a contrite heart.
Lord God of Hosts, be with us yet,
Lest we forget — lest we forget!

Far-called our navies melt away —
  On dune and headland sinks the fire —
Lo, all our pomp of yesterday
  Is one with Nineveh and Tyre!
Judge of the Nations, spare us yet,
Lest we forget — lest we forget!

If, drunk with sight of power, we loose
  Wild tongues that have not Thee in awe —
Such boasting as the Gentiles use
  Or lesser breeds without the Law —
Lord God of Hosts, be with us yet,
Lest we forget — lest we forget!

For heathen heart that puts her trust
  In reeking tube and iron shard,
All valiant dust that builds on dust,
  And guarding calls not Thee to guard —
For frantic boast and foolish word,
Thy mercy on Thy People, Lord!
                    Amen.
                        Rudyard Kipling

MISCELLANEOUS SONGS AND BALLADS

XLVI

Barbara Allen

All in the merry month of May,
  When green buds they were swelling,
Young Jemmy Grove on his death-bed lay
  For love o' Barbara Allen.

He sent his man unto her then,
  To the town where she was dwelling:
"O haste and come to my master dear,
  If your name be Barbara Allen."

Slowly, slowly rase she up,
  And she cam' where he was lying;
And when she drew the curtain by,
  Says, "Young man, I think you're dying."

"O it's I am sick, and very, very sick,
  And it's a' for Barbara Allen."
"O the better for me ye'se never be,
  Tho' your heart's blude were a-spilling!

"O dinna ye min', young man," she says,
  "When the red wine ye were filling,
That ye made the healths gae round and round,
  And ye slighted Barbara Allen?"

He turn'd his face unto the wa',
   And death was wi' him dealing:
"Adieu, adieu, my dear friends a';
   Be kind to Barbara Allen."

As she was walking o'er the fields,
   She heard the dead-bell knelling;
And every jow the dead-bell gave,
   It cried, "Woe to Barbara Allen!"

"O mother, mother, mak' my bed,
   To lay me down in sorrow.
My love has died for me to-day,
   I'll die for him to-morrow."

Anonymous

XLVII

The Bailiff's Daughter of Islington

There was a youth, and a well-beloved youth,
   And he was a squire's son;
He loved a bailiff's daughter dear,
   That lived in Islington.

Yet she, being coy, would not believe
   That he did love her so,
Nor would she any countenance
   Unto this young man show.

But when his friends did understand
   His fond and foolish mind,
They sent him up to fair London,
   An apprentice him to bind.

And now he 's gone 't is seven long years,
    And never his love could see:
"O many a tear have I shed for her sake,
    When she little thought of me!"

One day the maids of Islington
    Went forth to sport and play;
And then the bailiff's daughter dear,
    She secretly stole away.

She pull'd off her pretty gown of pink,
    And put on ragged attire,
And to fair London she would go,
    For her true love to enquire.

And as she went along the road,
    The weather being hot and dry,
She sat her down on a grassy bank,
    And her true love came riding by.

She started up, with a color so red;
    Catching hold of his bridle-rein:
"One penny, one penny, kind sir," she said,
    "Would ease me of much pain."

"Before I give you one penny, sweetheart,
    Pray tell me where you were born."
"At Islington, kind sir," said she,
    "Where I have had many a scorn."

"I prithee, sweetheart, then tell to me,
    O tell me whether you know
The bailiff's daughter of Islington?"
    "She is dead, sir, long ago."

"If she be dead, then take my horse,
  My saddle and bridle also;
For I'll sail away for some far country,
  Where no man shall me know."

"O stay, good youth! O look, dear love!
  She standeth by thy side;
She's here alive, she is not dead,
  She's ready to be thy bride."

"O farewell grief, and welcome joy,
  Ten thousand times, therefore!
For now I have found mine own true love,
  Whom I thought I should never see more."

Anonymous

XLVIII

My True-Love hath my Heart

My true-love hath my heart, and I have his,
By just exchange one for the other given:
I hold his dear, and mine he cannot miss;
There never was a better bargain driven:
  My true-love hath my heart, and I have his.

His heart in me keeps him and me in one,
My heart in him his thoughts and senses guides:
He loves my heart, for once it was his own,
I cherish his because in me it bides:
  My true-love hath my heart, and I have his.

Sir Philip Sidney

XLIX

Who is Silvia?

Who is Silvia? what is she,
    That all our swains commend her?
Holy, fair, and wise is she;
    The heaven such grace did lend her,
That she might admired be.

Is she kind as she is fair?
    For beauty lives with kindness.
Love doth to her eyes repair,
    To help him of his blindness,
And, being helped, inhabits there.

Then to Silvia let us sing,
    That Silvia is excelling;
She excels each mortal thing
    Upon the dull earth dwelling:
To her let us garlands bring.

Shakespeare

L

Take, O, Take those Lips Away

Take, O, take those lips away,
    That so sweetly were forsworn;
And those eyes, the break of day,
    Lights that do mislead the morn:
But my kisses bring again,
        Bring again;
Seals of love, but sealed in vain,
        Sealed in vain.

Shakespeare

LI

Blow, Blow, Thou Winter Wind

> Blow, blow, thou winter wind,
> Thou art not so unkind
>   As man's ingratitude;
> Thy tooth is not so keen,
> Because thou art not seen,
>   Although thy breath be rude.
>
> Heigh ho! sing, heigh ho! unto the green holly:
> Most friendship is feigning, most loving mere folly:
>   Then, heigh ho, the holly!
>   This life is most jolly.
>
> Freeze, freeze, thou bitter sky,
> That dost not bite so nigh
>   As benefits forgot:
> Though thou the waters warp,
> Thy sting is not so sharp
>   As friend remembered not.
> Heigh ho! sing, heigh ho! etc.

Shakespeare

LII

To Celia

> Drink to me only with thine eyes,
>   And I will pledge with mine;
> Or leave a kiss but in the cup
>   And I'll not look for wine.

The thirst that from the soul doth rise,
  Doth ask a drink divine;
But might I of Jove's nectar sup,
  I would not change for thine.

I sent thee late a rosy wreath,
  Not so much honoring thee
As giving it a hope that there
  It could not wither'd be;
But thou thereon didst only breathe
  And sent'st it back to me;
Since when it grows, and smells, I swear,
  Not of itself but thee!

Ben Jonson

LIII

You Gentlemen of England

You Gentlemen of England,
  That live at home at ease,
How little do you think upon
  The dangers of the seas;
Give ear unto the mariners,
  And they will plainly show
All the cares and the fears
  When the stormy winds do blow.

The sailor must have courage,
  No danger must he shun;
In every kind of weather
  His course he still must run;

Now mounted on the top-mast,
    How dreadful 't is below!
Then we ride, as the tide,
    When the stormy winds do blow.

If enemies oppose us,
    And England is at war
With any foreign nation,
    We fear not wound nor scar.
To humble them, come on, lads,
    Their flags we 'll soon lay low;
Clear the way for the fray,
    Tho' the stormy winds do blow.

Sometimes in Neptune's bosom
    Our ship is toss'd by waves,
And every man expecting
    The sea to be our graves;
Then up aloft she 's mounted,
    And down again so low,
In the waves, on the seas,
    When the stormy winds do blow.

But when the danger 's over,
    And safe we come on shore,
The horrors of the tempest
    We think about no more;
The flowing bowl invites us,
    And joyfully we go,
All the day drink away,
    Tho' the stormy winds do blow.

        The words altered from *Martin Parker*

LIV

Sally in our Alley

Of all the girls that are so smart
   There 's none like pretty Sally;
She is the darling of my heart,
   And she lives in our alley.
There is no lady in the land
   Is half so sweet as Sally;
She is the darling of my heart,
   And she lives in our alley.

Her father he makes cabbage-nets
   And through the streets does cry 'em;
Her mother she sells laces long
   To such as please to buy 'em;
But sure such folks could ne'er beget
   So sweet a girl as Sally!
She is the darling of my heart,
   And she lives in our alley.

When she is by, I leave my work,
   I love her so sincerely;
My master comes like any Turk,
   And bangs me most severely —
But let him bang his bellyful,
   I 'll bear it all for Sally;
She is the darling of my heart,
   And she lives in our alley.

Of all the days that 's in the week
   I dearly love but one day —

Sally in our Alley

And that's the day that comes betwixt
   A Saturday and Monday;
For then I'm drest all in my best
   To walk abroad with Sally;
She is the darling of my heart,
   And she lives in our alley.

My master carries me to church,
   And often am I blamèd
Because I leave him in the lurch
   As soon as text is namèd;
I leave the church in sermon-time
   And slink away to Sally;
She is the darling of my heart,
   And she lives in our alley.

When Christmas comes about again
   O then I shall have money;
I'll hoard it up, and box it all,
   I'll give it to my honey;
I would it were ten thousand pound,
   I'd give it all to Sally;
She is the darling of my heart,
   And she lives in our alley.

My master and the neighbors all
   Make game of me and Sally;
And, but for her, I'd better be
   A slave and row a galley;
But when my seven long years are out
   O then I'll marry Sally, —
O then we'll wed, and then we'll bed,
   But not in our alley!

H. Carey

LV

The Vicar of Bray

In good King Charles's golden days,
    When loyalty no harm meant,
A zealous high-churchman was I,
    And so I got preferment,
To teach my flock, I never miss'd,
    Kings were by God appointed,
And lost all those that dare resist,
    Or touch the Lord's anointed.
And this is law that I'll maintain,
    Until my dying day, Sir,
That whatsoever king shall reign,
    I'll still be Vicar of Bray, Sir.

When royal James possess'd the crown,
    And Popery came in fashion,
The penal laws I hooted down,
    And read the Declaration:
The Church of Rome I found would fit
    Full well my constitution.
And I had been a Jesuit,
    But for the Revolution.
And this is law, etc.

When William was our king declar'd,
    To ease the nation's grievance,
With this new wind about I steer'd,
    And swore to him allegiance.
Old principles I did revoke,
    Set conscience at a distance;

Passive obedience was a joke,
    A jest was non-resistance.
And this is law, etc.

When royal Anne became our queen,
    The Church of England's glory,
Another face of things was seen,
    And I became a Tory:
Occasional conformists base,
    I blam'd their moderation;
And thought the Church in danger was,
    By such prevarication.
And this is law, etc.

When George in pudding-time came o'er,
    And moderate men look'd big, Sir,
My principles I chang'd once more,
    And so became a Whig, Sir;
And thus preferment I procur'd
    From our new faith's-defender;
And almost every day abjur'd
    The Pope and the Pretender.
And this is law, etc.

Th' illustrious house of Hanover,
    And Protestant succession,
To them I do allegiance swear —
    While they can hold possession;
For in my faith and loyalty
    I never more will falter,
And George my lawful king shall be —
    Until the times do alter.
And this is law, etc.

Anonymous

LVI

The Lass of Richmond Hill

On Richmond Hill there lives a lass,
   More sweet than May-day morn,
Whose charms all other maids' surpass.
   A rose without a thorn.
This lass so neat, with smiles so sweet,
   Has won my right good will,
I 'd crowns resign to call her mine
   Sweet lass of Richmond Hill!
Sweet lass of Richmond Hill! Sweet lass of Richmond Hill!
   I 'd crowns resign to call her mine;
     Sweet lass of Richmond Hill!

Ye Zephyrs gay, that fan the air,
   And wanton through the grove,
Oh! whisper to my charming fair,
   I die for her, and love.
This lass so neat, etc.

How happy will the shepherd be,
   Who calls this nymph his own;—
Oh! may her choice be fix'd on me,
   Mine 's fix'd on her alone.
This lass so neat, etc.

McNally

LVII

A Wet Sheet and a Flowing Sea

A wet sheet and a flowing sea,
   A wind that follows fast
And fills the white and rustling sail
   And bends the gallant mast;
And bends the gallant mast, my boys,
   While like the eagle free
Away the good ship flies, and leaves
   Old England on the lee.

O for a soft and gentle wind!
   I heard a fair one cry;
But give to me the snoring breeze
   And white waves heaving high;
And white waves heaving high, my lads,
   The good ship tight and free —
The world of waters is our home,
   And merry men are we.

There 's tempest in yon hornèd moon,
   And lightning in yon cloud;
But hark the music, mariners!
   The wind is piping loud;
The wind is piping loud, my boys,
   The lightning flashes free —
While the hollow oak our palace is,
   Our heritage the sea.

A. Cunningham

LVIII

Poor Tom Bowling

Here, a sheer hulk, lies poor Tom Bowling,
    The darling of our crew,
No more he'll hear the tempest howling,
    For Death has broach'd him to:
His form was of the manliest beauty,
    His heart was kind and soft;
Faithful below he did his duty,
    And now he's gone aloft.

Tom never from his word departed,
    His virtues were so rare;
His friends were many, and true-hearted,
    His Poll was kind and fair:
And then he'd sing so blithe and jolly, —
    Ah, many's the time and oft!
But mirth is turn'd to melancholy,
    For Tom is gone aloft.

Yet shall poor Tom find pleasant weather,
    When He who all commands
Shall give, to call life's crew together,
    The word to pipe all hands.
Thus Death, who kings and tars despatches,
    In vain Tom's life has doff'd;
For though his body's under hatches,
    His soul is gone aloft.

C. Dibdin

BOOK THIRD — POEMS OF SCOTLAND: HISTORICAL AND PATRIOTIC

LIX

This is my Own, my Native Land

Breathes there the man, with soul so dead,
Who never to himself hath said,
  This is my own, my native land!
Whose heart hath ne'er within him burn'd,
As home his footsteps he hath turn'd,
  From wandering on a foreign strand!
If such there breathe, go, mark him well;
For him no minstrel raptures swell;
High though his titles, proud his name,
Boundless his wealth as wish can claim:
Despite those titles, power, and pelf,
The wretch, concentred all in self,
Living, shall forfeit fair renown,
And, doubly dying, shall go down
To the vile dust, from whence he sprung,
Unwept, unhonor'd, and unsung.

O Caledonia! stern and wild,
Meet nurse for a poetic child!

Land of brown heath and shaggy wood,
Land of the mountain and the flood,
Land of my sires! what mortal hand
Can e'er untie the filial band,
That knits me to thy rugged strand!
Still, as I view each well-known scene,
Think what is now, and what hath been,
Seems as, to me, of all bereft,
Sole friends thy woods and streams were left;
And thus I love them better still,
Even in extremity of ill.
By Yarrow's streams still let me stray,
Though none should guide my feeble way;
Still feel the breeze down Ettrick break,
Although it chill my wither'd cheek;
Still lay my head by Teviot Stone,
Though there, forgotten and alone,
The Bard may draw his parting groan.

Sir Walter Scott

LX

Bannockburn

ROBERT BRUCE'S ADDRESS TO HIS ARMY

1314

Scots, wha hae wi' Wallace bled —
Scots, wham Bruce has aften led —
Welcome to your gory bed,
    Or to victorie!

Now 's the day, and now 's the hour;
See the front o' battle lower;
See approach proud Edward's power —
    Chains and slaverie!

Wha will be a traitor knave?
Wha can fill a coward's grave?
Wha sae base as be a slave?
    Let him turn and flee!

Wha for Scotland's king and law
Freedom's sword will strongly draw,
Freeman stand or freeman fa' —
    Let him follow me!

By oppression's woes and pains!
By your sons in servile chains!
We will drain our dearest veins,
    But they shall be free!

Lay the proud usurpers low!
Tyrants fall in every foe!
Liberty 's in every blow!
    Let us do, or die!

Robert Burns

LXI

Gathering Song of Donald the Black

1431

Pibroch of Donuil Dhu, pibroch of Donuil,
Wake thy wild voice anew, summon Clan-Conuil.
Come away, come away, hark to the summons!
Come in your war array, gentles and commons.

Come from deep glen, and from mountain so rocky,
The war-pipe and pennon are at Inverlochy.
Come every hill-plaid, and true heart that wears one,
Come every steel blade, and strong hand that bears one.

Leave untended the herd, the flock without shelter;
Leave the corpse uninterred, the bride at the altar;
Leave the deer, leave the steer, leave nets and barges:
Come with your fighting gear, broadswords and targes.

Come as the winds come, when forests are rended;
Come as the waves come, when navies are stranded:
Faster come, faster come, faster and faster,
Chief, vassal, page, and groom, tenant and master.

Fast they come, fast they come; see how they gather!
Wide waves the eagle plume, blended with heather.
Cast your plaids, draw your blades, forward each man set!
Pibroch of Donuil Dhu, knell for the onset!

Sir Walter Scott

LXII

The Flowers of the Forest; or, The Battle of Floden

1513

PART FIRST

I 've heard them lilting,
    At our yews' milking, —
Lasses a' lilting afore break of day;
    But now there 's a moaning
    On ilka green loaning
The Flowers of the Forest are a' wede away.

The Flowers of the Forest

At the bughts, in the morning,
  Nae blithe lads are scorning;
The lasses are lonely, and dowie, and wae:
  Nae daffing, nae gabbing,
  But sighing and sabbing,
Ilk lass takes her leglin, and hies her away.

At e'en in the gloaming,
  Nae swankies are roaming,
'Bout stacks wi' the lasses, at bogle to play;
  But ilk ane sits dreary,
  Lamenting her deary, —
The Flowers of the Forest are a' wede away.

In har'st, at the shearing,
  Nae younkers are jeering,
The bandsters are runkled, lieard, and gray;
  At fair and at preaching,
  Nae wooing, nae fleeching,
The Flowers of the Forest are a' wede away.

O dool for the order,
  Sent them to the border,
The English for anes by guile got the day;
  The Flowers of the Forest,
  That aye shone the fairest,
The prime of our land lies cauld in the clay.
  And now there 's a' moaning,
  On ilka green loaning,
The women and bairns are dowie and wae;
  There 'll be nae mair lilting,
  At our yews' milking,
The Flowers of the Forest are a' wede away.

Jane Elliott

Part Second

I 've seen the smiling,
Of Fortune beguiling,
I 've felt all her favors, and found her decay;
Sweet were her blessings,
Most kind her caressings,
But now they are dead, or a' fled away.
I 've seen the Forest,
Adorn'd of the foremost,
With flowers of the fairest, most pleasant, and gay.
Sae bonny their blooming,
Their scent sae perfuming,
But now they are wither'd, and a' wede away.

I 've seen the morning,
With gold hills adorning,
And the red storm roaring before middle-day.
I 've seen Tweed streaming,
With sunbeams a-shining,
Turn drumlie and dark as he roll'd on his way; —
O fickle Fortune,
Why this cruel sporting,
Why still thus perplex us, poor sons of a day?
No more thy frowns fear me,
No more thy smiles cheer me,
Since the Flowers of the Forest are a' wede away.

Alison Rutherford
(*Mrs. Patr. Cockburn of Ormiston*)

LXIII

Blue Bonnets over the Border

c. 1560

March, march, Ettrick and Teviotdale;
　Why the deil dinna ye march forward in order?
March, march, Eskdale and Liddesdale,
　All the Blue Bonnets are bound for the Border:
　　Many a banner spread
　　Flutters above your head,
Many a crest that is famous in story.
　　Mount and make ready then,
　　Sons of the mountain glen;
Fight for the Queen and our old Scottish glory.

Come from the hills where your hirsels are grazing,
　Come from the glen of the buck and the roe;
Come to the crag where the beacon is blazing,
　Come with the buckler, the lance, and the bow.
　　Trumpets are sounding,
　　War-steeds are bounding,
Stand to your arms, and march in good order;
　　England shall many a day
　　Tell of the bloody fray,
When the Blue Bonnets came over the Border.

Sir Walter Scott

LXIV

The Execution of Montrose

1650

Come hither, Evan Cameron,
   Come, stand beside my knee —
I hear the river roaring down
   Towards the wintry sea.
There's shouting on the mountain-side,
   There's war within the blast —
Old faces look upon me,
   Old forms go trooping past;
I hear the pibroch wailing
   Amidst the din of fight,
And my dim spirit wakes again
   Upon the verge of night.

'T was I that led the Highland host
   Through wild Lochaber's snows,
What time the plaided clans came down
   To battle with Montrose.
I've told thee how the Southrons fell
   Beneath the broad claymore,
And how we smote the Campbell clan,
   By Inverlochy's shore.
I've told thee how we swept Dundee,
   And tamed the Lindsays' pride;
But never have I told thee yet
   How the great Marquis died.

A traitor sold him to his foes;
   O deed of deathless shame!

I charge thee, boy, if e'er thou meet
  With one of Assynt's name —
Be it upon the mountain's side,
  Or yet within the glen,
Stand he in martial gear alone,
  Or backed by armèd men —
Face him as thou wouldst face the man
  Who wronged thy sire's renown;
Remember of what blood thou art,
  And strike the caitiff down!

They brought him to the Watergate,
  Hard bound with hempen span,
As though they held a lion there,
  And not a fenceless man.
They set him high upon a cart —
  The hangman rode below —
They drew his hands behind his back,
  And bared his noble brow.
Then, as a hound is slipped from leash,
  They cheered, the common throng,
And blew the note with yell and shout,
  And bade him pass along.

It would have made a brave man's heart
  Grow sad and sick that day,
To watch the keen, malignant eyes
  Bent down on that array.
There stood the Whig west-country lords,
  In balcony and bow;
There sat the gaunt and withered dames,
  And their daughters all a-row.

And every open window
    Was full as full might be
With black-robed Covenanting carles,
    That goodly sport to see!

But when he came, though pale and wan,
    He looked so great and high,
So noble was his manly front,
    So calm his steadfast eye; —
The rabble rout forebore to shout,
    And each man held his breath,
For well they knew the hero's soul
    Was face to face with death.
And then a mournful shudder
    Through all the people crept,
And some that came to scoff at him
    Now turned aside and wept.

But onwards — always onwards,
    In silence and in gloom,
The dreary pageant labored,
    Till it reached the house of doom.
Then first a woman's voice was heard
    In jeer and laughter loud,
And an angry cry and a hiss arose
    From the heart of the tossing crowd:
Then as the Græme looked upwards,
    He saw the ugly smile
Of him who sold his king for gold —
    The master-fiend Argyle!

The Marquis gazed a moment,
    And nothing did he say,

But the cheek of Argyle grew ghastly pale
    And he turned his eyes away.
The painted harlot by his side,
    She shook through every limb,
For a roar like thunder swept the street,
    And hands were clenched at him;
And a Saxon soldier cried aloud,
    "Back, coward, from thy place!
For seven long years thou hast not dared
    To look him in the face."

Had I been there with sword in hand,
    And fifty Camerons by,
That day through high Dunedin's streets
    Had pealed the slogan-cry.
Not all their troops of trampling horse,
    Nor might of mailèd men —
Not all the rebels in the south
    Had borne us backwards then!
Once more his foot on highland heath
    Had trod as free as air,
Or I, and all who bore my name,
    Been laid around him there!

It might not be. They placed him next
    Within the solemn hall,
Where once the Scottish kings were throned
    Amidst their nobles all.
But there was dust of vulgar feet
    On that polluted floor,
And perjured traitors filled the place
    Where good men sate before.

With savage glee came Warristoun,
  To read the murderous doom;
And then uprose the great Montrose
  In the middle of the room.

"Now, by my faith, as belted knight,
  And by the name I bear,
And by the bright Saint Andrew's cross
  That waves above us there —
Yea, by a greater, mightier oath —
  And oh, that such should be! —
By that dark stream of royal blood
  That lies 'twixt you and me —
I have not sought in battle-field
  A wreath of such renown,
Nor dared I hope on my dying day
  To win the martyr's crown!

"There is a chamber far away
  Where sleep the good and brave,
But a better place ye have named for me
  Than by my father's grave.
For truth and right, 'gainst treason's might,
  This hand hath always striven,
And ye raise it up for a witness still
  In the eye of earth and heaven.
Then nail my head on yonder tower —
  Give every town a limb —
And God who made shall gather them:
  I go from you to Him!"

The morning dawned full darkly,
  The rain came flashing down,

And the jagged streak of the levin-bolt
  Lit up the gloomy town :
The thunder crashed across the heaven,
  The fatal hour was come ;
Yet aye broke in with muffled beat,
  The 'larum of the drum.
There was madness on the earth below
  And anger in the sky,
And young and old, and rich and poor,
  Came forth to see him die.

Ah, God! that ghastly gibbet!
  How dismal 't is to see
The great, tall, spectral skeleton,
  The ladder and the tree!
Hark! hark! it is the clash of arms —
  The bells begin to toll —
"He is coming! he is coming!
  God's mercy on his soul!"
One last, long peal of thunder —
  The clouds are cleared away,
And the glorious sun once more looks down
  Amidst the dazzling day.

"He is coming! he is coming!"
  Like a bridegroom from his room
Came the hero from his prison
  To the scaffold and the doom.
There was glory on his forehead,
  There was lustre in his eye,
And he never walked to battle
  More proudly than to die ;

There was color in his visage
  Though the cheeks of all were wan,
And they marveled as they saw him pass,
  That great and goodly man!

He mounted up the scaffold,
  And he turned him to the crowd;
But they dared not trust the people,
  So he might not speak aloud.
But he looked upon the heavens,
  And they were clear and blue,
And in the liquid ether
  The eye of God shone through.
Yet a black and murky battlement
  Lay resting on the hill,
As though the thunder slept within —
  All else was calm and still.

The grim Geneva ministers
  With anxious scowl drew near,
As you have seen the ravens flock
  Around the dying deer.
He would not deign them word nor sign,
  But alone he bent the knee;
And veiled his face for Christ's dear grace
  Beneath the gallows-tree.
Then radiant and serene he rose,
  And cast his cloak away:
For he had ta'en his latest look
  Of earth and sun and day.

A beam of light fell o'er him,
  Like a glory round the shriven,

And he climbed the lofty ladder
  As it were the path to heaven.
Then came a flash from out the cloud,
  And a stunning thunder-roll;
And no man dared to look aloft,
  For fear was on every soul.
There was another heavy sound,
  A hush and then a groan;
And darkness swept across the sky —
  The work of death was done!

William Edmonstoune Aytoun

LXV

The Bonnets o' Bonnie Dundee

1689

To the Lords o' Convention 't was Claverhouse who spoke,
Ere the king's crown go down, there are crowns to be broke;
Then each cavalier who loves honor and me
Let him follow the bonnets o' bonnie Dundee!

    Come fill up my cup, come fill up my can;
    Come saddle my horses, and call out my men;
    Come open the Westport and let us gae free,
    And it's room for the bonnets o' bonnie Dundee!

Dundee he is mounted, he rides up the street,
The bells are rung backward, the drums they are beat;
But the provost, douce man, said, "Just e'en let him be,
The gude toun is weel rid o' that deil o' Dundee!"

As he rode doun the sanctified bends of the Bow,
Ilk carline was flyting and shaking her pow;
But the young plants o' grace they looked cowthie and slee,
Thinking, Luck to thy bonnet, thou bonnie Dundee!

With sour-featured whigs the Grass-Market was thranged,
As if half the west had set tryst to be hanged;
There was spite in each look, there was fear in each ee,
As they watched for the bonnets o' bonnie Dundee.

These cowls of Kilmarnock had spits and had spears,
And lang-hafted gullies to kill cavaliers;
But they shrunk to close-heads, and the causeway was free
At the toss o' the bonnet o' bonnie Dundee.

He spurred to the foot o' the proud castle rock,
And with the gay Gordon he gallantly spoke:
"Let Mons Meg and her marrows speak twa words or three,
For the love o' the bonnet o' bonnie Dundee."

The Gordon demands of him which way he goes.
"Where'er shall direct me the shade o' Montrose!
Your grace in short space shall hear tidings of me,
Or that low lies the bonnet o' bonnie Dundee.

"There are hills beyond Pentland and lands beyond Forth;
If there's lords in the lowland, there's chiefs in the north;
There are wild Duniewassals three thousand times three
Will cry 'Hey!' for the bonnet o' bonnie Dundee.

"There's brass on the target of barkened bull-hide,
There's steel in the scabbard that dangles beside;
The brass shall be burnished, the steel shall flash free,
At a toss o' the bonnet o' bonnie Dundee.

"Then awa' to the hills, to the lea, to the rocks,
Ere I own a usurper I'll couch with the fox:
And tremble, false whigs, in the midst o' your glee,
Ye hae no seen the last o' my bonnet and me."

He waved his proud hand, and the trumpets were blown,
The kettle-drums clashed, and the horsemen rode on,
Till on Ravelston's cliffs and on Clermiston's lea
Died away the wild war-notes o' bonnie Dundee.

Come fill up my cup, come fill up my can,
Come saddle the horses, and call up the men;
Come open your doors and let me gae free,
For it's up with the bonnets o' bonnie Dundee.

Sir Walter Scott

LXVI

The Old Scottish Cavalier

1689–1746

Come, listen to another song,
   Should make your heart beat high,
Bring crimson to your forehead,
   And the lustre to your eye; —
It is a song of olden time,
   Of days long since gone by,
And of a baron stout and bold
   As e'er wore sword on thigh!
     Like a brave old Scottish cavalier,
       All of the olden time!

He kept his castle in the North,
　　Hard by the thundering Spey;
And a thousand vassals dwelt around,
　　All of his kindred they.
And not a man of all that clan
　　Had ever ceased to pray
For the Royal race they loved so well,
　　Though exiled far away
　　　　From the steadfast Scottish cavaliers,
　　　　　　All of the olden time!

His father drew the righteous sword
　　For Scotland and her claims,
Among the loyal gentlemen
　　And chiefs of ancient names,
Who swore to fight or fall beneath
　　The standard of King James,
And died at Killiecrankie Pass,
　　With the glory of the Græmes,
　　　　Like a true old Scottish cavalier,
　　　　　　All of the olden time!

He never owned the foreign rule,
　　No master he obeyed;
But kept his clan in peace at home
　　From foray and from raid;
And when they asked him for his oath,
　　He touched his glittering blade,
And pointed to his bonnet blue,
　　That bore the white cockade:
　　　　Like a leal old Scottish cavalier,
　　　　　　All of the olden time!

The Old Scottish Cavalier

At length the news ran through the land, —
  THE PRINCE had come again!
That night the fiery cross was sped
  O'er mountain and through glen;
And our old Baron rose in might,
  Like a lion from his den,
And rode away across the hills
  To Charlie and his men,
    With the valiant Scottish cavaliers,
      All of the olden time!

He was the first that bent the knee
  When the Standard waved abroad;
He was the first that charged the foe
  On Preston's bloody sod;
And ever in the van of fight
  The foremost still he trod,
Until on bleak Culloden's heath
  He gave his soul to God,
    Like a good old Scottish cavalier,
      All of the olden time!

Oh! never shall we know again
  A heart so stout and true —
The olden times have passed away,
  And weary are the new:
The fair White Rose has faded
  From the garden where it grew,
And no fond tears, save those of heaven,
  The glorious bed bedew
    Of the last old Scottish cavalier,
      All of the olden time!

William Edmonstoune Aytoun

LXVII

The Lament of Flora Macdonald
1746

Far over yon hills of the heather sae green,
   An' doun by the Corrie that sings to the sea,
The bonnie young Flora sat sighing her lane,
   The dew on her plaid an' the tear in her e'e.
She look'd at a boat wi' the breezes that swung,
   Away on the wave, like a bird of the main;
An' aye as it lessen'd she sighed an' she sung,
   "Fareweel to the lad I shall ne'er see again;
Fareweel to my hero, the gallant an' young,
   Fareweel to the lad I shall ne'er see again!

"The moorcock that crows on the brows o' Ben-Connal,
   He kens o' his bed in a sweet mossy hame;
The eagle that soars o'er the cliffs o' Clan-Ronald,
   Unawed and unhunted his eyrie can claim;
The solan can sleep on the shelve of the shores;
   The cormorant roost on his rock of the sea;
But, ah! there is one whose hard fate I deplore,
   Nor house, ha', nor hame in his country has he;
The conflict is past, and our name is no more,
   There's nought left but sorrow for Scotland an' me!

"The target is torn from the arm of the just,
   The helmet is cleft on the brow of the brave,
The claymore forever in darkness must rust;
   But red is the sword of the stranger and slave;
The hoof of the horse, and the foot of the proud,
   Have trod o'er the plumes on the bonnet of blue;

Why slept the red bolt in the breast of the cloud
   When tyranny reveled in blood of the true?
Fareweel, my young hero, the gallant and good!
   The crown of thy fathers is torn from thy brow."

                      Arranged by *James Hogg*

LXVIII

Wae's Me for Prince Charlie

1746

A wee bird cam' to our ha' door,
   He warbled sweet an' clearly,
An' aye the o'er-come o' his sang
   Was "Wae's me for Prince Charlie!"
Oh! when I heard the bonnie, bonnie bird,
   The tears cam' drappin' rarely,
I took my bannet aff my head,
   For weel I lo'ed Prince Charlie.

Quoth I, "My bird, my bonnie, bonnie bird,
   Is that a sang ye borrow,
Are these some words ye've learnt by heart,
   Or a lilt o' dool an' sorrow?"
"Oh! no, no, no," the wee bird sang,
   "I've flown sin' mornin' early,
But sic a day o' wind an' rain —
   Oh! wae's me for Prince Charlie!

"On hills that are, by right, his ain,
   He roves a lanely stranger,
On every side he's pressed by want,
   On every side is danger;

Yestreen I met him in a glen,
  My heart maist burstit fairly,
For sadly changed indeed was he —
  Oh! wae's me for Prince Charlie!

"Dark night cam' on, the tempest roared
  Loud o'er the hills an' valleys,
An' where was 't that your Prince lay doun,
  Wha's hame should been a palace?
He rowed him in a Highland plaid,
  Which covered him but sparely,
An' slept beneath a bush o' broom —
  Oh! wae's me for Prince Charlie!"

But now the bird saw some redcoats,
  An' he shook his wings wi' anger,
"Oh! this is no a land for me;
  I'll tarry here nae langer!"
He hovered on the wing a while
  Ere he departed fairly,
But weel I mind the fareweel strain
  Was, "Wae's me for Prince Charlie!"

Attributed to William Glen

LXIX

The Campbells are Comin'

The Campbells are comin', Oho, Oho,
The Campbells are comin', Oho, Oho,
The Campbells are comin' to bonnie Lochleven,
The Campbells are comin', Oho, Oho!

Upon the Lomonds, I lay, I lay,
Upon the Lomonds, I lay, I lay,
I lookit down to bonnie Lochleven,
And saw three bonnie perches play.
    The Campbells are comin', etc.

Great Argyle he goes before,
He makes his cannons and guns to roar;
Wi' sound o' trumpet, fife, and drum,
The Campbells are comin', Oho, Oho!
    The Campbells are comin', etc.

The Campbells they are a' wi' arms,
Their loyal faith and truth to show,
Wi' banners rattlin' in the wind
The Campbells are comin', Oho, Oho!
    The Campbells are comin', etc.

Anonymous

LXX

The Blue Bell of Scotland

Oh, where? and oh, where is your Highland laddie gone?
Oh, where? and oh, where is your Highland laddie gone?
He's gone to fight the French for King George upon the
    throne,
And it's oh, in my heart how I wish him safe at home!
  He's gone to fight the French for King George upon the
    throne,
  And it's oh, in my heart how I wish him safe at home!

Oh, where? and oh, where does your Highland laddie dwell?
Oh, where? and oh, where does your Highland laddie dwell?

He dwells in merrie Scotland, at the sign of the Blue Bell;
And it's oh, in my heart that I lo'e my laddie well!
  He dwells in merrie Scotland, etc.

What clothes, in what clothes is your Highland laddie clad?
What clothes, in what clothes is your Highland laddie clad?
His bonnet's of the Saxon green, his waistcoat's of the plaid,
And it's oh, in my heart that I lo'e my Highland lad!
  His bonnet's of the Saxon green, etc.

Suppose, oh suppose that your Highland lad should die?
Suppose, oh suppose that your Highland lad should die?
The bagpipes shall play o'er him, I'll lay me doun and cry;
And it's oh, in my heart, that I wish he may not die!
  The bagpipes shall play o'er him, etc.

Anonymous

MISCELLANEOUS SONGS AND BALLADS

LXXI

Annie Laurie

c. 1700

Maxwelton braes are bonnie,
  Where early fa's the dew;
An' it's there that Annie Laurie
  Gi'ed me her promise true;
Gi'ed me her promise true,
  Which ne'er forgot sall be;

And for bonnie Annie Laurie
　　I 'd lay me doun and dee.

Her brow is like the snaw-drift,
　　Her throat is like the swan,
Her face it is the fairest
　　That e'er the sun shone on;
That e'er the sun shone on —
　　An' dark blue is her ee;
An' for bonnie Annie Laurie
　　I 'd lay me doun and dee.

Like dew on the gowan lying
　　Is the fa' o' her fairy feet;
Like simmer breezes sighing,
　　Her voice is low an' sweet;
Her voice is low an' sweet —
　　An' she 's a' the world to me;
An' for bonnie Annie Laurie
　　I 'd lay me doun and dee.

William Douglas of Fingland
and *Lady John Scott*

LXXII

Lochaber No More

c. 1720

Farewell to Lochaber, and farewell, my Jean,
Where heartsome with thee I 've mony days been;
For Lochaber no more, Lochaber no more,
We 'll may be return to Lochaber no more.

These tears that I shed, they are a' for my dear,
And no for the dangers attending on weir';
Tho' bore on rough seas to a far bloody shore,
May be to return to Lochaber no more.

Tho' hurricanes rise, and rise every wind,
They'll ne'er make a tempest like that in my mind.
Tho' loudest of thunder on louder waves roar,
That's naething like leaving my love on the shore.
To leave thee behind me, my heart is sair pain'd:
By ease that's inglorious, no fame can be gain'd;
And beauty and love's the reward of the brave,
And I must deserve it before I can crave.

Then glory, my Jeanie, maun plead my excuse,
Since honor commands me, how can I refuse?
Without it I ne'er can have honor for thee;
And without thy favor, I'd better not be.
I gae then, my lass, to win honor and fame,
And if I should luck to come gloriously hame,
A heart I'll bring to thee with love running o'er,
And then I'll leave thee and Lochaber no more.

Allan Ramsay

LXXIII

There's Nae Luck about the House

And are ye sure the news is true?
    And are ye sure he's weel?
Is this a time to talk o' wark?
    Ye jauds fling by your wheel!
Is this a time to think o' wark,
    When Colin's at the door?

There's Nae Luck about the House

Rax doun my cloak, I'll to the quay,
    And see him come ashore.
For there's nae luck about the house,
    There's nae luck at a',
There's nae luck about the house,
    When our guidman's awa'.

Rise up and mak' a clean fireside,
    Put on the muckle pot;
Gie little Kate her button goun,
    And Jock his Sunday's coat;
And mak' their shoon as black as slaes,
    Their hose as white as snaw;
It's a' to pleasure our guidman,
    He likes to see them braw.
For there's nae luck, etc.

There's twa fat hens upo' the bauk
    Hae fed this month and mair,
Mak' haste and thraw their necks about,
    That Colin weel may fare:
And spread the table neat and clean,
    Gàr ilka thing look braw;
For wha can tell how Colin fared,
    When he was far awa'?
For there's nae luck, etc.

Come, gie me doun my bigonet,
    My bishop-satin goun;
And rin and tell the Bailie's wife
    That Colin's come to town:
My Turkey-slippers maun gae on,
    My hose o' pearl blue;

It's a' to pleasure our guidman,
  For he's baith leal and true.
For there's nae luck, etc.

Sae sweet his voice, sae smooth his tongue,
  His breath like caller air!
His very fit has music in't
  As he comes up the stair:
And will I see his face again?
  And will I hear him speak?
I'm dounricht dizzy wi' the thocht,
  In troth I'm like to greet.
For there's nae luck, etc.

The cauld blasts o' the winter wind,
  That thirlèd through my heart,
They're a' blawn by, I hae him safe,
  Till death we'll never part:
But what puts parting in my heid,
  It may be far awa';
The present moment is our ain,
  The neist we never saw!
For there's nae luck, etc.

Since Colin's weel, I'm weel content,
  I hae nae mair to crave;
Could I but live to mak' him blest,
  I'm blest aboon the lave.
And will I see his face again?
  And will I hear him speak?
I'm dounricht dizzy wi' the thocht,
  In troth I'm like to greet.
For there's nae luck, etc.

              Attributed to *William Julius Mickle*

LXXIV

A Red, Red Rose

O, my luve 's like a red, red rose,
    That 's newly sprung in June:
O, my luve 's like the melodie
    That 's sweetly play'd in tune.

As fair art thou, my bonnie lass,
    So deep in luve am I:
And I will luve thee still, my dear,
    Till a' the seas gang dry.

Till a' the seas gang dry, my dear,
    And the rocks melt wi' the sun:
I will luve thee still, my dear,
    While the sands o' life shall run.

And fare thee weel, my only luve,
    And fare thee weel awhile!
And I will come again, my luve,
    Tho' it were ten thousand mile.

Revised by Robert Burns

LXXV

For a' that, and a' that

Is there, for honest poverty
    That hangs his head, and a' that?
The coward-slave, we pass him by;
    We dare be poor for a' that!

> For a' that, and a' that,
>   Our toils obscure, and a' that:
> The rank is but the guinea's stamp,
>   The man's the gowd for a' that!
>
> What tho' on hamely fare we dine,
>   Wear hodden-grey, and a' that?
> Gie fools their silks, and knaves their wine,
>   A man's a man for a' that!
>   For a' that, and a' that,
>   Their tinsel show, and a' that:
>   The honest man, tho' e'er sae poor,
>   Is king o' men for a' that!
>
> Ye see yon birkie, ca'd a lord,
>   Wha struts, and stares, and a' that:
> Tho' hundreds worship at his word,
>   He's but a coof for a' that:
>   For a' that, and a' that,
>   His riband, star, and a' that:
>   The man of independent mind,
>   He looks and laughs at a' that!
>
> A prince can mak a belted knight,
>   A marquis, duke, and a' that;
> But an honest man's aboon his might:
>   Guid faith, he mauna fa' that!
>   For a' that, and a' that,
>   Their dignities, and a' that,
>   The pith o' sense, and pride o' worth,
>   Are higher rank than a' that.
>
> Then let us pray that come it may —
>   As come it will for a' that —

That sense and worth, o'er a' the earth,
    May bear the gree, and a' that:
      For a' that, and a' that,
        It's comin' yet for a' that,
    That man to man, the warld o'er,
      Shall brothers be for a' that!

Robert Burns

LXXVI

John Anderson, my Jo

John Anderson, my jo, John,
    When we were first acquent,
Your locks were like the raven,
    Your bonnie brow was brent;
But now your brow is beld, John,
    Your locks are like the snaw,
But blessings on your frosty pow,
    John Anderson, my jo.

John Anderson, my jo, John,
    We clamb the hill thegither;
And monie a canty day, John,
    We've had wi' ane anither:
Now we maun totter down, John,
    But hand-in-hand we'll go,
And sleep thegither at the foot,
    John Anderson, my jo.

Robert Burns

LXXVII

Afton Water

Flow gently, sweet Afton, among thy green braes,
Flow gently, I'll sing thee a song in thy praise;
My Mary's asleep by thy murmuring stream, —
Flow gently, sweet Afton, disturb not her dream.

Thou stock-dove whose echo resounds thro' the glen,
Ye wild whistling blackbirds in yon thorny den,
Thou green-crested lapwing, thy screaming forbear,
I charge you disturb not my slumbering fair.

How lofty, sweet Afton, thy neighboring hills,
Far mark'd with the courses of clear, winding rills;
There daily I wander as noon rises high,
My flocks and my Mary's sweet cot in my eye.

How pleasant thy banks and green valleys below,
Where wild in the woodlands the primroses blow;
There oft as mild ev'ning weeps over the lea,
The sweet-scented birk shades my Mary and me.

Thy crystal stream, Afton, how lovely it glides,
And winds by the cot where my Mary resides;
How wanton thy waters her snowy feet lave,
As gathering sweet flow'rets she stems thy clear wave.

Flow gently, sweet Afton, among thy green braes,
Flow gently, sweet river, the theme of my lays;
My Mary's asleep by thy murmuring stream, —
Flow gently, sweet Afton, disturb not her dream.

Robert Burns

LXXVIII

Ye Banks and Braes o' Bonnie Doon

Ye banks and braes o' bonnie Doon,
   How can ye bloom sae fair!
How can ye chant, ye little birds,
   And I sae fu' o' care!

Thou 'll break my heart, thou bonnie bird
   That sings upon the bough;
Thou minds me o' the happy days
   When my fause Luve was true.

Thou 'll break my heart, thou bonnie bird
   That sings beside thy mate;
For sae I sat, and sae I sang,
   And wist na o' my fate.

Aft hae I roved by bonnie Doon
   To see the woodbine twine,
And ilka bird sang o' its luve;
   And sae did I o' mine.

Wi' lightsome heart I pu'd a rose
   Frae aff its thorny tree;
And my fause luver staw the rose,
   But left the thorn wi' me.

Robert Burns

LXXIX

My Heart's in the Highlands

My heart's in the Highlands, my heart is not here;
My heart's in the Highlands a-chasing the deer;
Chasing the wild deer, and following the roe,
My heart's in the Highlands wherever I go.
Farewell to the Highlands, farewell to the North,
The birthplace of valor, the country of worth;
Wherever I wander, wherever I rove,
The hills of the Highlands forever I love.

Farewell to the mountains high cover'd with snow;
Farewell to the straths and green valleys below;
Farewell to the forests and wild-hanging woods;
Farewell to the torrents and loud-pouring floods.
My heart's in the Highlands, my heart is not here;
My heart's in the Highlands a-chasing the deer;
Chasing the wild deer, and following the roe,
My heart's in the Highlands wherever I go.

Robert Burns

LXXX

Jock of Hazeldean

"Why weep ye by the tide, ladie?
   Why weep ye by the tide?
I'll wed ye to my youngest son,
   And ye sall be his bride:
And ye sall be his bride, ladie,
   Sae comely to be seen" —

But aye she loot the tears down fa'
  For Jock of Hazeldean.

"Now let this wilfu' grief be done,
  And dry that cheek so pale;
Young Frank is chief of Errington
  And lord of Langley-dale;
His step is first in peaceful ha',
  His sword in battle keen"—
But aye she loot the tears down fa'
  For Jock of Hazeldean.

"A chain of gold ye sall not lack,
  Nor braid to bind your hair,
Nor mettled hound, nor managed hawk,
  Nor palfrey fresh and fair;
And you the foremost o' them a'
  Shall ride our forest-queen"—
But aye she loot the tears down fa'
  For Jock of Hazeldean.

The kirk was deck'd at morning-tide,
  The tapers glimmer'd fair;
The priest and bridegroom wait the bride,
  And dame and knight are there:
They sought her baith by bower and ha';
  The ladie was not seen!
She's o'er the Border, and awa'
  Wi' Jock of Hazeldean.

Sir Walter Scott

LXXXI

Lochinvar

O, young Lochinvar is come out of the west,
Through all the wide Border his steed was the best;
And save his good broadsword, he weapon had none,
He rode all unarmed, and he rode all alone.
So faithful in love, and so dauntless in war,
There never was knight like the young Lochinvar.

He staid not for brake, and he stopped not for stone,
He swam the Eske river where ford there was none;
But ere he alighted at Netherby gate,
The bride had consented, the gallant came late:
For a laggard in love, and a dastard in war,
Was to wed the fair Ellen of young Lochinvar.

So boldly he entered the Netherby Hall,
Among bridesmen and kinsmen, and brothers, and all:
Then spake the bride's father, his hand on his sword,
(For the poor craven bridegroom said never a word,)
"O come ye in peace here, or come ye in war,
Or to dance at our bridal, young Lord Lochinvar?"

"I long wooed your daughter, my suit you denied;
Love swells like the Solway, but ebbs like its tide —
And now am I come, with this lost love of mine,
To lead but one measure, drink one cup of wine.
There are maidens in Scotland more lovely by far,
That would gladly be bride to the young Lochinvar."

The bride kissed the goblet: the knight took it up,
He quaffed off the wine, and he threw down the cup.

Lochinvar

She looked down to blush, and she looked up to sigh,
With a smile on her lips and a tear in her eye.
He took her soft hand, ere her mother could bar, —
"Now tread we a measure!" said young Lochinvar.

So stately his form, and so lovely her face,
That never a hall such a galliard did grace;
While her mother did fret, and her father did fume,
And the bridegroom stood dangling his bonnet and plume;
And the bride-maidens whispered, "'T were better by far
To have matched our fair cousin with young Lochinvar."

One touch to her hand, and one word in her ear,
When they reached the hall-door, and the charger stood near;
So light to the croupe the fair lady he swung,
So light to the saddle before her he sprung.
"She is won! we are gone over bank, bush, and scaur;
They'll have fleet steeds that follow," quoth young Lochinvar.

There was mounting 'mong Græmes of the Netherby clan;
Forsters, Fenwicks, and Musgraves, they rode and they ran:
There was racing and chasing on Cannobie Lee,
But the lost bride of Netherby ne'er did they see.
So daring in love, and so dauntless in war,
Have ye e'er heard of gallant like young Lochinvar?

Sir Walter Scott

LXXXII

When the Kye Comes Hame

Come all ye jolly shepherds
  That whistle through the glen,
I 'll tell ye of a secret
  That courtiers dinna ken:
What is the greatest bliss
  That the tongue o' man can name?
'T is to woo a bonnie lassie
  When the kye comes hame.
When the kye comes hame,
  When the kye comes hame,
'Tween the gloamin' and the mirk,
  When the kye comes hame.

'T is not beneath the coronet,
  Nor canopy of state,
'T is not on couch of velvet,
  Nor arbor of the great:
'T is beneath the spreading birk,
  In the dell without a name,
Wi' a bonnie, bonnie lassie
  When the kye comes hame.

There the blackbird bigs his nest
  For the mate he lo'es to see,
And up upon the tapmost bough,
  O, a happy bird is he!
Then he pours his melting ditty,
  And love 't is a' the theme,

And he'll woo his bonnie lassie
   When the kye comes hame.

When the bluart bears a pearl,
   And the daisy turns a pea,
And the bonnie lucken gowan
   Has fauldit up his e'e,
Then the laverock frae the blue lift
   Doops down, and thinks nae shame
To woo his bonnie lassie
   When the kye comes hame.

Then since all nature joins
   In this love without alloy,
Wha wad prove a traitor
   To Nature's dearest joy?
O, wha wad choose a crown,
   Wi' its perils and its fame,
And miss his bonnie lassie
   When the kye comes hame?

See yonder pawky shepherd
   That lingers on the hill —
His yowes are in the fauld,
   And his lambs are lying still;
Yet he downa gang to rest,
   For his heart is in a flame
To meet his bonnie lassie
   When the kye comes hame.

When the little wee bit heart
   Rises high in the breast,
An' the little wee bit starn
   Rises red in the east,

O, there's a joy so dear
  That the heart can hardly frame,
Wi' a bonnie, bonnie lassie
  When the kye comes hame.

James Hogg

LXXXIII

Jessie, the Flower of Dumblane

The sun has gane down o'er the lofty Benlomond,
  And left the red clouds to preside o'er the scene,
While lanely I stray in the calm simmer gloamin'
  To muse on sweet Jessie, the flower o' Dumblane.
How sweet is the brier, wi' its saft faulding blossom,
  And sweet is the birk, wi' its mantle o' green;
Yet sweeter and fairer, and dear to this bosom,
  Is lovely young Jessie, the flower o' Dumblane.

She's modest as ony, and blythe as she's bonny;
  For guileless simplicity marks her its ain;
And far be the villain, divested o' feeling,
  Wha 'd blight, in its bloom, the sweet flower o' Dumblane.
Sing on, thou sweet mavis, thy hymn to the e'ening,
  Thou 'rt dear to the echoes of Calderwood glen;
Sae dear to this bosom, sae artless and winning,
  Is charming young Jessie, the flower o' Dumblane.

How lost were my days till I met wi' my Jessie,
  The sports o' the city seemed foolish and vain;
I ne'er saw a nymph I could ca' my dear lassie,
  Till charm'd wi' sweet Jessie, the flower o' Dumblane.

Though mine were the station o' loftiest grandeur,
    Amidst its profusion I 'd languish in pain;
And reckon as naething the height o' its splendor,
    If wanting sweet Jessie, the flower o' Dumblane.

Robert Tannahill

LXXXIV

The Bonnie Banks o' Loch Lomond

By yon bonnie banks and by yon bonnie braes,
Where the sun shines bright on Loch Lomon',
Where me and my true love were ever wont to gae,
On the bonnie, bonnie banks o' Loch Lomon'.
    O ye 'll tak the high road and I 'll tak the low road,
    And I 'll be in Scotland afore ye;
    But me and my true love will never meet again
    On the bonnie, bonnie banks o' Loch Lomon'.

'T was there that we parted in yon shady glen,
On the steep, steep side o' Ben Lomon',
Where in purple hue the Hieland hills we view,
And the moon coming out in the gloamin'. — *Cho.*

The wee birdies sing and the wild flowers spring,
And in sunshine the waters are sleepin';
But the broken heart it kens nae second spring again
Though the waefu' may cease from their greetin.' — *Cho.*

Anonymous

LXXXV

The Land o' the Leal

I 'm wearin' awa', Jean,
Like snaw-wreaths in thaw, Jean;
I 'm wearin' awa'
  To the land o' the leal.
There 's nae sorrow there, Jean,
There 's neither cauld nor care, Jean.
The day is aye fair
  In the land o' the leal.

Ye 've been leal and true, Jean,
Your task is ended noo, Jean,
And I 'll welcome you
  To the land o' the leal.
Our bonnie bairn 's there, Jean,
She was baith guid and fair, Jean,
And we grudged her sair
  To the land o' the leal.

Sorrow's sel' wears past, Jean,
And joy is comin' fast, Jean,
Joy that 's aye to last
  In the land o' the leal.
Then dry that glist'nin' e'e, Jean,
My soul langs to be free, Jean,
And angels wait on me
  To the land o' the leal.

A' our friends are gane, Jean,
We 've lang been left alane, Jean,

We 'll a' meet again
  In the land o' the leal.
Now, fare ye weel, my ain Jean,
This warld's care is vain, Jean,
We 'll meet and aye be fain
  In the land o' the leal.

Lady Nairne

LXXXVI

Auld Lang Syne

Should auld acquaintance be forgot,
  And never brought to min'?
Should auld acquaintance be forgot,
  And days o' lang syne?
    For auld lang syne, my dear,
      For auld lang syne, —
    We 'll tak a cup o' kindness yet,
      For auld lang syne.

We twa hae run about the braes,
  And pu'd the gowans fine;
But we 've wandered mony a weary foot
  Sin' auld lang syne.
    For auld lang syne, my dear, etc.

We twa hae paidl't i' the burn
  Frae mornin' sun till dine;
But seas between us braid hae roared
  Sin' auld lang syne.
    For auld lang syne, my dear, etc.

And here 's a hand, my trusty fiere,
    And gie 's a hand o' thine;
And we 'll tak a right guid willie-waught
    For auld lang syne.
        For auld lang syne, my dear, etc.

And surely ye 'll be your pint-stowp,
    And surely I 'll be mine;
And we 'll tak a cup o' kindness yet,
    For auld lang syne.
        For auld lang syne, my dear, etc.

Robert Burns

BOOK FOURTH — POEMS OF IRELAND: HISTORICAL AND PATRIOTIC

LXXXVII

The Green Little Shamrock of Ireland

1806

There 's a dear little plant that grows in our isle,
   'T was St. Patrick himself, sure, that set it;
And the sun on his labor with pleasure did smile,
   And with dew from his eye often wet it.
It thrives through the bog, through the brake, and the mireland;
And its name is the dear little shamrock of Ireland —
   The sweet little shamrock, the dear little shamrock,
   The sweet little, green little, shamrock of Ireland!

This dear little plant still grows in our land,
   Fresh and fair as the daughters of Erin,
Whose smiles can bewitch, whose eyes can command,
   In what climate they chance to appear in;
For they shine through the bog, through the brake, and the mireland;
Just like their own dear little shamrock of Ireland.
   The sweet little shamrock, the dear little shamrock,
   The sweet little, green little, shamrock of Ireland!

This dear little plant that springs from our soil,
  When its three little leaves are extended,
Betokens that each for the other should toil,
  And ourselves by ourselves be befriended, —
And still through the bog, through the brake, and the mireland,
From one root should branch, like the shamrock of Ireland.
  The sweet little shamrock, the dear little shamrock,
  The sweet little, green little, shamrock of Ireland!

Andrew Cherry

LXXXVIII

The Irish Wife

(EARL DESMOND'S APOLOGY)

1376

I would not give my Irish wife
  For all the dames of the Saxon land;
I would not give my Irish wife
  For the Queen of France's hand;
For she to me is dearer
  Than castles strong, or lands, or life —
An outlaw, so I 'm near her,
  To love till death my Irish wife.

Oh, what would be this home of mine?
  A ruined, hermit-haunted place,
But for the light that still will shine
  Upon its walls from Kathleen's face!

The Irish Wife

What comfort in a mine of gold?
   What pleasure in a royal life?
If the heart within lay dead and cold,
   If I could not wed my Irish wife.

I knew the laws forbade the banns,
   I knew my King abhorred her race:
Who never bent before their clans
   Must bow before their ladies' grace.
Take all my forfeited domain,
   I cannot wage with kinsmen strife, —
Take knightly gear and noble name,
   And I will keep my Irish wife.

My Irish wife has clear blue eyes,
   My heaven by day, my stars by night,
And, twin-like, truth and fondness lie
   Within her swelling bosom white.
My Irish wife has golden hair —
   Apollo's harp had once such strings, —
Apollo's self might pause to hear
   Her birdlike carol when she sings.

I would not give my Irish wife
   For all the dames of the Saxon land;
I would not give my Irish wife
   For the Queen of France's hand.
For she to me is dearer
   Than castles strong, or lands, or life;
In death I would lie near her,
   And rise beside my Irish wife.

Thomas D'Arcy McGee

LXXXIX

Dark Rosaleen

[From the Irish. *c.* 1590]

O my Dark Rosaleen,
    Do not sigh, do not weep!
The priests are on the ocean green,
    They march along the Deep.
There's wine . . . from the royal Pope,
    Upon the ocean green;
And Spanish ale shall give you hope,
    My Dark Rosaleen!
    My own Rosaleen!
Shall glad your heart, shall give you hope,
Shall give you health, and help, and hope,
    My Dark Rosaleen!

Over hills and through dales
    Have I roamed for your sake;
All yesterday I sailed with sails
    On river and on lake.
The Erne, . . . at its highest flood,
    I dashed across unseen,
For there was lightning in my blood,
    My Dark Rosaleen!
    My own Rosaleen!
O! there was lightning in my blood,
Red lightning lightened through my blood,
    My Dark Rosaleen!

All day long, in unrest,
    To and fro, do I move,

The very soul within my breast
   Is wasted for you, love!
The heart . . . in my bosom faints
   To think of you, my Queen,
My life of life, my saint of saints,
   My Dark Rosaleen!
   My own Rosaleen!
To hear your sweet and sad complaints,
My life, my love, my saint of saints,
   My Dark Rosaleen!

Woe and pain, pain and woe,
   Are my lot, night and noon,
To see your bright face clouded so,
   Like to the mournful moon.
But yet . . . will I rear your throne
   Again in golden sheen;
'T is you shall reign, shall reign alone,
   My Dark Rosaleen!
   My own Rosaleen!
'T is you shall have the golden throne,
'T is you shall reign, and reign alone,
   My Dark Rosaleen!

Over dews, over sands,
   Will I fly for your weal:
Your holy, delicate white hands
   Shall girdle me with steel.
At home . . . in your emerald bowers,
   From morning's dawn till e'en,
You'll pray for me, my flower of flowers,
   My Dark Rosaleen!
   My fond Rosaleen!

You'll think of me through daylight's hours,
My virgin flower, my flower of flowers,
   My Dark Rosaleen?

I could scale the blue air,
   I could plough the high hills,
O, I could kneel all night in prayer,
   To heal your many ills!
And one . . . beamy smile from you
   Would float like light between
My toils and me, my own, my true,
   My Dark Rosaleen!
   My fond Rosaleen!
Would give me life and soul anew,
A second life, a soul anew,
   My Dark Rosaleen!

O! the Erne shall run red
   With redundance of blood,
The earth shall rock beneath our tread,
   And flames warp hill and wood,
And gun-peal and slogan cry,
   Wake many a glen serene,
Ere you shall fade, ere you shall die,
   My Dark Rosaleen!
   My own Rosaleen!
The Judgment Hour must first be nigh,
Ere you can fade, ere you can die,
   My Dark Rosaleen!

James Clarence Mangan

XC

The Battle of the Boyne

1690

July the first, in Oldbridge town, there was a grievous battle,
Where many a man lay on the ground by cannons that did rattle.
King James he pitched his tents between the lines for to retire ;
But King William threw his bomb-balls in, and set them all on fire.

Thereat enraged they vowed revenge upon King William's forces,
And oft did vehemently cry that they would stop their courses.
A bullet from the Irish came and grazed King William's arm,
They thought his majesty was slain, yet it did him little harm.

Duke Schomberg then, in friendly care, his King would often caution
To shun the spot where bullets hot retained their rapid motion ;
But William said, he don't deserve the name of Faith's defender,
Who would not venture life and limb to make a foe surrender.

When we the Boyne began to cross, the enemy they descended ;
But few of our brave men were lost, so stoutly we defended ;
The horse was the first that marchèd o'er, the foot soon followed after ;
But brave Duke Schomberg was no more by venturing over the water.

When valiant Schomberg he was slain, King William did accost
His warlike men for to march on and he would be foremost;
"Brave boys," he said, "be not dismayed for the loss of one commander,
For God will be our king this day, and I'll be general under."

Then stoutly we the Boyne did cross, to give the enemies battle:
Our cannon, to our foe's great cost, like thundering claps did rattle.
In majestic mien our Prince rode o'er, his men soon followed after,
With blow and shout put our foes to the rout the day we crossed the water.

The Protestants of Drogheda have reason to be thankful,
That they were not to bondage brought, they being but a handful,
First to the Tholsel they were brought, and tried at the Millmount after;
But brave King William set them free by venturing over the water.

The cunning French near to Duleek had taken up their quarters,
And fenced themselves on every side, still waiting for new orders;
But in the dead time of the night, they set the fields on fire,
And long before the morning light, to Dublin they did retire.

Then said King William to his men, after the French
    departed,
"I 'm glad" (said he) "that none of ye seem to be faint-
    hearted;
So sheath your swords and rest awhile, in time we 'll follow
    after";
Those words he uttered with a smile the day he crossed the
    water.

Come let us all with heart and voice applaud our lives'
    defender,
Who at the Boyne his valor showed and made his foe
    surrender.
To God above the praise we 'll give both now and ever
    after;
And bless the glorious memory of King William that crossed
    the water.

Attributed to *Captain Blacker*

XCI

After Aughrim

1691

Do you remember long ago,
    Kathaleen?
When your lover whispered low,
"Shall I stay or shall I go,
    Kathaleen?"
And you answered proudly, "Go!
And join King James and strike a blow
    For the Green."

Mavrone, your hair is white as snow,
    Kathaleen;
Your heart is sad and full of woe,
Do you repent you bade him go,
    Kathaleen?
But quick you answer proudly, "No!
For better die with Sarsfield so,
Than live a slave without a blow
    For the Green."

Arthur Gerald Geoghegan

XCII

The Shan Van Vocht

1797

The sainted isle of old,
  Says the *shan van vocht*,
The parent and the mould
Of the beautiful and bold,
Has her sainted heart waxed cold?
  Says the *shan van vocht*.

Oh! the French are on the say,
  Says the *shan van vocht*;
Oh! the French are in the bay;
They'll be here without delay,
And the Orange will decay,
  Says the *shan van vocht*.
    Oh! the French are in the bay,
    They'll be here by break of day,
    And the Orange will decay,
    Says the shan van vocht.

The Shan Van Vocht

And their camp it shall be where?
  Says the *shan van vocht;*
Their camp it shall be where?
  Says the *shan van vocht.*
On the Currach of Kildare;
The boys they will be there
With their pikes in good repair,
  Says the *shan van vocht.*
    To the Currach of Kildare
    The boys they will repair,
    And Lord Edward will be there,
    Says the shan van vocht.

Then what will the yeomen do?
  Says the *shan van vocht;*
What *will* the yeomen do?
  Says the *shan van vocht.*
What *should* the yeomen do,
But throw off the red and blue,
And swear that they'll be true
  To the *shan van vocht?*
    What should the yeomen do,
    But throw off the red and blue,
    And swear that they'll be true
    To the shan van vocht?

And what color will they wear?
  Says the *shan van vocht;*
What color will they wear?
  Says the *shan van vocht.*
What color *should* be seen,
Where our fathers' homes have been,
But our own immortal green?
  Says the *shan van vocht.*

What color should be seen,
Where our fathers' homes have been,
But our own immortal green?
Says the shan van vocht.

And will Ireland then be free?
  Says the *shan van vocht*;
Will Ireland then be free?
  Says the *shan van vocht*;
Yes! Ireland *shall* be free,
From the centre to the sea;
Then hurrah for liberty!
  Says the *shan van vocht*.
    Yes! Ireland SHALL *be free,*
    From the centre to the sea;
    Then hurrah for Liberty!
    Says the shan van vocht.

Anonymous

XCIII

The Wearing of the Green

1798

O Paddy dear, and did you hear the news that's going round?
The shamrock is forbid by law to grow on Irish ground;
St. Patrick's day no more we'll keep, his colors can't be seen,
For there's a bloody law agin' the wearing of the green.
I met with Napper Tandy, and he took me by the hand,
And he said, "How's poor old Ireland, and how does she stand?"

She's the most distressful country that ever yet was seen,
They are hanging men and women there for wearing of the green.

Then since the color we must wear is England's cruel red,
Sure Ireland's sons will ne'er forget the blood that they have shed:
You may take the shamrock from your hat and cast it on the sod,
But 't will take root and flourish still, though under foot 't is trod.
When the law can stop the blades of grass from growing as they grow,
And when the leaves in summer-time their color cease to show,
Then I will change the favor that I wear in my caubeen,
But till that day, please God, I 'll stick to wearing of the green.

But if at last our color should be torn from Ireland's heart,
Her sons with shame and sorrow from the dear old soil will part;
I 've heard whisper of a country that lies far beyond the sea,
Where rich and poor stand equal in the light of freedom's day: —
O Erin, must we leave you, driven by the tyrant's hand?
Must we ask a mother's blessing from a strange and distant land?
Where the cruel cross of England shall nevermore be seen,
And where, please God, we 'll live and die still wearing of the green.

Street Ballad

XCIV

The Memory of the Dead

1798

Who fears to speak of Ninety-Eight?
    Who blushes at the name?
When cowards mock the patriot's fate,
    Who hangs his head for shame?
He's all a knave or half a slave
    Who slights his country thus;
But a *true* man, like you, man,
    Will fill your glass with us.

We drink the memory of the brave,
    The faithful and the few —
Some lie far off beyond the wave,
    Some sleep in Ireland, too;
All, all are gone — but still lives on
    The fame of those who died;
All true men, like you, men,
    Remember them with pride.

Some on the shores of distant lands
    Their weary hearts have laid,
And by the stranger's heedless hands
    Their lonely graves were made;
But, though their clay be far away
    Beyond the Atlantic foam,
In true men, like you, men,
    Their spirit's still at home.

The Memory of the Dead

The dust of some is Irish earth;
   Among their own they rest;
And the same land that gave them birth
   Has caught them to her breast;
And we will pray that from their clay
   Full many a race may start
Of true men, like you, men,
   To act as brave a part.

They rose in dark and evil days
   To right their native land;
They kindled here a living blaze
   That nothing shall withstand.
Alas! that Might can vanquish Right —
   They fell, and passed away;
But true men, like you, men,
   Are plenty here to-day.

Then here's their memory — may it be
   For us a guiding light,
To cheer our strife for liberty,
   And teach us to unite!
Through good and ill, be Ireland's still,
   Though sad as theirs your fate;
And true men, like you, men,
   Like those of Ninety-Eight.

                              John Kells Ingram

XCV

The Geraldines

The Geraldines! the Geraldines! — 'tis full a thousand years
Since, 'mid the Tuscan vineyards, bright flashed their battle-spears;
When Capet seized the crown of France, their iron shields were known,
And their sabre dint struck terror on the banks of the Garonne;
Across the downs of Hastings they spurred hard by William's side,
And the grey sands of Palestine with Moslem blood they dyed;
But never then, nor thence till now, have falsehood or disgrace
Been seen to soil Fitzgerald's plume, or mantle in his face.

The Geraldines! the Geraldines! — 'tis true, in Strongbow's van,
By lawless force, as conquerors, their Irish reign began;
And, O! through many a dark campaign they proved their prowess stern,
In Leinster's plains, and Munster's vales, on king, and chief, and kerne:
But noble was the cheer within the halls so rudely won,
And generous was the steel-gloved hand that had such slaughter done!
How gay their laugh! how proud their mien! you'd ask no herald's sign —
Among a thousand you had known the princely Geraldine.

These Geraldines! these Geraldines! — not long our air they breathed,
Not long they fed on venison, in Irish water seethed,
Not often had their children been by Irish mothers nursed,
When from their full and genial hearts an Irish feeling burst!
The English monarchs strove in vain, by law, and force, and bribe,
To win from Irish thoughts and ways this "more than Irish" tribe;
For still they clung to fosterage, to Brehon, cloak, and bard:
What king dare say to Geraldine, "Your Irish wife discard?"

Ye Geraldines! ye Geraldines! how royally ye reigned
O'er Desmond broad and rich Kildare, and English arts disdained:
Your sword made knights, your banner waved, free was your bugle call
By Glyn's green slopes, and Dingle's tide, from Barrow's banks to Eochaill,[1]
What gorgeous shrines, what Brehon lore, what minstrel feasts there were
In and around Magh Nuadhaid's[2] keep, and palace-filled Adare!
But not for rite or feast ye stayed when friend or kin were pressed;
And foemen fled when "Crom abu" bespoke your lance in rest.

[1] Engl. Youghal.   [2] Engl. Maynooth.

Ye Geraldines! ye Geraldines! since Silken Thomas flung
King Henry's sword on council board, the English thanes
   among,
Ye never ceased to battle brave against the English sway,
Though axe and brand and treachery your proudest cut
   away.
Of Desmond's blood through woman's veins passed on the
   exhausted tide;
His title lives — a Sassanach churl usurps the lion's hide;
And though Kildare tower haughtily, there's ruin at the
   root,
Else why, since Edward fell to earth, had such a tree no
   fruit?

True Geraldines! brave Geraldines! as torrents mould the
   earth,
You channeled deep old Ireland's heart by constancy and
   worth:
When Ginckle leaguered Limerick, the Irish soldiers gazed
To see if in the setting sun dead Desmond's banner blazed!
And still it is the peasants' hope upon the Curragh's mere,
"They live who 'll see ten thousand men with good Lord
   Edward here."
So let them dream till brighter days, when, not by Edward's
   shade,
But by some leader true as he, their lines shall be arrayed!

These Geraldines! these Geraldines! rain wears away the
   rock,
And time may wear away the tribe that stood the battle's
   shock,
But ever, sure, while one is left of all that honored race,
In front of Ireland's chivalry is that Fitzgerald's place;

And though the last were dead and gone, how many a field
    and town,
From Thomas Court to Abbeyfeile, would cherish their
    renown!
And men will say of valor's rise, or ancient power's decline,
" 'T will never soar, it never shone, as did the Geraldine."

The Geraldines! the Geraldines! and are there any fears
Within the sons of conquerors for full a thousand years?
Can treason spring from out a soil bedewed with martyrs'
    blood?
Or has that grown a purling brook which long rushed down
    a flood?
By Desmond swept with sword and fire, by clan and keep
    laid low,
By Silken Thomas and his kin, by sainted Edward! No!
The forms of centuries rise up, and in the Irish line
COMMAND THEIR SONS TO TAKE THE POST THAT FITS
    THE GERALDINE!

Thomas Davis

XCVI

Soggarth Aroon

Am I the slave they say,
    Soggarth aroon?
Since you did show the way,
    Soggarth aroon,
Their slave no more to be,
While they would work with me
Old Ireland's slavery,
    Soggarth aroon.

Why not her poorest man,
    Soggarth aroon,
Try and do all he can,
    Soggarth aroon,
Her commands to fulfil
Of his own heart and will,
Side by side with you still,
    Soggarth aroon?

Loyal and brave to you,
    Soggarth aroon,
Yet be not slave to you,
    Soggarth aroon,
Nor, out of fear to you —
Stand up so near to you —
Och! out of fear to *you*,
    Soggarth aroon!

Who in the winter's night,
    Soggarth aroon,
When the cold blast did bite,
    Soggarth aroon,
Came to my cabin door,
And, on my earthen floor,
Knelt by me, sick and poor,
    Soggarth aroon?

Who, on the marriage day,
    Soggarth aroon,
Made the poor cabin gay,
    Soggarth aroon? —
And did both laugh and sing,
Making our hearts to ring,

>   At the poor christening,
>   Soggarth aroon?
>
> Who, as friend only met,
>   Soggarth aroon,
> Never did flout me yet,
>   Soggarth aroon?
> And when my heart was dim,
> Gave, while his eye did brim,
> What I should give to him,
>   Soggarth aroon?
>
> Och! you, and only you,
>   Soggarth aroon!
> And for this I was true to you,
>   Soggarth aroon;
> *In* love they 'll never shake,
> When for ould Ireland's sake,
> We a true part did take,
>   Soggarth aroon!

John Banim

XCVII

The Girl I Left behind Me

The dames of France are fond and free,
   And Flemish lips are willing,
And soft the maids of Italy,
   And Spanish eyes are thrilling;
Still, though I bask beneath their smile,
   Their charms fail to bind me,
And my heart falls back to Erin's Isle,
   To the girl I left behind me.

For she 's as fair as Shannon's side,
   And purer than its water,
But she refus'd to be my bride
   Though many a year I sought her;
Yet, since to France I sail'd away,
   Her letters oft remind me,
That I promis'd never to gainsay
   The girl I left behind me.

She says, "My own dear love, come home,
   My friends are rich and many,
Or else, abroad with you I 'll roam,
   A soldier stout as any;
If you 'll not come, nor let me go,
   I 'll think you have resign'd me," —
My heart nigh broke when I answer'd "No,"
   To the girl I left behind me.

For never shall my true love brave
   A life of war and toiling,
And never as a skulking slave
   I 'll tread my native soil on;
But, were it free or to be freed,
   The battle's close would find me
To Ireland bound, nor message need
   From the girl I left behind me.

Anonymous

MISCELLANEOUS SONGS AND BALLADS

XCVIII

The Harp that once through Tara's Halls

    The harp that once through Tara's halls
        The soul of music shed,
    Now hangs as mute on Tara's walls
        As if that soul were fled.
    So sleeps the pride of former days,
        So glory's thrill is o'er,
    And hearts that once beat high for praise
        Now feel that pulse no more.

    No more to chiefs and ladies bright
        The harp of Tara swells:
    The chord alone that breaks at night
        Its tale of ruin tells.
    Thus Freedom now so seldom wakes,
        The only throb she gives
    Is when some heart indignant breaks,
        To show that still she lives.

Thomas Moore

XCIX

The Meeting of the Waters

There is not in the wide world a valley so sweet
As that vale in whose bosom the bright waters meet;
Oh! the last ray of feeling and life must depart,
Ere the bloom of that valley shall fade from my heart.

Yet it *was* not that nature had shed o'er the scene
Her purest of crystal and brightest of green;
'T was *not* the soft magic of streamlet or hill —
Oh, no! — it was something more exquisite still.

'T was that friends, the beloved of my bosom, were near,
Who made every dear scene of enchantment more dear,
And who felt how the best charms of nature improve,
When we see them reflected from looks that we love.

Sweet vale of Avoca! how calm could I rest
In thy bosom of shade with the friends I love best,
Where the storms that we feel in this cold world should cease,
And our hearts, like thy waters, be mingled in peace!

Thomas Moore

C

Believe me, if all those endearing young charms

Believe me, if all those endearing young charms
   Which I gaze on so fondly to-day,
Were to change by to-morrow, and fleet in my arms,
   Like fairy-gifts fading away,
Thou wouldst still be adored, as this moment thou art,
   Let thy loveliness fade as it will;
And around the dear ruin each wish of my heart
   Would entwine itself verdantly still.

It is not while beauty and youth are thine own,
   And thy cheeks unprofaned by a tear,
That the fervor and faith of a soul may be known
   To which time will but make thee more dear;

No, the heart that has truly loved never forgets,
  But as truly loves on to the close,
As the sunflower turns on her god when he sets
  The same look which she turned when he rose.

Thomas Moore

CI

The Last Rose of Summer

'T is the last rose of summer
  Left blooming alone;
All her lovely companions
  Are faded and gone;
No flow'r of her kindred,
  No rose-bud is nigh,
To reflect back her blushes,
  Or give sigh for sigh.

I 'll not leave thee, thou lone one!
  To pine on the stem;
Since the lovely are sleeping,
  Go, sleep thou with them.
Thus kindly I scatter
  Thy leaves o'er the bed,
Where thy mates of the garden
  Lie scentless and dead.

So soon may *I* follow,
  When friendships decay,
And from Love's shining circle
  The gems drop away.

When true hearts lie wither'd,
   And fond ones are flown,
Oh! who would inhabit
   This bleak world alone?

Thomas Moore

CII

Oft, in the stilly night

Oft, in the stilly night,
   Ere Slumber's chain has bound me,
Fond Memory brings the light
   Of other days around me:
     The smiles, the tears,
     Of boyhood's years,
   The words of love then spoken;
     The eyes that shone,
     Now dimm'd and gone,
   The cheerful hearts now broken!
Thus, in the stilly night,
   Ere Slumber's chain has bound me
Sad Memory brings the light
   Of other days around me.

When I remember all
   The friends, so link'd together,
I 've seen around me fall
   Like leaves in wintry weather,
     I feel like one
     Who treads alone
   Some banquet-hall deserted,
     Whose lights are fled,
     Whose garlands dead,

   And all but he departed!
Thus in the stilly night,
   Ere Slumber's chain has bound me,
Sad Memory brings the light
   Of other days around me.

Thomas Moore

CIII

The Coolun

[FROM THE IRISH]

Oh, had you seen the Coolun
   Walking down by the cuckoo's street,
With the dew of the meadow shining
   On her milk-white twinkling feet,
Oh, my love she is and my colleen oge,
   And she dwells in Balnagar;
And she bears the palm of beauty bright
   From the fairest that in Erin are.

In Balnagar is the Coolun,
   Like the berry on the bough her cheek;
Bright beauty dwells for ever
   On her fair neck and ringlets sleek.
Oh, sweeter is her mouth's soft music
   Than the lark or thrush at dawn,
Or the blackbird in the greenwood singing
   Farewell to the setting sun.

Rise up, my boy, make ready
   To horse, for I forth would ride,
To follow the modest damsel
   Where she walks on the green hillside;

For ever since our youth were we plighted
   In faith, truth, and wedlock true.
O sweeter her voice is nine times over
   Than organ or cuckoo!

And ever since my childhood
   I've loved the dair and darling child;
But our people came between us,
   And with lucre our pure love defiled.
Oh, my woe it is and my bitter pain,
   And I weep it night and day
That the colleen bawn of my early love
   Is torn from my heart away.

Sir Samuel Ferguson

CIV

The Bells of Shandon

With deep affection and recollection
   I often think of the Shandon bells,
Whose sounds so wild would, in days of childhood,
   Fling round my cradle their magic spells —
On this I ponder, where'er I wander,
   And thus grow fonder, sweet Cork, of thee;
     With thy bells of Shandon,
     That sound so grand on
The pleasant waters of the river Lee.

I have heard bells chiming full many a clime in,
   Tolling sublime in cathedral shrine;
While at a glib rate brass tongues would vibrate,
   But all their music spoke naught like thine;

For memory, dwelling on each proud swelling
  Of thy belfry knelling its bold notes free,
    Made the bells of Shandon
    Sound far more grand on
The pleasant waters of the river Lee.

I have heard bells tolling "old Adrian's Mole" in,
  Their thunder rolling from the Vatican,
And cymbals glorious, swinging uproarious
  In the gorgeous turrets of Notre Dame;
But thy sounds were sweeter than the dome of Peter
  Flings o'er the Tiber, pealing solemnly: —
    Oh, the bells of Shandon,
    Sound far more grand on
The pleasant waters of the river Lee.

There's a bell in Moscow, — while on tower and kiosk, O!
  In St. Sophia the Turkman gets,
And loud in air, calls men to prayer,
  From the tapering summit of tall minarets, —
Such empty phantom I freely grant them,
  But there's an anthem more dear to me:
    'T is the bells of Shandon,
    That sound so grand on
The pleasant waters of the river Lee.

Francis Mahony

CV

Kathleen Mavourneen

Kathleen Mavourneen! the gray dawn is breaking,
  The horn of the hunter is heard on the hill,
The lark from her light wing the bright dew is shaking —
  Kathleen Mavourneen! what, slumbering still?

Oh! hast thou forgotten how soon we must sever?
  Oh! hast thou forgotten how soon we must part?
It may be for years and it may be for ever,
  Oh! why art thou silent, thou voice of my heart?

Kathleen Mavourneen! awake from thy slumbers,
  The blue mountains glow in the sun's golden light;
Ah! where is the spell that once hung on thy numbers?
  Arise in thy beauty, thou star of the night!
Mavourneen! Mavourneen! my sad tears are falling,
  To think that from Erin and thee I must part:
It may be for years, and it may be for ever,
  Then why art thou silent, thou voice of my heart?

Mrs. Crawford

CVI

The Lament of the Irish Emigrant

I'm sittin' on the stile, Mary, where we sat side by side
On a bright May mornin', long ago, when first you were my bride;
The corn was springin' fresh and green, and the lark sang loud and high;
And the red was on your lip, Mary, and the love-light in your eye.

The *place* is little changed, Mary, the day is bright as then,
The lark's loud song is in my ear, and the corn is green again:
But I miss the soft clasp of your hand, and your breath warm on my cheek,
And I still keep list'nin' for the words you nevermore will speak.

'T is but a step down yonder lane, and the little church stands near, —
The church where we were wed, Mary; I see the spire from here.
But the graveyard lies between, Mary, and my step might break your rest, —
For I 've laid you, darling, down to sleep, with your baby on your breast.

I 'm very lonely now, Mary, — for the poor make no new friends;
But, oh! they love the better still the few our Father sends!
And you were all *I* had, Mary — my blessin' and my pride:
There 's nothin' left to care for now, since my poor Mary died.

Yours was the good, brave heart, Mary, that still kept hopin' on,
When the trust in God had left my soul, and my arm's young strength was gone;
There was comfort ever on *your* lip, and the kind look on your brow, —
I bless you, Mary, for that same, though you cannot hear me now.

I thank you for the patient smile when your heart was fit to break, —
When the hunger pain was gnawing there, and you hid it for *my* sake;
I bless you for the pleasant word when your heart was sad and sore, —
Oh, I 'm thankful you are gone, Mary, where grief can't reach you more!

I'm bidding you a long farewell, my Mary, — kind and true!
But I'll not forget you, darling, in the land I'm goin' to;
They say there's bread and work for all, and the sun shines always there, —
But I'll not forget old Ireland, were it fifty times as fair!

And often in those grand old woods I'll sit, and shut my eyes,
And my heart will travel back again to the place where Mary lies;
And I'll think I see the little stile where we sat side by side,
And the springin' corn, and the bright May morn, when first you were my bride.

Lady Dufferin

CVII

Dear Land

When comes the day all hearts to weigh,
    If staunch they be, or vile,
Shall we forget the sacred debt
    We owe our mother isle?
My native heath is brown beneath,
    My native waters blue,
But crimson red o'er both shall spread,
    Ere I am false to you,
               Dear land —
    Ere I am false to you.

When I behold your mountains bold —
    Your noble lakes and streams —
A·mingled tide of grief and pride
    Within my bosom teems.

Dear Land

I think of all your long, dark thrall —
  Your martyrs brave and true;
And dash apart the tears that start —
  We must not *weep* for you,
                    Dear land —
  We must not *weep* for you.

My grandsire died his home beside;
  They seized and hanged him there;
His only crime, in evil time
  Your hallowed green to wear.
Across the main his brothers twain
  Were sent to pine and rue;
And still they turned, with hearts that burned,
  In hopeless love to you,
                    Dear land —
  In hopeless love to you.

My boyish ear still clung to hear
  Of Erin's pride of yore, —
Ere Norman foot had dared pollute
  Her independent shore —
Of chiefs, long dead, who rose to head
  Some gallant patriot few;
Till all my aim on earth became
  To strike one blow for you,
                    Dear land —
  To strike one blow for you.

What path is best your rights to wrest
  Let other heads divine;
By work or word, with voice or sword,
  To follow them be mine.

The breast that zeal and hatred steel,
  No terrors can subdue;
If death should come, that martyrdom
  Were sweet, endured for you,
                    Dear land —
  Were sweet, endured for you.

Sliabh Cuilinn

CVIII

O Bay of Dublin

O bay of Dublin! my heart you 're troublin',
  Your beauty haunts me like a fevered dream;
Like frozen fountains that the sun sets bubblin',
  My heart's blood warms when I but hear your name.
And never till this life pulse ceases,
  My earliest thought you 'll cease to be!
O there 's no one here knows how fair that place is,
  And no one cares how dear it is to me.

Sweet Wicklow mountains! the sunlight sleeping
  On your green banks is a picture rare:
You crowd around me like young girls peeping,
  And puzzling me to say which is most fair!
As though you 'd see your own sweet faces
  Reflected in that smooth and silver sea.
O! my blessing on those lovely places,
  Though no one cares how dear they are to me.

How often when at work I 'm sitting,
  And musing sadly on the days of yore,

I think I see my Katey knitting,
   And the children playing round the cabin door;
I think I see the neighbors' faces
   All gathered round, their long-lost friend to see.
O! though no one knows how fair that place is,
   Heaven knows how dear my poor home was to me.

Lady Dufferin

CIX

Killarney

By Killarney's lakes and fells,
   Emerald isles and winding bays,
Mountain paths and woodland dells,
   Memory ever fondly strays.
Bounteous Nature loves all lands;
   Beauty wanders everywhere,
Footprints leaves on many strands,
   But her home is surely there!
Angels fold their wings and rest
   In the Eden of the West,
Beauty's home, Killarney,
   Ever fair Killarney.

Inisfallen's ruined shrine
   May suggest a passing sigh,
But man's faith can ne'er decline,
   Such God's wonders passing by:
Castle Lough and Glenna Bay,
   Mountain Torc and Eagle's Nest;
Still at Muckross you must pray,
   Though the monks are now at rest;

Angels wonder not that man
   There would fain prolong life's span;
Beauty's home, Killarney,
   Ever fair Killarney.

No place else can charm the eye
   With such bright and varied tints,
Every rock that you pass by
   Verdure broiders or besprints,
Virgin there the green grass grows,
   Every morn Spring's natal day,
Bright-hued berries daff the snows,
   Smiling Winter's frown away.
Angels often pausing there,
   Doubt if Eden were more fair;
Beauty's home, Killarney,
   Ever fair Killarney.

Music there for Echo dwells,
   Makes each sound a harmony,
Many-voiced the chorus swells,
   Till it faints in ecstasy:
With the charmful tints below
   Seems the heaven above to vie,
All rich colors that we know
   Tinge the cloud-wreaths in the sky;
Wings of angels so might shine,
   Glancing back soft light divine —
Beauty's home, Killarney,
   Ever fair Killarney.

Edmund O'Rourke

CX

Song from the Backwoods

Deep in Canadian woods we 've met,
    From one bright island flown!
Great is the land we tread, but yet
    Our hearts are with our own.
And ere we leave this shanty small,
    While fades the autumn day,
We 'll toast old Ireland! dear old Ireland!
    Ireland, boys, hurray!

We 've heard her faults a hundred times,
    The new ones and the old,
In songs and sermons, rants and rhymes,
    Enlarged some fifty-fold.
But take them all, the great and small,
    And this we 've got to say: —
Here 's dear old Ireland! good old Ireland!
    Ireland, boys, hurray!

We know that brave and good men tried
    To snap her rusty chain,
That patriots suffered, martyrs died,
    And all, 't is said, in vain;
But no, boys, no! a glance will show
    How far they 've won their way —
Here 's good old Ireland! loved old Ireland!
    Ireland, boys, hurray!

We 've seen the wedding and the wake,
    The patron and the fair;

The stuff they take, the fun they make,
  And the heads they break down there,
With a loud "hurroo" and a "pillalu,"
  And a thundering "clear the way!"
Here's gay old Ireland! dear old Ireland!
  Ireland, boys, hurray!

And well we know in the cool grey eves,
  When the hard day's work is o'er,
How soft and sweet are the words that greet
  The friends who meet once more;
With "Mary machree!" and "My Pat! 'tis he!"
  And "My own heart night and day!"
Ah, fond old Ireland! dear old Ireland!
  Ireland, boys, hurray!

And happy and bright are the groups that pass
  From their peaceful homes, for miles
O'er fields, and roads, and hills, to Mass,
  When Sunday morning smiles!
And deep the zeal their true hearts feel
  When low they kneel and pray.
O, dear old Ireland! blest old Ireland!
  Ireland, boys, hurray!

But deep in Canadian woods we've met,
  And we never may see again
The dear old isle where our hearts are set,
  And our first fond hopes remain!
But come, fill up another cup,
  And with every sup let's say —
Here's loved old Ireland! good old Ireland!
  Ireland, boys, hurray!

T. D. Sullivan

CXI

To God and Ireland True

I sit beside my darling's grave
   Who in the prison died,
And though my tears fall thick and fast
   I think of him with pride;
Ay, softly fall my tears like dew,
For one to God and Ireland true.

"I love my God o'er all," he said,
   "And then I love my land,
And next I love my Lily sweet
   Who pledged me her white hand:
To each, to all, I'm ever true,
To God — to Ireland, and to you."

No tender nurse his hard bed smoothed,
   Or softly raised his head:
He fell asleep and woke in heaven
   Ere I knew he was dead;
Yet why should I my darling rue?
He was to God and Ireland true.

Oh, 't is a glorious memory;
   I'm prouder than a queen
To sit beside my hero's grave
   And think on what has been:
And O my darling, I am true
To God — to Ireland, and to you!

Ellen O'Leary

BOOK FIFTH — POEMS OF AMERICA: HISTORICAL AND PATRIOTIC

CXII

America

My country, 't is of thee,
Sweet Land of Liberty,
  Of thee I sing;
Land where my fathers died,
Land of the pilgrims' pride,
From every mountain-side
  Let Freedom ring.

My native country, thee,
Land of the noble free, —
  Thy name I love;
I love thy rocks and rills,
Thy woods and templed hills,
My heart with rapture thrills
  Like that above.

Let music swell the breeze,
And ring from all the trees,
  Sweet Freedom's song;
Let mortal tongues awake;
Let all that breathe partake;
Let rocks their silence break, —
  The sound prolong.

Our fathers' God, to Thee,
Author of Liberty,
    To Thee I sing;
Long may our land be bright
With Freedom's holy light;
Protect us by Thy might,
    Great God, our King.

S. F. Smith

CXIII

Columbus

1492

Behind him lay the gray Azores,
  Behind the Gates of Hercules;
Before him not the ghost of shores,
  Before him only shoreless seas.
The good mate said: "Now must we pray,
  For lo! the very stars are gone.
Brave Admiral, speak, what shall I say?"
  "Why, say, 'Sail on! sail on! and on!'"

"My men grow mutinous day by day;
  My men grow ghastly wan and weak."
The stout mate thought of home; a spray
  Of salt wave washed his swarthy cheek.
"What shall I say, brave Admiral, say,
  If we sight naught but seas at dawn?"
"Why, you shall say at break of day,
  'Sail on! sail on! sail on! and on!'"

They sailed and sailed, as winds might blow,
　Until at last the blanched mate said:
"Why, now not even God would know
　Should I and all my men fall dead.
These very winds forget their way,
　For God from these dread seas is gone.
Now speak, brave Admiral, speak and say"—
　He said: "Sail on! sail on! and on!"

They sailed. They sailed. Then spake the mate:
　"This mad sea shows his teeth to-night.
He curls his lip, he lies in wait,
　With lifted teeth, as if to bite!
Brave Admiral, say but one good word:
　What shall we do when hope is gone?"
The words leapt like a leaping sword:
　"Sail on! sail on! sail on! and on!"

Then, pale and worn, he kept his deck,
　And peered through darkness. Ah, that night
Of all dark nights! And then a speck—
　A light! A light! A light! A light!
It grew, a starlit flag unfurled!
　It grew to be Time's burst of dawn.
He gained a world; he gave that world
　Its grandest lesson: "On! sail on!"

Joaquin Miller

CXIV

The Landing of the Pilgrim Fathers in New England

1620

The breaking waves dashed high
  On a stern and rock-bound coast,
And the woods against a stormy sky
  Their giant branches tossed;

And the heavy night hung dark,
  The hills and waters o'er,
When a band of exiles moored their bark
  On the wild New England shore.

Not as the conqueror comes,
  They, the true-hearted, came;
Not with the roll of the stirring drums,
  And the trumpet that sings of fame;

Not as the flying come,
  In silence and in fear;
They shook the depths of the desert gloom
  With their hymns of lofty cheer.

Amidst the storm they sang,
  And the stars heard, and the sea;
And the sounding aisles of the dim woods rang
  To the anthem of the free.

The ocean eagle soared
  From his nest by the white waves' foam;
And the rocking pines of the forest roared —
  This was their welcome home.

There were men with hoary hair
   Amidst that pilgrim band:
Why had they come to wither there,
   Away from their childhood's land?

There was woman's fearless eye,
   Lit by her deep love's truth;
There was manhood's brow, serenely high,
   And the fiery heart of youth.

What sought they thus afar?
   Bright jewels of the mine?
The wealth of seas, the spoils of war?
   They sought a faith's pure shrine!

Ay, call it holy ground,
   The soil where first they trod;
They have left unstained what there they found —
   Freedom to worship God.

Felicia Hemans

CXV

The Pilgrim Fathers

The Pilgrim Fathers, — where are they?
   The waves that brought them o'er
Still roll in the bay, and throw their spray
   As they break along the shore;
Still roll in the bay, as they rolled that day
   When the *Mayflower* moored below,
When the sea around was black with storms,
   And white the shore with snow.

The mists that wrapped the Pilgrim's sleep
  Still brood upon the tide;
And his rocks yet keep their watch by the deep
  To stay its waves of pride.
But the snow-white sail that he gave to the gale,
  When the heavens looked dark, is gone, —
As an angel's wing through an opening cloud
  Is seen, and then withdrawn.

The pilgrim exile, — sainted name!
  The hill whose icy brow
Rejoiced, when he came, in the morning's flame,
  In the morning's flame burns now.
And the moon's cold light, as it lay that night
  On the hillside and the sea,
Still lies where he laid his houseless head, —
  But the Pilgrim! where is he?

The Pilgrim Fathers are at rest:
  When summer's throned on high,
And the world's warm breast is in verdure drest,
  Go, stand on the hill where they lie.
The earliest ray of the golden day
  On that hallowed spot is cast;
And the evening sun, as he leaves the world,
  Looks kindly on that spot last.

The Pilgrim spirit has not fled:
  It walks in noon's broad light;
And it watches the bed of the glorious dead,
  With the holy stars by night.
It watches the bed of the brave who have bled,
  And still guards this ice-bound shore,
Till the waves of the bay, where the *Mayflower* lay,
  Shall foam and freeze no more.

John Pierpont

CXVI

The Thanksgiving in Boston Harbor

"Praise ye the Lord!" The psalm to-day
  Still rises on our ears,
Borne from the hills of Boston Bay
  Through five times fifty years,
When Winthrop's fleet from Yarmouth crept
  Out to the open main,
And through the widening waters swept,
  In April sun and rain.
    "Pray to the Lord with fervent lips,"
      The leader shouted, "pray;"
    And prayer arose from all the ships
      As faded Yarmouth Bay.

They passed the Scilly Isles that day,
  And May-days came, and June,
And thrice upon the ocean lay
  The full orb of the moon.
And as that day on Yarmouth Bay,
  Ere England sunk from view,
While yet the rippling Solent lay
  In April skies of blue,
    "Pray to the Lord with fervent lips,"
      Each morn was shouted, "pray;"
    And prayer arose from all the ships,
      As first in Yarmouth Bay.

Blew warm the breeze o'er western seas,
  Through Maytime morns, and June,
Till hailed these souls the Isles of Shoals,
  Low 'neath the summer moon;

And as Cape Ann arose to view,
  And Norman's Woe they passed,
The wood-doves came the white mists through,
  And circled round each mast.
    "Pray to the Lord with fervent lips,"
      Then called the leader, "pray;"
    And prayer arose from all the ships,
      As first in Yarmouth Bay.

Above the sea the hill-tops fair —
  God's towers — began to rise,
And odors rare breathe through the air,
  Like the balms of Paradise.
Through burning skies the ospreys flew,
  And near the pine-cooled shores
Danced airy boat and thin canoe,
  To flash of sunlit oars.
    "Pray to the Lord with fervent lips,"
      The leader shouted, "pray!"
    Then prayer arose, and all the ships
      Sailed into Boston Bay.

The white wings folded, anchors down,
  The sea-worn fleet in line,
Fair rose the hills where Boston town
  Should rise from clouds of pine;
Fair was the harbor, summit-walled,
  And placid lay the sea.
"Praise ye the Lord," the leader called;
  "Praise ye the Lord," spake he.
    "Give thanks to God with fervent lips,
      Give thanks to God to-day,"
    The anthem rose from all the ships
      Safe moored in Boston Bay.

The Thanksgiving in Boston Harbor

"Praise ye the Lord!" Primeval woods
  First heard the ancient song,
And summer hills and solitudes
  The echoes rolled along.
The Red Cross flag of England blew
  Above the fleet that day,
While Shawmut's triple peaks in view
  In amber hazes lay.
    "Praise ye the Lord with fervent lips,
      Praise ye the Lord to-day,"
    The anthem rose from all the ships
      Safe moored in Boston Bay.

The *Arabella* leads the song —
  The *Mayflower* sings below,
That erst the Pilgrims bore along
  The Plymouth reefs of snow.
Oh! never be that psalm forgot
  That rose o'er Boston Bay,
When Winthrop sang, and Endicott,
  And Saltonstall, that day:
    "Praise ye the Lord with fervent lips,
      Praise ye the Lord to-day;"
    And praise arose from all the ships,
      Like prayers in Yarmouth Bay.

That psalm our fathers sang we sing,
  That psalm of peace and wars,
While o'er our heads unfolds its wing
  The flag of forty stars.
And while the nation finds a tongue
  For nobler gifts to pray,
'T will ever sing the song they sung
  That first Thanksgiving Day:

> "Praise ye the Lord with fervent lips,
>   Praise ye the Lord to-day;"
> So rose the song from all the ships,
>   Safe moored in Boston Bay.

Our fathers' prayers have changed to psalms,
  As David's treasures old
Turned, on the Temple's giant arms,
  To lily-work of gold.
Ho! vanished ships from Yarmouth's tide,
  Ho! ships of Boston Bay,
Your prayers have crossed the centuries wide
  To this Thanksgiving Day!
>   We pray to God with fervent lips,
>   We praise the Lord to-day,
>   As prayers arose from Yarmouth ships,
>   But psalms from Boston Bay.

Hezekiah Butterworth

CXVII

Concord Hymn

[COMMEMORATING BATTLE OF 1775]

By the rude bridge that arched the flood,
  Their flag to April's breeze unfurled,
Here once the embattled farmers stood,
  And fired the shot heard round the world.

The foe long since in silence slept;
  Alike the conqueror silent sleeps;
And Time the ruined bridge has swept
  Down the dark stream which seaward creeps.

On the green bank, by this soft stream,
    We set to-day a votive stone;
That memory may their dead redeem,
    When, like our sires, our sons are gone.

Spirit, that made those heroes dare
    To die, and leave their children free,
Bid Time and Nature gently spare
    The shaft we raise to them and thee.

Ralph Waldo Emerson

CXVIII

Warren's Address

Stand! the ground 's your own, my braves!
Will ye give it up to slaves?
Will ye look for greener graves?
    Hope ye mercy still?
What 's the mercy despots feel?
Hear it in that battle-peal!
Read it on yon bristling steel!
    Ask it, — ye who will.

Fear ye foes who kill for hire?
Will ye to your homes retire?
Look behind you! — they 're a-fire!
    And, before you, see
Who have done it! From the vale
On they come! — and will ye quail?
Leaden rain and iron hail
    Let their welcome be!

In the God of battles trust!
Die we may, — and die we must;
But, oh, where can dust to dust
    Be consign'd so well,
As where Heaven its dews shall shed
On the martyr'd patriot's bed,
And the rocks shall raise their head
    Of his deeds to tell?

John Pierpont

CXIX

The Maryland Battalion

1776

Spruce Macaronis, and pretty to see,
Tidy and dapper and gallant were we;
Blooded, fine gentlemen, proper and tall,
Bold in a fox-hunt and gay at a ball;
Prancing soldados so martial and bluff,
Billets for bullets, in scarlet and buff, —
But our cockades were clasped with a mother's low prayer,
And the sweethearts that braided the sword-knots were fair.

There was grummer of drums humming hoarse in the hills,
And the bugle sang fanfaron down by the mills;
By Flatbush the bagpipes were droning amain,
And keen cracked the rifles in Martense's lane;
For the Hessians were flecking the hedges with red,
And the grenadiers' tramp marked the roll of the dead.

Three to one, flank and rear, flashed the files of St. George,
The fierce gleam of their steel as the glow of a forge.

The Maryland Battalion

The brutal boom-boom of their swart cannoneers
Was sweet music compared with the taunt of their cheers—
For the brunt of their onset, our crippled array,
And the light of God's leading gone out in the fray!

Oh, the rout on the left and the tug on the right!
The mad plunge of the charge and the wreck of the flight!
When the cohorts of Grant held stout Stirling at strain,
And the mongrels of Hesse went tearing the slain;
When at Freeke's Mill the flumes and the sluices ran red,
And the dead choked the dyke and the marsh choked the dead!

"O Stirling, good Stirling! how long must we wait?
Shall the shout of your trumpet unleash us too late?
Have you never a dash for brave Mordecai Gist,
With his heart in his throat, and his blade in his fist?
Are we good for no more than to prance in a ball,
When the drums beat the charge and the clarions call?"

Tralara! Tralara! Now praise we the Lord
For the clang of His call and the flash of His sword!
Tralara! Tralara! Now forward to die;
For the banner, hurrah! and for sweethearts, good-bye!
"Four hundred wild lads!" Maybe so. I'll be bound
'T will be easy to count us, face up, on the ground.
If we hold the road open, tho' Death take the toll,
We'll be missed on parade when the States call the roll—
When the flags meet in peace and the guns are at rest,
And fair Freedom is singing Sweet Home in the West.

John W. Palmer

CXX

"Columbia, Columbia, to Glory Arise"

1777

Columbia, Columbia, to glory arise,
The queen of the world, and the child of the skies!
Thy genius commands thee; with rapture behold,
While ages on ages thy splendors unfold.
Thy reign is the last, and the noblest of time,
Most fruitful thy soil, most inviting thy clime;
Let the crimes of the east ne'er encrimson thy name,
Be freedom, and science, and virtue thy fame.

To conquest and slaughter let Europe aspire;
Whelm nations in blood, and wrap cities in fire;
Thy heroes the rights of mankind shall defend,
And triumph pursue them, and glory attend.
A world is thy realm: for a world be thy laws,
Enlarged as thine empire, and just as thy cause;
On Freedom's broad basis, that empire shall rise,
Extend with the main, and dissolve with the skies.

Fair Science her gates to thy sons shall unbar,
And the east see thy morn hide the beams of her star.
New bards, and new sages, unrival'd shall soar
To fame unextinguish'd, when time is no more;
To thee, the last refuge of virtue designed,
Shall fly from all nations the best of mankind;
Here, grateful to heaven, with transport shall bring
Their incense, more fragrant than odors of spring.

Nor less shall thy fair ones to glory ascend,
And genius and beauty in harmony blend;

The graces of form shall awake pure desire,
And the charms of the soul ever cherish the fire;
Their sweetness unmingled, their manners refined,
And virtue's bright image, instamp'd on the mind,
With peace, and soft rapture, shall teach life to glow,
And light up a smile in the aspect of woe.

Thy fleets to all regions thy power shall display,
The nations admire, and the ocean obey;
Each shore to thy glory its tribute unfold,
And the east and the south yield their spices and gold.
As the day-spring unbounded, thy splendor shall flow,
And earth's little kingdoms before thee shall bow:
While the ensigns of union, in triumph unfurl'd,
Hush the tumult of war, and give peace to the world.

Thus, as down a lone valley, with cedars o'erspread,
From war's dread confusion I pensively stray'd —
The gloom from the face of fair heaven retired;
The winds ceased to murmur; the thunders expired;
Perfumes, as of Eden, flow'd sweetly along,
And a voice, as of angels, enchantingly sung:
"Columbia, Columbia, to glory arise,
The queen of the world, and the child of the skies."

Timothy Dwight

CXXI

Song of Marion's Men

1780–1781

Our band is few but true and tried,
   Our leader frank and bold;
The British soldier trembles
   When Marion's name is told.

Our fortress is the good greenwood,
　　Our tent the cypress-tree;
We know the forest round us,
　　As seamen know the sea.
We know its walls of thorny vines,
　　Its glades of reedy grass,
Its safe and silent islands
　　Within the dark morass.

Woe to the English soldiery
　　That little dread us near!
On them shall light at midnight
　　A strange and sudden fear
When, waking to their tents on fire,
　　They grasp their arms in vain,
And they who stand to face us
　　Are beat to earth again;
And they who fly in terror deem
　　A mighty host behind,
And hear the tramp of thousands
　　Upon the hollow wind.

Then sweet the hour that brings release
　　From danger and from toil:
We talk the battle over,
　　And share the battle's spoil.
The woodland rings with laugh and shout,
　　As if a hunt were up,
And woodland flowers are gathered
　　To crown the soldier's cup.
With merry songs we mock the wind
　　That in the pine-top grieves,
And slumber long and sweetly
　　On beds of oaken leaves.

Song of Marion's Men

Well knows the fair and friendly moon
  The band that Marion leads —
The glitter of their rifles,
  The scampering of their steeds.
'T is life to guide the fiery barb
  Across the moonlight plain;
'T is life to feel the night-wind
  That lifts the tossing mane.
A moment in the British camp —
  A moment — and away
Back to the pathless forest,
  Before the peep of day.

Grave men there are by broad Santee,
  Grave men with hoary hairs;
Their hearts are all with Marion,
  For Marion are their prayers.
And lovely ladies greet our band,
  With kindliest welcoming,
With smiles like those of summer,
  And tears like those of spring.
For them we wear these trusty arms,
  And lay them down no more
Till we have driven the Briton,
  Forever from our shore.

William Cullen Bryant

CXXII

Eutaw Springs

1781

At Eutaw Springs the valiant died:
   Their limbs with dust are covered o'er;
Weep on, ye springs, your tearful tide;
   How many heroes are no more!

If in this wreck of ruin they
   Can yet be thought to claim a tear,
O smite thy gentle breast, and say
   The friends of freedom slumber here!

Thou, who shalt trace this bloody plain,
   If goodness rules thy generous breast,
Sigh for the wasted rural reign;
   Sigh for the shepherds sunk to rest!

Stranger, their humble graves adorn;
   You too may fall, and ask a tear:
'T is not the beauty of the morn
   That proves the evening shall be clear.

They saw their injured country's woe,
   The flaming town, the wasted field;
Then rushed to meet the insulting foe;
   They took the spear — but left the shield.

Led by thy conquering standards, Greene,
   The Britons they compelled to fly:
None distant viewed the fatal plain,
   None grieved in such a cause to die —

But, like the Parthians famed of old,
   Who, flying, still their arrows threw,

These routed Britons, full as bold,
  Retreated, and retreating slew.

Now rest in peace our patriot band;
  Though far from nature's limits thrown,
We trust they find a happier land,
  A brighter Phœbus of their own.

Philip Freneau

CXXIII

Carmen Bellicosum

In their ragged regimentals
Stood the old Continentals,
    Yielding not,
When the grenadiers were lunging,
And like hail fell the plunging
    Cannon-shot;
    When the files
    Of the isles,
From the smoky night-encampment, bore the banner of the rampant
    Unicorn;
And grummer, grummer, grummer, rolled the roll of the drummer
    Through the morn!

Then with eyes to the front all,
And with guns horizontal,
    Stood our sires;
And the balls whistled deadly,
And in streams flashing redly
    Blazed the fires:

As the roar
On the shore
Swept the strong battle-breakers o'er the green-sodded acres
Of the plain;
And louder, louder, louder, cracked the black gunpowder,
Cracking amain!

Now like smiths at their forges
Worked the red St. George's
Cannoneers,
And the villainous saltpetre
Rung a fierce, discordant metre
Round their ears;
As the swift
Storm-drift,
With hot sweeping anger, came the horse-guards' clangor
On our flanks.
Then higher, higher, higher, burned the old-fashioned fire
Through the ranks!

Then the bare-headed Colonel
Galloped through the white infernal
Powder-cloud;
And his broadsword was swinging,
And his brazen throat was ringing
Trumpet-loud;
Then the blue
Bullets flew,
And the trooper-jackets redden at the touch of the leaden
Rifle-breath;
And rounder, rounder, rounder, roared the iron six-pounder,
Hurling death!

Guy Humphrey McMaster

CXXIV

The Sword of Bunker Hill

He lay upon his dying bed;
  His eye was growing dim,
When with a feeble voice he called
  His weeping son to him:
"Weep not, my boy!" the vet'ran said,
  "I bow to Heaven's high will,—
But quickly from yon antlers bring
  The sword of Bunker Hill."

The sword was brought, the soldier's eye
  Lit with a sudden flame;
And as he grasp'd the ancient blade,
  He murmured WARREN'S name:
Then said, "My boy, I leave you gold,—
  But what is richer still,
I leave you, mark me, mark me now—
  The sword of Bunker Hill.

"'T was on that dread, immortal day,
  I dared the Briton's band,
A Captain raised this blade on me—
  I tore it from his hand;
And while the glorious battle raged,
  It lightened freedom's will—
For, boy, the God of freedom blessed
  The sword of Bunker Hill.

"Oh, keep the sword!"— his accents broke—
  A smile — and he was dead—
But his wrinkled hand still grasped the blade
  Upon that dying bed.

The son remains; the sword remains —
  Its glory growing still —
And twenty millions bless the sire,
  And sword of Bunker Hill.

William Ross Wallace

CXXV

Washington's Statue

The quarry whence thy form majestic sprung
  Has peopled earth with grace,
Heroes and gods that elder bards have sung,
  A bright and peerless race;
But from its sleeping veins ne'er rose before
  A shape of loftier name
Than his, who Glory's wreath with meekness wore,
  The noblest son of Fame.

Sheathed is the sword that Passion never stained;
  His gaze around is cast,
As if the joys of Freedom, newly gained,
  Before his vision passed;
As if a nation's shout of love and pride
  With music filled the air,
And his calm soul was lifted on the tide
  Of deep and grateful prayer;
As if the crystal mirror of his life
  To fancy sweetly came,
With scenes of patient toil and noble strife,
  Undimmed by doubt or shame;
As if the lofty purpose of his soul
  Expression would betray, —

The high resolve Ambition to control,
    And thrust her crown away!
O, it was well in marble firm and white
    To carve our hero's form,
Whose angel guidance was our strength in fight,
    Our star amid the storm!
Whose matchless truth has made his name divine,
    And human freedom sure,
His country great, his tomb earth's dearest shrine,
    While man and time endure!
And it is well to place his image there
    Upon the soil he blest:
Let meaner spirits, who its councils share,
    Revere that silent guest!
Let us go up with high and sacred love
    To look on his pure brow,
And as, with solemn grace, he points above,
    Renew the patriot's vow!

Henry Theodore Tuckerman

CXXVI

Hail, Columbia

1798

Hail, Columbia! happy land!
Hail, ye heroes! heaven-born band!
Who fought and bled in Freedom's cause,
Who fought and bled in Freedom's cause,
And when the storm of war was gone,
Enjoyed the peace your valor won.

Let independence be your boast,
Ever mindful what it cost;
Ever grateful for the prize,
Let its altar reach the skies.

Chorus

> Firm, united, let us be,
> Rallying round our Liberty;
> As a band of brothers joined,
> Peace and safety we shall find.

Immortal patriots! rise once more:
Defend your rights, defend your shore:
Let no rude foe, with impious hand,
Let no rude foe, with impious hand,
Invade the shrine where sacred lies
Of toil and blood the well-earned prize.
While offering peace, sincere and just,
In Heaven we place a manly trust,
That truth and justice will prevail,
And every scheme of bondage fail. — *Cho.*

Sound, sound the trump of fame!
Let WASHINGTON'S great name
Ring thro' the world with loud applause,
Ring thro' the world with loud applause;
Let every clime to Freedom dear
Listen with a joyful ear.
With equal skill, and godlike pow'r,
He governs in the fearful hour
Of horrid war, or guides with ease
The happier time of honest peace. — *Cho.*

Behold the chief who now commands,
Once more to serve his country stands!
The rock on which the storm will beat,
The rock on which the storm will beat;
But armed in virtue, firm and true,
His hopes are fixed on Heaven and you.
When hope was sinking in dismay,
When glooms obscured Columbia's day,
His steady mind, from changes free,
Resolved on death or Liberty.— *Cho.*

Joseph Hopkinson

CXXVII

The "Constitution's" Last Fight

1815

A Yankee ship and a Yankee crew —
  Constitution, where ye bound for?
Wherever, my lad, there's fight to be had
  Acrost the Western ocean.

Our captain was married in Boston town
  And sailed next day to sea;
For all must go when the State says so;
  Blow high, blow low, sailed we.

"Now, what shall I bring for a bridal gift
  When my home-bound pennant flies?
The rarest that be on land or sea
  It shall be my lady's prize."

"There 's never a prize on sea or land
  Could bring such joy to me
As my true love sound and homeward bound
  With a king's ship under his lee."

The Western ocean is wide and deep,
  And wild its tempests blow,
But bravely rides *Old Ironsides*,
  A-cruising to and fro.

We cruised to the east and we cruised to north,
  And southing far went we,
And at last off Cape de Verd we raised
  Two frigates sailing free.

Oh, God made man, and man made ships,
  But God makes very few
Like him who sailed our ship that day,
  And fought her, one to two.

He gained the weather gauge of both,
  He held them both a-lee;
And gun for gun, till set of sun,
  He spoke them fair and free;

Till the night fog fell on spar and sail,
  And ship, and sea, and shore,
And our only aim was the bursting flame
  And the hidden cannon's roar.

Then a long rift in the mist showed up
  The stout *Cyane*, close-hauled
To swing in our wake and our quarter rake,
  And a boasting Briton bawled:

The "Constitution's" Last Fight

"Starboard and larboard, we 've got him fast
   Where his heels won't take him through;
Let him luff or wear, he 'll find us there, —
   Ho, Yankee, which will you do?"

We did not luff and we did not wear,
   But braced our topsails back,
Till the sternway drew us fair and true
   Broadsides athwart her track.

Athwart her track and across her bows
   We raked her fore and aft,
And out of the fight and into the night
   Drifted the beaten craft.

The slow *Levant* came up too late;
   No need had we to stir;
Her decks we swept with fire, and kept
   The flies from troubling her.

We raked her again, and her flag came down, —
   The haughtiest flag that floats, —
And the lime-juice dogs lay there like logs,
   With never a bark in their throats.

With never a bark and never a bite,
   But only an oath to break,
As we squared away for Praya Bay
   With our prizes in our wake.

Parole they gave and parole they broke,
   What matters the cowardly cheat,
If the captain's bride was satisfied
   With the one prize laid at her feet?

A Yankee ship and a Yankee crew —
   Constitution, where ye bound for?
Wherever the British prizes be,
Though it's one to two, or one to three, —
Old Ironsides means victory,
   Acrost the Western ocean.

                              James Jeffrey Roche

CXXVIII

"Old Ironsides"

Ay, tear her tattered ensign down!
   Long has it waved on high,
And many an eye has danced to see
   That banner in the sky;
Beneath it rung the battle shout,
   And burst the cannon's roar; —
The meteor of the ocean air
   Shall sweep the clouds no more.

Her deck, once red with heroes' blood,
   Where knelt the vanquished foe,
When winds were hurrying o'er the flood,
   And waves were white below,
No more shall feel the victor's tread,
   Or know the conquered knee;
The harpies of the shore shall pluck
   The eagle of the sea!

O, better that her shattered hulk
   Should sink beneath the wave;
Her thunders shook the mighty deep,
   And there should be her grave;

Nail to the mast her holy flag,
 Set every threadbare sail,
And give her to the god of storms,
 The lightning and the gale!

Oliver Wendell Holmes

CXXIX

The Warship of 1812

She was no armored cruiser of twice six thousand tons,
With the thirty foot of metal that make your modern guns;
She did n't have a free board of thirty foot in clear,
An' she did n't need a million repairin' fund each year.
She had no rackin' engines to ramp an' stamp an' strain,
To work her steel-clad turrets an' break her hull in twain;
She did not have electric lights, — the battle-lantern's glare
Was all the light the 'tween decks had, — an' God's own good fresh air.

She had no gapin' air-flumes to throw us down our breath,
An' we did n't batten hatches to smother men to death;
She did n't have five hundred smiths — two hundred men would do —
In the old-time Yankee frigate for an old-time Yankee crew,
An' a fightin' Yankee captain, with his old-time Yankee clothes,
A-cursin' Yankee sailors with his old-time Yankee oaths.
She was built of Yankee timber and manned by Yankee men,
An' fought by Yankee sailors — Lord send their like again!

With the wind abaft the quarter and the sea foam flyin' free,
An' every tack and sheet housed taut and braces eased to lee,
You could hear the deep sea thunder from the knightheads where it broke,
As she trailed her lee guns under a blindin' whirl o' smoke.

She did n't run at twenty knots, — she was n't built to run, —
An' we did n't need a half a watch to handle every gun.
Our captain did n't fight his ship from a little pen o' steel;
He fought her from his quarter-deck, with two hands at the wheel,
An' we fought in Yankee fashion, half naked, — stripped to board, —
An' when they hauled their red flag down we praised the Yankee Lord.
We fought like Yankee sailors, an' we 'll do it, too, again;
You 've changed the ships an' methods, but you can't change Yankee men!

Philadelphia Record

CXXX

The Star-Spangled Banner

1814

Oh, say, can you see, by the dawn's early light,
    What so proudly we hailed at the twilight's last gleaming?
Whose broad stripes and bright stars, thro' the clouds of the fight,
    O'er the ramparts we watched were so gallantly streaming?

And the rockets' red glare, the bombs bursting in air,
  Gave proof thro' the night that our flag was still there;
Oh, say, does that star-spangled banner yet wave
  O'er the land of the free, and the home of the brave?

Chorus

  Oh, say, does the Star-Spangled Banner yet wave
  O'er the land of the free and the home of the brave?

On that shore dimly seen thro' the mists of the deep,
  Where the foe's haughty host in dread silence reposes,
What is that which the breeze, o'er the towering steep,
  As it fitfully blows, now conceals, now discloses?
Now it catches the gleam of the morning's first beam,
  In full glory reflected now shines in the stream;
'T is the star-spangled banner; oh, long may it wave
  O'er the land of the free, and the home of the brave!
        — *Cho.*

And where is that band who so vauntingly swore,
  Mid the havoc of war and the battle's confusion,
A home and a country they 'd leave us no more?
  Their blood has washed out their foul footsteps' pollution.
No refuge could save the hireling and slave
  From terror of flight or the gloom of the grave;
And the star-spangled banner in triumph doth wave
  O'er the land of the free, and the home of the brave.
        — *Cho.*

Oh! thus be it ever, when freemen shall stand
  Between their loved home, and the war's desolation!
Blest with victory and peace, may the heav'n-rescued land
  Praise the Power that made and preserved us a nation.

Then conquer we must, when our cause it is just,
  And this be our motto, "*In God is our trust!*"
And the star-spangled banner in triumph shall wave
  O'er the land of the free, and the home of the brave.
— Cho.

Francis Scott Key

CXXXI

Columbia, the Gem of the Ocean

O Columbia, the gem of the ocean,
  The home of the brave and the free,
The shrine of each patriot's devotion,
  A world offers homage to thee!
Thy mandates make heroes assemble,
  When Liberty's form stands in view;
Thy banners make Tyranny tremble,
  When borne by the red, white, and blue.

Chorus

  When borne by the red, white, and blue,
  When borne by the red, white, and blue,
  Thy banners make Tyranny tremble,
  When borne by the red, white, and blue.

When war winged its wide desolation
  And threatened the land to deform,
The ark then of Freedom's foundation,
  Columbia, rode safe thro' the storm;
With her garlands of vict'ry around her,
  When so proudly she bore her brave crew,
With her flag proudly floating before her,
  The boast of the red, white, and blue. *— Cho.*

The wine cup, the wine cup bring hither,
    And fill you it true to the brim;
May the wreaths they have won never wither,
    Nor the star of their glory grow dim!
May the service united ne'er sever,
    But they to their colors prove true!
The Army and Navy forever!
    Three cheers for the red, white, and blue! — *Cho.*

D. T. Shaw

CXXXII

The American Flag

1819

When Freedom from her mountain height
    Unfurled her standard to the air,
She tore the azure robe of night,
    And set the stars of glory there.
She mingled with its gorgeous dyes
The milky baldric of the skies,
And striped its pure celestial white
With streakings of the morning light;
Then from his mansion in the sun
She called her eagle bearer down,
And gave into his mighty hand
The symbol of her chosen land.

Majestic monarch of the cloud,
    Who rear'st aloft thy regal form,
To hear the tempest trumpings loud
And see the lightning lances driven,
    When strive the warriors of the storm,

And rolls the thunder-drum of heaven,
Child of the sun! to thee 't is given
　To guard the banner of the free,
To hover in the sulphur smoke,
To ward away the battle stroke,
And bid its blendings shine afar,
Like rainbows on the cloud of war,
　The harbingers of victory!

Flag of the brave! thy folds shall fly,
The sign of hope and triumph high,
When speaks the signal trumpet tone,
And the long line comes gleaming on.
Ere yet the life-blood, warm and wet,
Has dimmed the glistening bayonet,
Each soldier eye shall brightly turn
To where thy sky-born glories burn,
And, as his springing steps advance,
Catch war and vengeance from the glance.
And when the cannon-mouthings loud
Heave in wild wreaths the battle shroud,
And gory sabres rise and fall
Like shoots of flame on midnight's pall,
Then shall thy meteor glances glow,
　And cowering foes shall shrink beneath
Each gallant arm that strikes below
　That lovely messenger of death.

Flag of the seas! on ocean wave
Thy stars shall glitter o'er the brave;
When death, careering on the gale,
Sweeps darkly round the bellied sail,
And frighted waves rush wildly back
Before the broadside's reeling rack,

Each dying wanderer of the sea
Shall look at once to heaven and thee,
And smile to see thy splendors fly
In triumph o'er his closing eye.

Flag of the free heart's hope and home!
　By angel hands to valor given;
Thy stars have lit the welkin dome,
　And all thy hues were born in heaven.
Forever float that standard sheet!
　Where breathes the foe but falls before us,
With Freedom's soil beneath our feet,
　And Freedom's banner streaming o'er us?

Joseph Rodman Drake

CXXXIII

God Bless our Native Land

God bless our native land!
Firm may she ever stand,
　Through storm and night:
When the wild tempests rave,
Ruler of wind and wave,
Do Thou our country save
　By Thy great might!

For her our prayers shall rise
To God, above the skies;
　On Him we wait:
Thou who art ever nigh,
Guarding with watchful eye,
To Thee aloud we cry,
　"God save the State!"

C. T. Brooks (1834) and *J. S. Dwight* (1844)

CXXXIV

The Defence of the Alamo

1840

Santa Ana came storming, as a storm might come;
  There was rumble of cannon; there was rattle of blade;
There was cavalry, infantry, bugle, and drum, —
  Full seven thousand, in pomp and parade,
The chivalry, flower of Mexico;
And a gaunt two hundred in the Alamo!

And thirty lay sick, and some were shot through;
  For the siege had been bitter, and bloody, and long.
"Surrender, or die!" — "Men, what will you do?"
  And Travis, great Travis, drew sword, quick and strong;
Drew a line at his feet . . . "Will you come? Will you go?
I die with my wounded, in the Alamo."

Then Bowie gasped, "Lead me over that line!"
  Then Crockett, one hand to the sick, one hand to his gun,
Crossed with him; then never a word or a sign
  Till all, sick or well, all, all save but one,
One man. Then a woman stepped, praying, and slow
Across; to die at her post in the Alamo.

Then that one coward fled, in the night, in that night
  When all men silently prayed and thought
Of home; of to-morrow; of God and the right,
  Till dawn: and with dawn came Travis's cannon shot,
In answer to insolent Mexico,
From the old bell-tower of the Alamo.

Then came Santa Ana; a crescent of flame!
  Then the red "escalade"; then the fight hand to hand;
Such an unequal fight as never had name
  Since the Persian hordes butchered that doomed Spartan
    band.
All day, — all day and all night, and the morning? so slow
Through the battle smoke mantling the Alamo.

Now silence! Such silence! Two thousand lay dead
  In a crescent outside! And within? Not a breath
Save the gasp of a woman, with gory gashed head,
  All alone, all alone there, waiting for death;
And she but a nurse. Yet when shall we know
Another like this of the Alamo?

Shout "Victory, victory, victory ho!"
  I say 't is not always to the hosts that win;
I say that the victory, high or low,
  Is given the hero who grapples with sin,
Or legion or single; just asking to know
When duty fronts death in his Alamo.

Joaquin Miller

CXXXV

The Bivouac of the Dead

1847

The muffled drum's sad roll has beat
  The soldier's last tattoo;
No more on Life's parade shall meet
  That brave and fallen few.

On Fame's eternal camping-ground
    Their silent tents are spread,
And Glory guards, with solemn round,
    The bivouac of the dead.

No rumor of the foe's advance
    Now swells upon the wind;
No troubled thought at midnight haunts
    Of loved ones left behind;
No vision of the morrow's strife
    The warrior's dream alarms;
No braying horn nor screaming fife
    At dawn shall call to arms.

Their shivered swords are red with rust,
    Their plumèd heads are bowed;
Their haughty banner, trailed in dust,
    Is now their martial shroud.
And plenteous funeral tears have washed
    The red stains from each brow,
And the proud forms, by battle gashed,
    Are free from anguish now.

The neighing troop, the flashing blade,
    The bugle's stirring blast,
The charge, the dreadful cannonade,
    The din and shout, are past;
Nor war's wild note nor glory's peal
    Shall thrill with fierce delight
Those breasts that nevermore may feel
    The rapture of the fight.

Like the fierce northern hurricane
    That sweeps his great plateau,

Flushed with the triumph yet to gain,
    Came down the serried foe.
Who heard the thunder of the fray
    Break o'er the field beneath,
Knew well the watchword of that day
    Was "Victory or Death."

Long had the doubtful conflict raged
    O'er all that stricken plain,
For never fiercer fight had waged
    The vengeful blood of Spain;
And still the storm of battle blew,
    Still swelled the gory tide;
Not long, our stout old chieftain knew,
    Such odds his strength could bide.

'T was in that hour his stern command
    Called to a martyr's grave
The flower of his beloved land,
    The nation's flag to save.
By rivers of their fathers' gore
    His firstborn laurels grew,
And well he deemed the sons would pour
    Their lives for glory too.

Full many a norther's breath has swept
    O'er Angostura's plain,
And long the pitying sky has wept
    Above its mouldered slain.
The raven's scream, or eagle's flight,
    Or shepherd's pensive lay,
Alone awakes each sullen height
    That frowned o'er that dread fray.

Sons of the Dark and Bloody Ground,
   Ye must not slumber there,
Where stranger steps and tongues resound
   Along the heedless air.
Your own proud land's heroic soil
   Shall be your fitter grave :
She claims from war his richest spoil —
   The ashes of her brave.

Thus 'neath their parent turf they rest,
   Far from the gory field,
Borne to a Spartan mother's breast
   On many a bloody shield ;
The sunshine of their native sky
   Smiles sadly on them here,
And kindred eyes and hearts watch by
   The heroes' sepulchre.

Rest on, embalmed and sainted dead !
   Dear as the blood ye gave ;
No impious footstep here shall tread
   The herbage of your grave ;
Nor shall your glory be forgot
   While Fame her record keeps,
Or Honor points the hallowed spot
   Where Valor proudly sleeps.

Yon marble minstrel's voiceless stone
   In deathless song shall tell,
When many a vanished age hath flown,
   The story how ye fell ;
Nor wreck, nor change, nor winter's blight,
   Nor Time's remorseless doom,
Shall dim one ray of glory's light
   That gilds your deathless tomb.

Theodore O'Hara

CXXXVI

John Brown's Body

John Brown's body lies a-mould'ring in the grave,
John Brown's body lies a-mould'ring in the grave,
John Brown's body lies a-mould'ring in the grave,
    His soul is marching on!

Chorus

    Glory! Glory Hallelujah!
    Glory! Glory Hallelujah!
    Glory! Glory Hallelujah!
    His soul is marching on.

He's gone to be a soldier in the army of the Lord!
He's gone to be a soldier in the army of the Lord!
He's gone to be a soldier in the army of the Lord!
    His soul is marching on. — *Cho.*

John Brown's knapsack is strapped upon his back.
    His soul is marching on. — *Cho.*

His pet lambs will meet him on the way,
    And they'll go marching on. — *Cho.*

They'll hang Jeff Davis to a sour apple tree,
    As they go marching on. — *Cho.*

Now for the Union let's give three rousing cheers,
    As we go marching on.
        Hip, hip, hip, hip, Hurrah!

Anonymous

CXXXVII

Battle-Hymn of the Republic

1861

Mine eyes have seen the glory of the coming of the Lord:
He is trampling out the vintage where the grapes of wrath
  are stored;
He hath loosed the fateful lightning of His terrible swift
  sword:
    His truth is marching on.

I have seen Him in the watch-fires of a hundred circling
  camps;
They have builded Him an altar in the evening dews and
  damps;
I have read His righteous sentence by the dim and flaring
  lamps.
    His day is marching on.

I have read a fiery gospel, writ in burnished rows of steel:
"As ye deal with my contemners, so with you my grace
  shall deal;
Let the Hero, born of woman, crush the serpent with His heel,
    Since God is marching on."

He has sounded forth the trumpet that shall never call
  retreat;
He is sifting out the hearts of men before His judgment-seat:
Oh! be swift, my soul, to answer Him, be jubilant, my
  feet!
    Our God is marching on.

In the beauty of the lilies Christ was born across the sea,
With a glory in His bosom that transfigures you and me:
As He died to make men holy, let us die to make men free,
    While God is marching on.

Julia Ward Howe

CXXXVIII

The Battle-Cry of Freedom

Yes, we 'll rally 'round the flag, boys, we 'll rally once again,
  Shouting the battle-cry of freedom;
We will rally from the hillside, we 'll gather from the plain,
  Shouting the battle-cry of freedom.

Chorus

  The Union forever, hurrah, boys, hurrah!
    Down with the traitor, up with the star,
  While we rally 'round the flag, boys, rally once again,
    Shouting the battle-cry of freedom.

We are springing to the call of our brothers gone before,
  Shouting the battle-cry of freedom,
And we 'll fill the vacant ranks with a million freemen more,
  Shouting the battle-cry of freedom. — *Cho.*

We will welcome to our numbers the loyal, true, and brave,
  Shouting the battle-cry of freedom,
And altho' they may be poor, not a man shall be a slave,
  Shouting the battle-cry of freedom. — *Cho.*

So we 're springing to the call from the East and from the West,
  Shouting the battle-cry of freedom,
And we 'll hurl the rebel crew from the land we love the best,
  Shouting the battle-cry of freedom. — *Cho.*

George F. Root

CXXXIX

The Reveille

Hark! I hear the tramp of thousands,
    And of armèd men the hum;
Lo! a nation's hosts have gathered
    Round the quick-alarming drum,
        Saying, "Come,
        Freemen, come!
Ere your heritage be wasted," said the quick-alarming drum.

"Let me of my heart take counsel:
    War is not of life the sum;
Who shall stay and reap the harvest
    When the autumn days shall come?"
        But the drum
        Echoed, "Come!
Death shall reap the braver harvest," said the solemn-sounding drum.

"But when won the coming battle,
    What of profit springs therefrom?
What if conquest, subjugation,
    Even greater ills become?"
        But the drum
        Answered, "Come!
You must do the sum to prove it," said the Yankee-answering drum.

"What if, mid the cannon's thunder,
    Whistling shot, and bursting bomb,
When my brothers fall around me,
    Should my heart grow cold and numb?"

>   But the drum
>   Answered, "Come!
> Better there in death united, than in life a recreant —
>   Come!"
>
>   Thus they answered, — hoping, fearing,
>   Some in faith, and doubting some, —
>   Till a trumpet-voice, proclaiming,
>   Said, "My chosen people, come!"
>   Then the drum,
>   Lo! was dumb;
> For the great heart of the nation, throbbing, answered,
>   "Lord, we come!"

Bret Harte

CXL

The "Cumberland"

1862

> At anchor in Hampton Roads we lay,
>   On board of the *Cumberland*, sloop-of-war;
> And at times from the fortress across the bay
>   The alarum of drums swept past,
>   Or a bugle blast
> From the camp on the shore.
>
> Then far away to the south uprose
>   A little feather of snow-white smoke,
> And we knew that the iron ship of our foes
>   Was steadily steering its course
>   To try the force
> Of our ribs of oak.

Down upon us heavily runs,
    Silent and sullen, the floating fort;
Then comes a puff of smoke from her guns,
        And leaps the terrible death,
            With fiery breath,
    From each open port.

We are not idle, but send her straight
    Defiance back in a full broadside!
As hail rebounds from a roof of slate,
        Rebounds our heavier hail
           From each iron scale
    Of the monster's hide.

"Strike your flag!" the rebel cries,
    In his arrogant old plantation strain.
"Never!" our gallant Morris replies;
        "It is better to sink than to yield!"
        And the whole air pealed
    With the cheers of our men.

Then, like a kraken huge and black,
    She crushed our ribs in her iron grasp!
Down went the *Cumberland* all a wrack,
        With a sudden shudder of death,
        And the cannon's breath
    For her dying gasp.

Next morn, as the sun rose over the bay,
    Still floated our flag at the mainmast head
Lord, how beautiful was Thy day!
        Every waft of the air
        Was a whisper of prayer,
    Or a dirge for the dead.

Ho! brave hearts that went down in the seas!
  Ye are at peace in the troubled stream;
Ho! brave land! with hearts like these,
    Thy flag, that is rent in twain,
      Shall be one again,
  And without a seam!

Henry Wadsworth Longfellow

CXLI

Kearney at Seven Pines

1862

So that soldierly legend is still on its journey, —
  That story of Kearney who knew not to yield!
'T was the day when with Jameson, fierce Berry, and Birney,
  Against twenty thousand he rallied the field.
Where the red volleys poured, where the clamor rose highest,
  Where the dead lay in clumps through the dwarf oak and pine,
Where the aim from the thicket was surest and nighest, —
  No charge like Phil Kearney's along the whole line.

When the battle went ill, and the bravest were solemn,
  Near the dark Seven Pines, where we still held our ground,
He rode down the length of the withering column,
  And his heart at our war-cry leapt up with a bound.
He snuffed, like his charger, the wind of the powder, —
  His sword waved us on, and we answered the sign;
Loud our cheer as we rushed, but his laugh rang the louder;
  "There's the devil's own fun, boys, along the whole line!"

How he strode his brown steed! How we saw his blade
    brighten
  In the one hand still left, — and the reins in his teeth!
He laughed like a boy when the holidays heighten,
  But a soldier's glance shot from his visor beneath.
Up came the reserves to the mellay infernal,
  Asking where to go in, — through the clearing or pine?
"Oh, anywhere! Forward! 'T is all the same, Colonel;
  You 'll find lovely fighting along the whole line!"

Oh, evil the black shroud of night at Chantilly,
  That hid him from sight of his brave men and tried!
Foul, foul sped the bullet that clipped the white lily,
  The flower of our knighthood, the whole army's pride!
Yet we dream that he still — in that shadowy region
  Where the dead form their ranks at the wan drummer's
    sign —
Rides on, as of old, down the length of his legion,
  And the word still is Forward! along the whole line.

Edmund Clarence Stedman

CXLII

Barbara Frietchie

1862

Up from the meadows rich with corn,
Clear in the cool September morn,

The clustered spires of Frederick stand
Green-walled by the hills of Maryland.

Round about them orchards sweep,
Apple and peach tree fruited deep,

Fair as the garden of the Lord
To the eyes of the famished rebel horde,

On that pleasant morn of the early fall
When Lee marched over the mountain wall,

Over the mountains winding down,
Horse and foot, into Frederick town.

Forty flags with their silver stars,
Forty flags with their crimson bars,

Flapped in the morning wind: the sun
Of noon looked down, and saw not one.

Up rose old Barbara Frietchie then,
Bowed with her fourscore years and ten;

Bravest of all in Frederick town,
She took up the flag the men hauled down;

In her attic window the staff she set,
To show that one heart was loyal yet.

Up the street came the rebel tread,
Stonewall Jackson riding ahead.

Under his slouched hat left and right
He glanced; the old flag met his sight.

"Halt!" — the dust-brown ranks stood fast.
"Fire!" — out blazed the rifle-blast.

It shivered the window, pane and sash;
It rent the banner with seam and gash.

Quick, as it fell, from the broken staff
Dame Barbara snatched the silken scarf.

She leaned far out on the window-sill,
And shook it forth with a royal will.

"Shoot, if you must, this old gray head,
But spare your country's flag," she said.

A shade of sadness, a blush of shame,
Over the face of the leader came;

The nobler nature within him stirred
To life at that woman's deed and word:

"Who touches a hair of yon gray head
Dies like a dog! March on!" he said.

All day long through Frederick street
Sounded the tread of marching feet:

All day long that free flag tost
Over the heads of the rebel host.

Ever its torn folds rose and fell
On the loyal winds that loved it well;

And through the hill-gaps sunset light
Shone over it with a warm good-night.

Barbara Frietchie's work is o'er,
And the Rebel rides on his raids no more.

Honor to her! and let a tear
Fall, for her sake, on Stonewall's bier.

Over Barbara Frietchie's grave,
Flag of Freedom and Union, wave!

Peace and order and beauty draw
Round thy symbol of light and law;

And ever the stars above look down
On thy stars below in Frederick town!

John Greenleaf Whittier

CXLIII

Vicksburg

1862–1863

For sixty days and upwards,
   A storm of shell and shot
Rained round us in a flaming shower,
   But still we faltered not.
"If the noble city perish,"
   Our grand young leader said,
"Let the only walls the foe shall scale
   Be the ramparts of the dead!"

For sixty days and upwards,
   The eye of heaven waxed dim;
And even throughout God's holy morn,
   O'er Christian prayer and hymn,

Arose a hissing tumult,
   As if the fiends in air
Strove to engulf the voice of faith
   In the shrieks of their despair.

There was wailing in the houses,
   There was trembling on the marts,
While the tempest raged and thundered,
   Mid the silent thrill of hearts;
But the Lord, our shield, was with us,
   And ere a month had sped,
Our very women walked the streets
   With scarce one throb of dread.

And the little children gambolled,
   Their faces purely raised,
Just for a wondering moment,
   As the huge bombs whirled and blazed;
Then turned with silvery laughter
   To the sports which children love,
Thrice-mailed in the sweet, instinctive thought
   That the good God watched above.

Yet the hailing bolts fell faster,
   From scores of flame-clad ships,
And about us, denser, darker,
   Grew the conflict's wild eclipse,
Till a solid cloud closed o'er us,
   Like a type of doom and ire,
Whence shot a thousand quivering tongues
   Of forked and vengeful fire.

But the unseen hands of angels
   Those death-shafts warned aside,

And the dove of heavenly mercy
    Ruled o'er the battle tide;
In the houses ceased the wailing,
    And through the war-scarred marts
The people strode, with step of hope,
    To the music in their hearts.

                        Paul Hamilton Hayne

CXLIV

Keenan's Charge [1]

1863

I

The sun had set;
The leaves with dew were wet:
Down fell a bloody dusk
On the woods, that second of May,
Where Stonewall's corps, like the beast of prey,
Tore through, with angry tusk.

"They 've trapped us, boys!"
Rose from our flank a voice.
With a rush of steel and smoke
On came the rebels straight,
Eager as love and wild as hate;
And our line reeled and broke:

Broke and fled.
No one stayed — but the dead!
With curses, shrieks, and cries,
Horses and wagons and men
Tumbled back through the shuddering glen,
And above us the fading skies.

---

[1] From *Dreams and Days*, by permission of Charles Scribner's Sons.

There 's one hope still, —
Those batteries parked on the hill!
"Battery, wheel!" (mid the roar)
"Pass pieces; fix prolonge to fire
Retiring. Trot!" In the panic dire
A bugle rings "Trot!" — and no more.

The horses plunged,
The cannon lurched and lunged,
To join the hopeless rout.
But suddenly rode a form
Calmly in front of the human storm,
With a stern, commanding shout:

"Align those guns!"
(We knew it was Pleasonton's.)
The cannoneers bent to obey,
And worked with a will at his word:
And the black guns moved as if *they* had heard.
But ah the dread delay!

"To wait is crime;
O God, for ten minutes' time!"
The General looked around.
There Keenan sat, like a stone,
With his three hundred horse alone,
Less shaken than the ground.

"Major, your men?"
"Are soldiers, General." "Then
Charge, Major! Do your best:
Hold the enemy back, at all cost,
Till my guns are placed, — else the army is lost.
You die to save the rest!"

II

By the shrouded gleam of the western skies,
Brave Keenan looked into Pleasonton's eyes
For an instant, — clear, and cool, and still;
Then, with a smile, he said: "I will."

"Cavalry, charge!" Not a man of them shrank.
Their sharp, full cheer, from rank on rank,
Rose joyously, with a willing breath, —
Rose like a greeting hail to death.
Then forward they sprang, and spurred and clashed;
Shouted the officers, crimson-sashed;
Rode well the men, each brave as his fellow,
In their faded coats of the blue and yellow;
And above in the air, with an instinct true,
Like a bird of war their pennon flew.

With clank of scabbards and thunder of steeds,
And blades that shine like sunlit reeds,
And strong brown faces bravely pale
For fear their proud attempt shall fail,
Three hundred Pennsylvanians close
On twice ten thousand gallant foes.

Line after line the troopers came
To the edge of the wood that was ringed with flame;
Rode in and sabred and shot — and fell;
Nor came one back his wounds to tell.
And full in the midst rose Keenan, tall
In the gloom, like a martyr awaiting his fall,
While the circle-stroke of his sabre, swung
'Round his head, like a halo there, luminous hung.
Line after line — ay, whole platoons,
Struck dead in their saddles — of brave dragoons

By the maddened horses were onward borne
And into the vortex flung, trampled and torn;
As Keenan fought with his men, side by side.
So they rode, till there were no more to ride.

But over them, lying there, shattered and mute,
What deep echo rolls? — 'T is a death-salute
From the cannon in place; for, heroes, you braved
Your fate not in vain: the army was saved!

Over them now — year following year —
Over their graves the pine-cones fall,
And the whippoorwill chants his spectre-call;
But they stir not again; they raise no cheer:
They have ceased. But their glory shall never cease,
Nor their light be quenched in the light of peace.
The rush of their charge is resounding still
That saved the army at Chancellorsville.

George Parsons Lathrop

CXLV

Gettysburg

1863

Wave, wave your glorious battle-flags, brave soldiers of the North,
And from the fields your arms have won to-day go proudly forth!
For now, O comrades dear and leal — from whom no ills could part,
Through the long years of hopes and fears, the nation's constant heart —

Men who have driven so oft the foe, so oft have striven in
    vain,
Yet ever in the perilous hour have crossed his path again,—
At last we have our heart's desire, from them we met have
    wrung
A victory that round the world shall long be told and sung!
It was the memory of the past that bore us through the fray,
That gave the grand old army strength to conquer on this
    day!

Oh, now forget how dark and red Virginia's rivers flow,
The Rappahannock's tangled wilds, the glory and the woe;
The fever-hung encampments, where our dying knew full
    sore
How sweet the north-wind to the cheek it soon shall cool no
    more;
The fields we fought, and gained, and lost; the lowland sun
    and rain
That wasted us, that bleached the bones of our unburied
    slain!
There was no lack of foes to meet, of deaths to die no lack,
And all the hawks of heaven learned to follow on our track;
But henceforth, hovering southward, their flight shall mark
    afar
The paths of yon retreating host that shun the northern
    star.

At night before the closing fray, when all the front was still,
We lay in bivouac along the cannon-crested hill.
Ours was the dauntless Second Corps; and many a soldier
    knew
How sped the fight, and sternly thought of what was yet
    to do.

Guarding the centre there, we lay, and talked with bated breath
Of Buford's stand beyond the town, of gallant Reynolds' death,
Of cruel retreats through pent-up streets by murderous volleys swept, —
How well the Stone, the Iron, brigades their bloody outposts kept:
'T was for the Union, for the Flag, they perished, heroes all,
And we swore to conquer in the end, or even like them to fall.

And passed from mouth to mouth the tale of that grim day just done,
The fight by Round Top's craggy spur — of all the deadliest one;
It saved the left: but on the right they pressed us back too well,
And like a field in Spring the ground was ploughed with shot and shell.
There was the ancient graveyard, its hummocks crushed and red,
And there, between them, side by side, the wounded and the dead:
The mangled corpses fallen above — the peaceful dead below,
Laid in their graves, to slumber here, a score of years ago;
It seemed their waking, wandering shades were asking of our slain,
What brought such hideous tumult now where they so still had lain!

Bright rose the sun of Gettysburg that morrow morning tide,
And call of trump and roll of drum from height to height
    replied.
Hark! from the east already goes up the rattling din;
The Twelfth Corps, winning back their ground, right well
    the day begin!
They whirl fierce Ewell from their front! Now we of the
    Second pray,
As right and left the brunt have borne, the centre might
    to-day.
But all was still from hill to hill for many a breathless hour,
While for the coming battle-shock Lee gathered in his
    power;
And back and forth our leaders rode, who knew not rest or
    fear,
And along the lines, where'er they came, went up the ringing
    cheer.

'T was past the hour of nooning; the Summer skies were
    blue;
Behind the covering timber the foe was hid from view;
So fair and sweet with waving wheat the pleasant valley lay,
It brought to mind our Northern homes and meadows far
    away;
When the whole western ridge at once was fringed with fire
    and smoke,
Against our lines from seven score guns the dreadful tempest
    broke!
Then loud our batteries answer, and far along the crest,
And to and fro the roaring bolts are driven east and west;
Heavy and dark around us glooms the stifling sulphur cloud,
And the cries of mangled men and horse go up beneath its
    shroud.

The guns are still: the end is nigh: we grasp our arms anew
Oh, now let every heart be stanch and every aim be true!
For look! from yonder wood that skirts the valley's further marge,
The flower of all the Southern host move to the final charge.
By heaven! it is a fearful sight to see their double rank
Come with a hundred battle-flags — a mile from flank to flank!
Tramping the grain to earth, they come, ten thousand men abreast;
Their standards wave — their hearts are brave — they hasten not, nor rest,
But close the gaps our cannon make, and onward press, and nigher,
And, yelling at our very front, again pour in their fire.

Now burst our sheeted lightnings forth, now all our wrath has vent!
They die, they wither; through and through their wavering lines are rent.
But these are gallant, desperate men, of our own race and land,
Who charge anew, and welcome death, and fight us hand to hand:
Vain, vain! give way, as well ye may — the crimson die is cast!
Their bravest leaders bite the dust, their strength is failing fast;
They yield, they turn, they fly the field: we smite them as they run;
Their arms, their colors, are our spoil; the furious fight is done!
Across the plain we follow far and backward push the fray:
Cheer! cheer! the grand old Army at last has won the day!

Hurrah! the day has won the cause! No gray-clad host henceforth
Shall come with fire and sword to tread the highways of the North!
'T was such a flood as when ye see, along the Atlantic shore,
The great Spring-tide roll grandly in with swelling surge and roar:
It seems no wall can stay its leap or balk its wild desire
Beyond the bound that Heaven hath fixed to higher mount, and higher;
But now, when whitest lifts its crest, most loud its billows call,
Touched by the Power that led them on, they fall, and fall, and fall.
Even thus, unstayed upon his course, to Gettysburg the foe
His legions led, and fought, and fled, and might no further go.

Full many a dark-eyed Southern girl shall weep her lover dead;
But with a price the fight was ours — we too have tears to shed!
The bells that peal our triumph forth anon shall toll the brave,
Above whose heads the cross must stand, the hill-side grasses wave!
Alas! alas! the trampled grass shall thrive another year,
The blossoms on the apple-boughs with each new Spring appear,
But when our patriot-soldiers fall, Earth gives them up to God;
Though their souls rise in clearer skies, their forms are as the sod;
Only their names and deeds are ours — but, for a century yet,
The dead who fell at Gettysburg the land shall not forget.

God send us peace! and where for aye the loved and lost recline
Let fall, O South, your leaves of palm — O North, your sprigs of pine!
But when, with every ripened year, we keep the harvest home,
And to the dear Thanksgiving-feast our sons and daughters come, —
When children's children throng the board in the old homestead spread,
And the bent soldier of these wars is seated at the head,
Long, long the lads shall listen to hear the gray-beard tell
Of those who fought at Gettysburg and stood their ground so well:
" 'T was for the Union and the Flag," the veteran shall say,
" Our grand old Army held the ridge, and won that glorious day!"

Edmund Clarence Stedman

CXLVI

Three Hundred Thousand More

We are coming, Father Abraham, three hundred thousand more,
From Mississippi's winding stream and from New England's shore;
We leave our ploughs and workshops, our wives and children dear,
With hearts too full for utterance, with but a silent tear;
We dare not look behind us, but steadfastly before:
We are coming, Father Abraham, three hundred thousand more!

If you look across the hilltops that meet the northern sky,
Long moving lines of rising dust your vision may descry;
And now the wind, an instant, tears the cloudy veil aside,
And floats aloft our spangled flag in glory and in pride,
And bayonets in the sunlight gleam, and bands brave music pour:
We are coming, Father Abraham, three hundred thousand more!

If you look all up our valleys where the growing harvests shine,
You may see our sturdy farmer boys fast forming into line;
And children from their mothers' knees are pulling at the weeds,
And learning how to reap and sow against their country's needs;
And a farewell group stands weeping at every cottage door;
We are coming, Father Abraham, three hundred thousand more!

You have called us, and we're coming, by Richmond's bloody tide
To lay us down, for Freedom's sake, our brothers' bones beside,
Or from foul treason's savage grasp to wrench the murderous blade,
And in the face of foreign foes its fragments to parade.
Six hundred thousand loyal men and true have gone before:
We are coming, Father Abraham, three hundred thousand more!

James Sloane Gibbons

CXLVII

Tramp, Tramp, Tramp

In the prison cell I sit,
   Thinking, mother dear, of you,
And our bright and happy home so far away,
   And the tears they fill my eyes,
   Spite of all that I can do,
Tho' I try to cheer my comrades and be gay.

Chorus

Tramp, tramp, tramp, the boys are marching,
   Oh, cheer up, comrades, they will come,
And beneath the starry flag we shall breathe the air again,
   Of freedom in our own beloved home.

In the battle front we stood
   When the fiercest charge they made,
And they swept us off a hundred men or more,
   But before we reached their lines
   They were beaten back dismayed,
And we heard the cry of vict'ry o'er and o'er. — *Cho.*

So, within the prison cell,
   We are waiting for the day
That shall come to open wide the iron door,
   And the hollow eye grows bright,
   And the poor heart almost gay,
As we think of seeing friends and home once more. — *Cho.*

George F. Root

CXLVIII

Farragut

MOBILE BAY, 5 AUGUST, 1864

Farragut, Farragut,
   Old Heart of Oak,
Daring Dave Farragut,
   Thunderbolt stroke,
Watches the hoary mist
   Lift from the bay,
Till his flag, glory-kissed,
   Greets the young day.

Far, by gray Morgan's walls,
   Looms the black fleet.
Hark, deck to rampart calls
   With the drums' beat!
Buoy your chains overboard,
   While the steam hums;
Men! to the battlement,
   Farragut comes.

See, as the hurricane
   Hurtles in wrath
Squadrons of clouds amain
   Back from its path!
Back to the parapet,
   To the guns' lips,
Thunderbolt Farragut
   Hurls the black ships.

Now through the battle's roar
   Clear the boy sings,

"By the mark fathoms four,"
  While his lead swings.
Steady the wheelmen five
  "Nor' by east keep her,"
"Steady," but two alive:
  How the shells sweep her!

Lashed to the mast that sways
  Over red decks,
Over the flame that plays
  Round the torn wrecks,
Over the dying lips
  Framed for a cheer,
Farragut leads his ships,
  Guides the line clear.

On by heights cannon-browed,
  While the spars quiver;
Onward still flames the cloud
  Where the hulks shiver.
See, yon fort's star is set,
  Storm and fire past.
Cheer him, lads, — Farragut,
  Lashed to the mast!

Oh! while Atlantic's breast
  Bears a white sail,
While the Gulf's towering crest
  Tops a green vale;
Men thy bold deeds shall tell,
  Old Heart of Oak,
Daring Dave Farragut,
  Thunderbolt stroke!

William Tuckey Meredith

CXLIX

Marching through Georgia

1864

Bring the good old bugle, boys! we 'll sing another song, —
Sing it with a spirit that will start the world along, —
Sing it as we used to sing it, fifty thousand strong,
While we were marching through Georgia.

Chorus

    Hurrah, hurrah! we bring the jubilee!
    Hurrah, hurrah! the flag that makes you free!
    So we sang the chorus from Atlanta to the sea,
    While we were marching through Georgia.

How the darkies shouted when they heard the joyful sound!
How the turkeys gobbled which our commissary found!
How the sweet potatoes even started from the ground,
While we were marching through Georgia! — *Cho.*

Yes, and there were Union men who wept with joyful tears
When they saw the honor'd flag they had not seen for years,
Hardly could they be restrained from breaking forth in tears
While we were marching through Georgia. — *Cho.*

"Sherman's dashing Yankee boys will never reach the coast!
So the saucy rebels said, — and 't was a handsome boast.
Had they not forgot, alas! to reckon on a host,
While we were marching through Georgia. — *Cho.*

So we made a thoroughfare for Freedom and her train,
Sixty miles in latitude, three hundred to the main;
Treason fled before us, for resistance was in vain,
While we were marching through Georgia. — *Cho.*

Henry Clay Work

CL

Sheridan's Ride

1864

Up from the South at break of day,
Bringing to Winchester fresh dismay,
The affrighted air with a shudder bore,
Like a herald in haste, to the chieftain's door,
The terrible grumble, and rumble, and roar,
Telling the battle was on once more,
And Sheridan twenty miles away.

And wider still those billows of war
Thundered along the horizon's bar;
And louder yet into Winchester rolled
The roar of that red sea uncontrolled,
Making the blood of the listener cold,
As he thought of the stake in that fiery fray,
And Sheridan twenty miles away.

But there is a road from Winchester town,
A good broad highway leading down;
And there, through the flush of the morning light,
A steed as black as the steeds of night
Was seen to pass, as with eagle flight,
As if he knew the terrible need;
He stretched away with his utmost speed;
Hills rose and fell; but his heart was gay,
With Sheridan fifteen miles away.

Still sprung from those swift hoofs, thundering South,
The dust, like smoke from the cannon's mouth;

Or a trail of a comet, sweeping faster and faster,
Foreboding to traitors the doom of disaster.
The heart of the steed and the heart of the master
Were beating like prisoners assaulting their walls,
Impatient to be where the battle-field calls;
Every nerve of the charger was strained to full play,
With Sheridan only ten miles away.

Under his spurning feet the road
Like an arrowy Alpine river flowed,
And the landscape sped away behind
Like an ocean flying before the wind;
And the steed, like a bark fed with furnace ire,
Swept on with his wild eye full of fire.
But lo! he is nearing his heart's desire;
He is snuffing the smoke of the roaring fray,
With Sheridan only five miles away.

The first that the General saw were the groups
Of stragglers, and then the retreating troops.
What was done? what to do? A glance told him both.
Then, striking his spurs, with a terrible oath,
He dashed down the line, mid a storm of huzzas,
And the wave of retreat checked its course there, because
The sight of the master compelled it to pause.
With foam and with dust the black charger was gray;
By the flash of his eye, and the red nostril's play,
He seemed to the whole great army to say,
" I have brought you Sheridan all the way
From Winchester down to save the day!"

Hurrah! hurrah for Sheridan!
Hurrah! hurrah for horse and man!
And when their statues are placed on high,
Under the dome of the Union sky,

The American soldier's Temple of Fame, —
There with the glorious General's name,
Be it said, in letters both bold and bright,
" Here is the steed that saved the day
By carrying Sheridan into the fight,
From Winchester, twenty miles away!"

Thomas Buchanan Read

CLI

The Old Man and Jim

Old man never had much to say —
   'Ceptin' to Jim, —
And Jim was the wildest boy he had,
   And the old man jes' wrapped up in him!
Never heerd him speak but once
Er twice in my life, — and first time was
When the army broke out, and Jim he went,
The old man backin' him, fer three months;
And all 'at I heerd the old man say
Was, jes' as we turned to start away, —
   " Well, good-by, Jim:
   Take keer of yourse'f!"

'Peared like he was more satisfied
   Jes' *lookin'* at Jim
And likin' him all to hisse'f-like, see? —
   Cause he was jes' wrapped up in him!
And over and over I mind the day
The old man come and stood round in the way
While we was drillin', a-watchin' Jim;

The Old Man and Jim

And down at the deepot a-heerin' him say, —
  "Well, good-by, Jim:
  Take keer of yourse'f!"

Never was nothin' about the farm
  Disting'ished Jim;
Neighbors all ust to wonder why
  The old man 'peared wrapped up in him:
But when Cap. Biggler, he writ back
'At Jim was the bravest boy he had
In the whole dern rigiment, white er black,
And his fightin' good as his farmin' bad, —
'At he had led, with a bullet clean
Bored through his thigh, and carried the flag
Through the bloodiest battle you ever seen, —
The old man wound up a letter to him
'At Cap. read to us, 'at said, — "Tell Jim
  Good-by;
  And take keer of hisse'f!"

Jim come home jes' long enough
  To take the whim
'At he'd like to go back in the calvery —
  And the old man jes' wrapped up in him!
Jim 'lowed 'at he'd had sich luck afore,
Guessed he'd tackle her three years more.
And the old man give him a colt he'd raised,
And follered him over to Camp Ben Wade,
And laid around fer a week er so,
Watchin' Jim on dress-parade;
'Tel finally he rid away,
And last he heerd was the old man say, —
  "Well, good-by, Jim:
  Take keer of yourse'f!"

Tuk the papers, the old man did,
   A-watchin' fer Jim,
Fully believin' he 'd make his mark
   Some way — jes' wrapped up in him!
And many a time the word 'ud come
'At stirred him up like the tap of a drum:
At Petersburg, fer instunce, where
Jim rid right into their cannons there,
And tuk 'em, and p'inted 'em t'other way,
And socked it home to the boys in gray,
As they skooted fer timber, and on and on —
Jim a lieutenant, — and one arm gone, —
And the old man's words in his mind all day, —
   "Well, good-by, Jim:
   Take keer of yourse'f!"

Think of a private, now perhaps,
   We 'll say like Jim,
'At 's clumb clean up to the shoulder-straps —
   And the old man jes' wrapped up in him!
Think of him — with the war plum' through,
And the glorious old Red-White-and-Blue
A-laughin' the news down over Jim,
And the old man, bendin' over him —
The surgeon turnin' away with tears
'At had n't leaked fer years and years,
As the hand of the dyin' boy clung to
His Father's, the old voice in his ears,
   "Well, good-by, Jim:
   Take keer of yourse'f!"

James Whitcomb Riley

CLII

Roll-Call

"Corporal Green!" the Orderly cried;
  "Here!" was the answer, loud and clear,
  From the lips of a soldier who stood near, —
And "Here!" was the word the next replied.

"Cyrus Drew!" — then a silence fell;
  This time no answer followed the call;
  Only his rear-man had seen him fall:
Killed or wounded — he could not tell.

There they stood in the failing light,
  These men of battle, with grave, dark looks,
  As plain to be read as open books,
While slowly gathered the shades of night.

The fern on the hillsides was splashed with blood,
  And down in the corn, where the poppies grew,
  Were redder stains than the poppies knew,
And crimson-dyed was the river's flood.

For the foe had crossed from the other side,
  That day, in the face of a murderous fire
  That swept them down in its terrible ire;
And their life-blood went to color the tide.

"Herbert Cline!" — At the call there came
  Two stalwart soldiers into the line,
  Bearing between them this Herbert Cline,
Wounded and bleeding, to answer his name.

"Ezra Kerr!"—and a voice answered "Here!"
  "Hiram Kerr!"—but no man replied.
  They were brothers, these two; the sad wind sighed,
And a shudder crept through the cornfield near.

"Ephraim Deane!"—then a soldier spoke:
  "Deane carried our regiment's colors," he said,
  "Where our ensign was shot; I left him dead
Just after the enemy wavered and broke.

"Close to the roadside his body lies;
  I paused a moment and gave him to drink;
  He murmured his mother's name, I think,
And Death came with it and closed his eyes."

'T was a victory,—yes; but it cost us dear:—
  For that company's roll, when called at night,
  Of a hundred men who went into the fight,
Numbered but twenty that answered *"Here!"*

Nathaniel Graham Shepherd

CLIII

Dixie

1861

Southrons, hear your country call you!
Up, lest worse than death befall you!
To arms! To arms! To arms, in Dixie!
Lo! all the beacon-fires are lighted,—
Let all hearts be now united!
    To arms! To arms! To arms, in Dixie!
      Advance the flag of Dixie!
        Hurrah! hurrah!

Dixie

For Dixie's land we take our stand,
    And live or die for Dixie!
        To arms!   To arms!
    And conquer peace for Dixie!
        To arms!   To arms!
    And conquer peace for Dixie.

Hear the Northern thunders mutter!
Northern flags in South winds flutter!
Send them back your fierce defiance!
Stamp upon the accursed alliance!

Fear no danger!   Shun no labor!
Lift up rifle, pike, and sabre!
Shoulder pressing close to shoulder,
Let the odds make each heart bolder!

How the South's great heart rejoices
At your cannons' ringing voices!
For faith betrayed, and pledges broken,
Wrongs inflicted, insults spoken.

Strong as lions, swift as eagles,
Back to their kennels hunt these beagles!
Cut the unequal bonds asunder!
Let them hence each other plunder!

Swear upon your country's altar
Never to submit or falter,
Till the spoilers are defeated,
Till the Lord's work is completed.

Halt not till our Federation
Secures among earth's powers its station!

Then at peace, and crowned with glory,
Hear your children tell the story!

If the loved ones weep in sadness,
Victory soon shall bring them gladness, —
   To arms!
Exultant pride soon banish sorrow,
Smiles chase tears away to-morrow.
  To arms! To arms! To arms, in Dixie!
   Advance the flag of Dixie!
    Hurrah! hurrah!
For Dixie's land we take our stand,
  And live or die for Dixie!
   To arms! To arms!
  And conquer peace for Dixie!
   To arms! To arms!
  And conquer peace for Dixie!

Albert Pike (for the original see Page 354)

CLIV

My Maryland

1861

The despot's heel is on thy shore,
   Maryland!
His torch is at thy temple door,
   Maryland!
Avenge the patriotic gore
That flecked the streets of Baltimore,
And be the battle-queen of yore,
   Maryland, my Maryland!

My Maryland

Hark to an exiled son's appeal,
    Maryland!
My Mother State, to thee I kneel,
    Maryland!
For life and death, for woe and weal,
Thy peerless chivalry reveal,
And gird thy beauteous limbs with steel,
    Maryland, my Maryland!

Thou wilt not cower in the dust,
    Maryland!
Thy beaming sword shall never rust,
    Maryland!
Remember Carroll's sacred trust,
Remember Howard's warlike thrust,
And all thy slumberers with the just,
    Maryland, my Maryland!

Come! 't is the red dawn of the day,
    Maryland!
Come with thy panoplied array,
    Maryland!
With Ringgold's spirit for the fray,
With Watson's blood at Monterey,
With fearless Lowe and dashing May,
    Maryland, my Maryland!

Dear Mother, burst the tyrant's chain,
    Maryland!
Virginia should not call in vain,
    Maryland!
She meets her sisters on the plain, —
"Sic semper!" 't is the proud refrain

That baffles minions back amain,
>	Maryland!
Arise in majesty again,
>	Maryland, my Maryland!

Come! for thy shield is bright and strong,
>	Maryland!
Come! for thy dalliance does thee wrong,
>	Maryland!
Come to thine own heroic throng,
Stalking with Liberty along,
And chant thy dauntless slogan-song,
>	Maryland, my Maryland!

I see the blush upon thy cheek,
>	Maryland!
For thou wast ever bravely meek,
>	Maryland!
But lo! there surges forth a shriek,
From hill to hill, from creek to creek,
Potomac calls to Chesapeake,
>	Maryland, my Maryland!

Thou wilt not yield the Vandal toll,
>	Maryland!
Thou wilt not crook to his control,
>	Maryland!
Better the fire upon thee roll,
Better the shot, the blade, the bowl,
Than crucifixion of the soul,
>	Maryland, My Maryland!

I hear the distant thunder hum,
>	Maryland!

The Old Line's bugle, fife, and drum,
   Maryland!
She is not dead, nor deaf, nor dumb;
Huzza! she spurns the Northern scum!
She breathes! She burns! She'll come! She'll come!
   Maryland, My Maryland!

James Ryder Randall

CLV

The Bonnie Blue Flag

We are a band of brothers, and native to the soil,
Fighting for the property we gain'd by honest toil;
And when our rights were threatened, the cry rose near and far,
Hurrah for the Bonnie Blue Flag that bears a single star!

Chorus

Hurrah! hurrah! for Southern rights, hurrah!
Hurrah for the Bonnie Blue Flag that bears a single star!

First gallant South Carolina so nobly made the stand,
Then came Alabama, who took her by the hand;
Next quickly Mississippi, Georgia, and Florida,
All raised on high the Bonnie Blue Flag that bears a single star. — *Cho*.

And here's to brave Virginia! the old Dominion State
That with the young Confed'racy at length has link'd her fate;
Impell'd by her example, now other states prepare
To hoist on high the Bonnie Blue Flag that bears a single star. — *Cho*.

Then here's to our Confed'racy, for strong we are and brave!
Like patriots of old, we'll fight our heritage to save;
And rather than submit to shame, to die we would prefer,
So cheer for the Bonnie Blue Flag that bears a single star.
— *Cho.*

H. McCarthy, or *Annie Chambers Ketchum*

CLVI

A Georgia Volunteer

Far up the lonely mountain-side
  My wandering footsteps led;
The moss lay thick beneath my feet,
  The pine sighed overhead.
The trace of a dismantled fort
  Lay in the forest nave,
And in the shadow near my path
  I saw a soldier's grave.

The bramble wrestled with the weed
  Upon the lowly mound;—
The simple head-board, rudely writ,
  Had rotted to the ground;
I raised it with a reverent hand,
  From dust its words to clear,
But time had blotted all but these—
  "A Georgia Volunteer!"

I saw the toad and scaly snake
  From tangled covert start,
And hide themselves among the weeds
  Above the dead man's heart;

But undisturbed, in sleep profound,
   Unheeding, there he lay;
His coffin but the mountain soil,
   His shroud Confederate gray.

I heard the Shenandoah roll
   Along the vale below,
I saw the Alleghanies rise
   Towards the realms of snow.
The "Valley Campaign" rose to mind —
   Its leader's name — and then
I knew the sleeper had been one
   Of Stonewall Jackson's men.

Yet whence he came, what lip shall say —
   Whose tongue will ever tell
What desolated hearths and hearts
   Have been because he fell?
What sad-eyed maiden braids her hair,
   Her hair which he held dear?
One lock of which perchance lies with
   The Georgia Volunteer!

What mother, with long watching eyes,
   And white lips cold and dumb,
Waits with appalling patience for
   Her darling boy to come?
Her boy! whose mountain grave swells up
   But one of many a scar,
Cut on the face of our fair land
   By gory-handed war.

What fights he fought, what wounds he wore,
   Are all unknown to fame;

Remember, on his lonely grave
    There is not e'en a name!
That he fought well and bravely too,
    And held his country dear
We know, else he had never been
    A Georgia Volunteer.

He sleeps — what need to question now
    If he were wrong or right?
He knows, ere this, whose cause was just
    In God the Father's sight.
He wields no warlike weapons now,
    Returns no foeman's thrust —
Who but a coward would revile
    An honest soldier's dust?

Roll, Shenandoah, proudly roll,
    Adown thy rocky glen,
Above thee lies the grave of one
    Of Stonewall Jackson's men.
Beneath the cedar and the pine,
    In solitude austere,
Unknown, unnamed, forgotten, lies
    A Georgia Volunteer.

Mary Ashley Townsend

CLVII

Stonewall Jackson's Way

Come, stack arms, men! Pile on the rails,
    Stir up the camp-fire bright;
No growling if the canteen fails,
    We'll make a roaring night.

Stonewall Jackson's Way

Here Shenandoah brawls along,
There burly Blue Ridge echoes strong,
To swell the Brigade's rousing song
  Of " Stonewall Jackson's Way."

We see him now — the queer slouched hat
  Cocked o'er his eye askew;
The shrewd, dry smile; the speech so pat,
  So calm, so blunt, so true.
The " Blue-light Elder " knows 'em well;
Says he, " That's Banks, he's fond of shell;
Lord save his soul! we'll give him — " well!
  That's " Stonewall Jackson's Way."

Silence! ground arms! kneel all! caps off!
  Old Massa's going to pray.
Strangle the fool that dares to scoff!
  Attention! it's his way.
Appealing from his native sod,
In *forma pauperis* to God:
" Lay bare Thine arm; stretch forth Thy rod!
  Amen!" That's " Stonewall's Way."

He's in the saddle now. Fall in!
  Steady! the whole brigade!
Hill's at the ford, cut off; we'll win
  His way out, ball and blade!
What matter if our shoes are worn?
What matter if our feet are torn?
" Quick step! we're with him before morn!"
  That's " Stonewall Jackson's Way."

The sun's bright lances rout the mists
  Of morning, and, by George!

Here's Longstreet, struggling in the lists,
  Hemmed in an ugly gorge.
Pope and his Dutchmen, whipped before;
"Bay'nets and grape!" hear Stonewall roar;
"Charge, Stuart! Pay off Ashby's score!"
  In "Stonewall Jackson's Way."

Ah, Maiden! wait and watch and yearn
  For news of Stonewall's band!
Ah, Widow! read, with eyes that burn,
  That ring upon thy hand.
Ah, Wife! sew on, pray on, hope on;
Thy life shall not be all forlorn;
The foe had better ne'er been born
  That gets in "Stonewall's Way."

John Williamson Palmer

CLVIII

The Conquered Banner

Furl that Banner, for 't is weary;
Round its staff 't is drooping dreary:
  Furl it, fold it, — it is best;
For there 's not a man to wave it,
And there 's not a sword to save it,
And there 's not one left to lave it
In the blood which heroes gave it,
And its foes now scorn and brave it:
  Furl it, hide it, — let it rest!

Take that Banner down! 't is tattered;
Broken is its staff and shattered;

And the valiant hosts are scattered,
  Over whom it floated high.
Oh, 't is hard for us to fold it,
Hard to think there 's none to hold it,
Hard that those who once unrolled it
  Now must furl it with a sigh!

Furl that Banner — furl it sadly!
Once ten thousands hailed it gladly,
And ten thousands wildly, madly,
  Swore it should forever wave;
Swore that foeman's sword should never
Hearts like theirs entwined dissever,
Till that flag should float forever
  O'er their freedom or their grave!

Furl it! for the hands that grasped it,
And the hearts that fondly clasped it,
  Cold and dead are lying low;
And that Banner — it is trailing,
While around it sounds the wailing
  Of its people in their woe.

For, though conquered, they adore it, —
Love the cold, dead hands that bore it,
Weep for those who fell before it,
Pardon those who trailed and tore it;
And oh, wildly they deplore it,
  Now to furl and fold it so!

Furl that Banner! True, 't is gory,
Yet 't is wreathed around with glory,
And 't will live in song and story
  Though its folds are in the dust!

For its fame on brightest pages,
Penned by poets and by sages,
Shall go sounding down the ages —
　　Furl its folds though now we must.

Furl that Banner, softly, slowly!
Treat it gently — it is holy,
　　For it droops above the dead.
Touch it not — unfold it never;
Let it droop there, furled forever, —
　　For its people's hopes are fled!

Abram Joseph Ryan

CLIX

Ode to the Confederate Dead

Sleep sweetly in your humble graves,
　　Sleep, martyrs of a fallen cause;
Though yet no marble column craves
　　The pilgrim here to pause.

In seeds of laurel in the earth
　　The blossom of your fame is blown,
And somewhere, waiting for its birth,
　　The shaft is in the stone!

Meanwhile, behalf the tardy years
　　Which keep in trust your storied tombs,
Behold! your sisters bring their tears
　　And these memorial blooms.

Small tributes! but your shades will smile
   More proudly on these wreaths to-day,
Than when some cannon-moulded pile
   Shall overlook this bay.

Stoop, angels, hither from the skies!
   There is no holier spot of ground
Than where defeated valor lies,
   By mourning beauty crowned!

Henry Timrod

CLX

Dirge for a Soldier

Close his eyes; his work is done!
   What to him is friend or foeman,
Rise of moon, or set of sun,
   Hand of man, or kiss of woman?
      Lay him low, lay him low,
      In the clover or the snow!
       What cares he? He cannot know:
         Lay him low!

As man may, he fought his fight,
   Proved his truth by his endeavor;
Let him sleep in solemn night,
   Sleep forever and forever.
      Lay him low, lay him low,
      In the clover or the snow!
       What cares he? He cannot know:
         Lay him low!

Fold him in his country's stars,
    Roll the drum and fire the volley!
What to him are all our wars,
    What but death bemocking folly?
      Lay him low, lay him low,
        In the clover or the snow!
      What cares he?   He cannot know:
        Lay him low!

Leave him to God's watching eye;
    Trust him to the hand that made him,
Mortal love weeps idly by;
    God alone has power to aid him.
      Lay him low, lay him low,
        In the clover or the snow!
      What cares he?   He cannot know:
        Lay him low!

G. H. Boker

CLXI

A Soldier's Grave

Break not his sweet repose —
Thou whom chance brings to this sequestered ground,
The sacred yard his ashes close,
But go thy way in silence; here no sound
Is ever heard but from the murmuring pines,
    Answering the sea's near murmur;
    Nor ever here comes rumor
Of anxious world or war's foregathering signs.
    The bleaching flag, the faded wreath,
    Mark the dead soldier's dust beneath,

And show the death he chose;
Forgotten save by her who weeps alone,
And wrote his fameless name on this low stone:
 Break not his sweet repose.

John Albee

CLXII

Driving Home the Cows

Out of the clover and blue-eyed grass
 He turned them into the river-lane;
One after another he let them pass,
 Then fastened the meadow-bars again.

Under the willows, and over the hill,
 He patiently followed their sober pace;
The merry whistle for once was still,
 And something shadowed the sunny face.

Only a boy! and his father had said
 He never could let his youngest go:
Two already were lying dead
 Under the feet of the trampling foe.

But after the evening work was done,
 And the frogs were loud in the meadow-swamp,
Over his shoulder he slung his gun
 And stealthily followed the foot-path damp.

Across the clover, and through the wheat,
 With resolute heart and purpose grim,
Though cold was the dew on his hurrying feet
 And the blind bat's flitting startled him.

Thrice since then had the lanes been white,
  And the orchards sweet with apple-bloom;
And now, when the cows came back at night,
  The feeble father drove them home.

For news had come to the lonely farm
  That three were lying where two had lain;
And the old man's tremulous, palsied arm
  Could never lean on a son's again.

The summer day grew cool and late.
  He went for the cows when the work was done;
But down the lane, as he opened the gate,
  He saw them coming one by one:

Brindle, Ebony, Speckle, and Bess,
  Shaking their horns in the evening wind;
Cropping the buttercups out of the grass —
  But who was it following close behind?

Loosely swung in the idle air
  The empty sleeve of army blue;
And worn and pale, from the crisping hair,
  Looked out a face that the father knew.

For Southern prisons will sometimes yawn,
  And yield their dead unto life again;
And the day that comes with a cloudy dawn
  In golden glory at last may wane.

The great tears sprang to their meeting eyes;
  For the heart must speak when the lips are dumb:
And under the silent evening skies
  Together they followed the cattle home.

Kate Putnam Osgood

CLXIII

The Brave at Home

The maid who binds her warrior's sash
   With smile that well her pain dissembles,
The while beneath her drooping lash
   One starry tear-drop hangs and trembles;
Though Heaven alone records the tear,
   And fame shall never know her story,
Her heart has shed a drop as dear
   As e'er bedewed the field of glory!

The wife who girds her husband's sword
   Mid little ones who weep or wonder,
And bravely speaks the cheering word,
   What though her heart be rent asunder,
Doomed nightly in her dreams to hear
   The bolts of death around him rattle,
Has shed as sacred blood as e'er
   Was poured upon the field of battle.

The mother who conceals her grief
   While to her breast her son she presses,
Then breathes a few brave words and brief,
   Kissing the patriot brow she blesses,
With no one but her secret God
   To know the pain that weighs upon her,
Sheds holy blood as e'er the sod
   Received on Freedom's field of honor!

Thomas Buchanan Read

CLXIV

The Blue and the Gray

By the flow of the inland river,
  Whence the fleets of iron have fled,
Where the blades of the grave-grass quiver,
  Asleep are the ranks of the dead:
    Under the sod and the dew,
      Waiting the judgment-day;
    Under the one, the Blue,
      Under the other, the Gray.

These in the robings of glory,
  Those in the gloom of defeat,
All with the battle-blood gory,
  In the dusk of eternity meet:
    Under the sod and the dew,
      Waiting the judgment-day;
    Under the laurel, the Blue,
      Under the willow, the Gray.

From the silence of sorrowful hours
  The desolate mourners go,
Lovingly laden with flowers
  Alike for the friend and the foe:
    Under the sod and the dew,
      Waiting the judgment-day;
    Under the roses, the Blue,
      Under the lilies, the Gray.

So with an equal splendor
  The morning sun-rays fall,

The Blue and the Gray

With a touch impartially tender,
  On the blossoms blooming for all:
    Under the sod and the dew,
      Waiting the judgment-day;
    Broidered with gold, the Blue,
      Mellowed with gold, the Gray.

So, when the summer calleth,
  On forest and field of grain,
With an equal murmur falleth
  The cooling drip of the rain:
    Under the sod and the dew,
      Waiting the judgment-day;
    Wet with the rain, the Blue,
      Wet with the rain, the Gray.

Sadly, but not with upbraiding,
  The generous deed was done,
In the storm of the years that are fading,
  No braver battle was won:
    Under the sod and the dew,
      Waiting the judgment-day;
    Under the blossoms, the Blue,
      Under the garlands, the Gray.

No more shall the war cry sever,
  Or the winding rivers be red;
They banish our anger forever
  When they laurel the graves of our dead!
    Under the sod and the dew,
      Waiting the judgment-day;
    Love and tears for the Blue,
      Tears and love for the Gray.

Francis Miles Finch

CLXV

Abraham Lincoln

Oh, slow to smite and swift to spare,
    Gentle and merciful and just!
Who, in the fear of God, didst bear
    The sword of power — a nation's trust.

In sorrow by thy bier we stand,
    Amid the awe that hushes all,
And speak the anguish of a land
    That shook with horror at thy fall.

Thy task is done — the bond are free;
    We bear thee to an honored grave,
Whose noblest monument shall be
    The broken fetters of the slave.

Pure was thy life; its bloody close
    Hath placed thee with the sons of light,
Among the noble host of those
    Who perished in the cause of right.

William Cullen Bryant

CLXVI

O Captain! My Captain! (Lincoln)

O Captain! my Captain! our fearful trip is done;
The ship has weather'd every rack, the prize we sought is won;
The port is near, the bells I hear, the people all exulting,
While follow eyes the steady keel, the vessel grim and daring:

O Captain! My Captain!

> But O heart! heart! heart!
> > O the bleeding drops of red,
> > > Where on the deck my Captain lies,
> > > Fallen cold and dead!

O Captain! my Captain! rise up and hear the bells;
Rise up — for you the flag is flung — for you the bugle trills;
For you bouquets and ribbon'd wreaths — for you the shores a-crowding;
For you they call, the swaying mass, their eager faces turning;
> Here Captain! dear father!
> > This arm beneath your head;
> > > It is some dream that on the deck
> > > You 've fallen cold and dead.

My Captain does not answer, his lips are pale and still;
My father does not feel my arm, he has no pulse nor will:
The ship is anchor'd safe and sound, its voyage closed and done;
From fearful trip the victor ship comes in with object won:
> Exult, O shores, and ring, O bells!
> > But I, with mournful tread,
> > > Walk the deck my Captain lies,
> > > Fallen cold and dead.

Walt Whitman

CLXVII

Lincoln

[FROM THE ODE RECITED AT THE HARVARD COMMEMORATION OF JULY 21, 1865]

Life may be given in many ways,
    And loyalty to Truth be sealed
As bravely in the closet as the field,
    So bountiful is Fate;
    But then to stand beside her,
    When craven churls deride her,
To front a lie in arms and not to yield,
    This shows, methinks, God's plan
    And measure of a stalwart man,
    Limbed like the old heroic breeds,
    Who stand self-poised on manhood's solid earth,
    Not forced to frame excuses for his birth,
Fed from within with all the strength he needs.

    Such was he, our Martyr-Chief,
    Whom late the Nation he had led,
    With ashes on her head,
Wept with the passion of an angry grief:
    Forgive me, if from present things I turn
    To speak what in my heart will beat and burn,
    And hang my wreath on his world-honored urn.
    Nature, they say, doth dote,
    And cannot make a man
    Save on some worn-out plan,
    Repeating us by rote:

For him her Old-World moulds aside she threw,
And, choosing sweet clay from the breast
    Of the unexhausted West,
With stuff untainted shaped a hero new,
Wise, steadfast in the strength of God, and true.
    How beautiful to see
Once more a shepherd of mankind indeed,
Who loved his charge, but never loved to lead;
One whose meek flock the people joyed to be,
    Not lured by any cheat of birth,
    But by his clear-grained human worth,
And brave old wisdom of sincerity!
    They knew that outward grace is dust;
    They could not choose but trust
In that sure-footed mind's unfaltering skill,
    And supple-tempered will
That bent like perfect steel to spring again and thrust.
His was no lonely mountain-peak of mind,
Thrusting to thin air o'er our cloudy bars,
A sea-mark now, now lost in vapor's blind;
Broad prairie rather, genial, level-lined,
Fruitful and friendly for all human kind,
Yet also nigh to heaven and loved of loftiest stars.
    Nothing of Europe here,
Or, then, of Europe fronting mornward still,
    Ere any names of Serf and Peer
    Could Nature's equal scheme deface
    And thwart her genial will;
Here was a type of the true elder race,
And one of Plutarch's men talked with us face to face.
    I praise him not; it were too late;
And some innative weakness there must be
In him who condescends to victory

Such as the Present gives, and cannot wait,
    Safe in himself as in a fate.
      So always firmly he:
      He knew to bide his time,
      And can fame abide,
Still patient in his simple faith sublime,
    Till the wise years decide.
    Great captains, with their guns and drums,
      Disturb our judgment for the hour,
      But at last silence comes!
These all are gone, and, standing like a tower,
    Our children shall behold his fame,
    The kindly-earnest, brave, foreseeing man,
    Sagacious, patient, dreading praise, not blame,
    New birth of our new soil, the first American.

James Russell Lowell

CLXVIII

The Republic

[FROM "THE BUILDING OF THE SHIP"]

Thou, too, sail on, O Ship of State!
Sail on, O UNION, strong and great!
Humanity with all its fears,
With all the hopes of future years,
Is hanging breathless on thy fate!
We know what Master laid thy keel,
What Workmen wrought thy ribs of steel,
Who made each mast, and sail, and rope,
What anvils rang, what hammers beat,
In what a forge and what a heat

Were shaped the anchors of thy hope!
Fear not each sudden sound and shock,
'T is of the wave and not the rock;
'T is but the flapping of the sail,
And not a rent made by the gale!
In spite of rock and tempest's roar,
In spite of false lights on the shore,
Sail on, nor fear to breast the sea!
Our hearts, our hopes, are all with thee,
Our hearts, our hopes, our prayers, our tears,
Our faith triumphant o'er our fears,
Are all with thee, — are all with thee!

Henry Wadsworth Longfellow

CLXIX

Centennial Hymn

1876

Our fathers' God! from out whose hand
The centuries fall like grains of sand,
We meet to-day, united, free,
And loyal to our land and Thee,
To thank Thee for the era done,
And trust Thee for the opening one.

Here, where of old, by Thy design,
The fathers spake that word of Thine
Whose echo is the glad refrain
Of rended bolt and falling chain,
To grace our festal time, from all
The zones of earth our guests we call.

Be with us while the New World greets
The Old World thronging all its streets,
Unveiling all the triumphs won
By art or toil beneath the sun;
And unto common good ordain
This rivalship of hand and brain.

Thou, who hast here in concord furled
The war flags of a gathered world,
Beneath our Western skies fulfil
The Orient's mission of good-will,
And, freighted with love's Golden Fleece,
Send back its Argonauts of peace.

For art and labor met in truce,
And beauty made the bride of use,
We thank Thee; but, withal, we crave
The austere virtues strong to save,
The honor proof to place or gold,
The manhood never bought nor sold!

Oh make Thou us, through centuries long,
In peace secure, in justice strong;
Around our gift of freedom draw
The safeguards of thy righteous law:
And, cast in some diviner mould,
Let the new cycle shame the old!

John Greenleaf Whittier

CLXX

America

[FROM THE NATIONAL ODE, JULY 4, 1876]

    Foreseen in the vision of sages,
      Foretold when martyrs bled,
    She was born of the longing of ages,
      By the truth of the noble dead
      And the faith of the living fed!
    No blood in her lightest veins
    Frets at remembered chains,
Nor shame of bondage has bowed her head.
      In her form and features still
      The unblenching Puritan will,
    Cavalier honor, Huguenot grace,
    The Quaker truth and sweetness,
And the strength of the danger-girdled race
Of Holland, blend in a proud completeness.
From the homes of all, where her being began,
    She took what she gave to Man;
      Justice, that knew no station,
        Belief, as soul decreed,
      Free air for aspiration,
    Free force for independent deed!
    She takes, but to give again,
As the sea returns the rivers in rain;
And gathers the chosen of her seed
From the hunted of every crown and creed.
    Her Germany dwells by a gentler Rhine;
    Her Ireland sees the old sunburst shine;
    Her France pursues some dream divine;

Her Norway keeps his mountain pine;
Her Italy waits by the western brine;
    And, broad-based under all,
Is planted England's oaken-hearted mood,
    As rich in fortitude
As e'er went worldward from the island-wall!
    Fused in her candid light,
To one strong race all races here unite;
Tongues melt in hers, hereditary foemen
Forget their sword and slogan, kith and clan.
    'T was glory, once, to be a Roman:
She makes it glory, now, to be a man!

Bayard Taylor

CLXXI

For Cuba

1898

    No precedent, ye say,
    To point the glorious way
Towards help for one downtrod in blood and tears?
    Brothers, 't is time there were!
    We bare our swords for her,
And set a model for the coming years!

    This act, to end her pain,
    Without a hope of gain,
Its like on history's page where can ye read?
    Humanity and God
    Call us to paths untrod!
On, brothers, on! we follow not, but lead!

Robert Mowry Bell

CLXXII

Answering to Roll-Call

This one fought with Jackson, and faced the fight with Lee;
That one followed Sherman as he galloped to the sea;
But they 're marchin' on together just as friendly as can be,
And they 'll answer to the roll-call in the mornin'!

    They 'll rally to the fight,
    In the stormy day and night,
  In bonds that no cruel fate shall sever;
     While the storm-winds waft on high
     Their ringing battle-cry:
  "Our country, — our country forever!"

The brave old flag above them is rippling down its red, —
Each crimson stripe the emblem of the blood by heroes shed;
It shall wave for them victorious or droop above them, — dead,
For they 'll answer to the roll-call in the mornin'!

    They 'll rally to the fight,
    In the stormy day and night,
  In bonds that no cruel fate shall sever;
     While their far-famed battle-cry
     Shall go ringing to the sky:
  "Our country, — our country forever!"

Frank L. Stanton

CLXXIII

The Men behind the Guns

A cheer and salute for the Admiral, and here's to the Captain bold,
And never forget the Commodore's debt when the deeds of might are told!
They stand to the deck through the battle's wreck when the great shells roar and screech —
And never they fear when the foe is near to practice what they preach:
But off with your hat and three times three for Columbia's true-blue sons,
The men below who batter the foe — the men behind the guns!

Oh, light and merry of heart are they when they swing into port once more,
When, with more than enough of the "green-backed stuff," they start for their leave-o'-shore;
And you'd think, perhaps, that the blue-bloused chaps who loll along the street
Are a tender bit, with salt on it, for some fierce "mustache" to eat —
Some warrior bold, with straps of gold, who dazzles and fairly stuns
The modest worth of the sailor boys — the lads who serve the guns.

But say not a word till the shot is heard that tells the fight is on,
Till the long, deep roar grows more and more from the ships of "Yank" and "Don,"

Till over the deep the tempests sweep of fire and bursting
  shell,
And the very air is a mad Despair in the throes of a living
  hell;
Then down, deep down, in the mighty ship, unseen by the
  midday suns,
You'll find the chaps who are giving the raps — the men
  behind the guns!

Oh, well they know how the cyclones blow that they loose
  from their cloud of death,
And they know is heard the thunder-word their fierce ten-
  incher saith;
The steel decks rock with the lightning shock, and shake
  with the great recoil,
And the sea grows red with the blood of the dead and reaches
  for his spoil —
But not till the foe has gone below or turns his prow and
  runs,
Shall the voice of peace bring sweet release to the men
  behind the guns!

John Jerome Rooney

CLXXIV

The War-Ship "Dixie"

They've named a cruiser *Dixie*, — that's whut the papers
  say, —
An' I hears they're goin' to man her with the boys that
  wore the gray;
Good news! It sorter thrills me, an' makes me want ter be
Whar the ban' is playin' "Dixie," an' the *Dixie* puts ter sea!

They 've named a cruiser *Dixie*. An', fellers, I 'll be boun'
You 're goin' ter see some fightin' when the *Dixie* swings
  aroun'!
Ef any o' them Spanish ships shall strike her east or west,
Jest let the ban' play "Dixie," an' the boys 'll do the rest!

I want to see that *Dixie*, — I want ter take my stan'
On the deck of her and holler: "Three cheers fer Dixie
  lan'!"
She means we 're all united, — the war hurts healed away,
An' "Way down South in Dixie" is national to-day!

I bet you she 's a good 'un! I 'll stake my last red cent
Thar ain't no better timber in the whole blame settlement!
An' all their shiny battle-ships beside that ship air tame,
Fer, when it comes to "Dixie" thar 's somethin' in a name!

Here 's three cheers an' a tiger, — as hearty as kin be;
An' let the ban' play "Dixie" when the *Dixie* puts ter sea!
She 'll make her way an' win the day from shinin' East to
  West —
Jest let the ban' play "Dixie," an' the boys 'll do the rest.

Frank L. Stanton

CLXXV

The Fighting Race

"Read out the names!" and Burke sat back,
  And Kelly drooped his head.
While Shea — they call him Scholar Jack —
  Went down the list of the dead.
Officers, seamen, gunners, marines,
  The crews of the gig and yawl,

The Fighting Race

The bearded man and the lad in his teens,
    Carpenters, coal passers — all.
Then, knocking the ashes from out his pipe,
    Said Burke in an offhand way:
"We're all in that dead man's list, by Cripe!
    Kelly and Burke and Shea."
"Well, here's to the *Maine*, and I'm sorry for Spain,"
    Said Kelly and Burke and Shea.

"Wherever there's Kellys there's trouble," said Burke.
    "Wherever fighting's the game,
Or a spice of danger in grown man's work,"
    Said Kelly, "you'll find my name."
"And do we fall short," said Burke, getting mad,
    "When it's touch and go for life?"
Said Shea, "It's thirty-odd years, bedad,
    Since I charged to drum and fife
Up Marye's Heights, and my old canteen
    Stopped a rebel ball on its way.
There were blossoms of blood on our sprigs of green —
    Kelly and Burke and Shea —
And the dead did n't brag." "Well, here's to the flag!"
    Said Kelly and Burke and Shea.

"I wish 't was in Ireland, for there's the place,"
    Said Burke, "that we'd die by right,
In the cradle of our soldier race,
    After one good stand-up fight.
My grandfather fell on Vinegar Hill,
    And fighting was not his trade;
But his rusty pike 's in the cabin still,
    With Hessian blood on the blade."
"Aye, aye," said Kelly, "the pikes were great
    When the word was 'clear the way!'

We were thick on the roll in ninety-eight —
    Kelly and Burke and Shea."
"Well, here 's to the pike and the sword and the like!"
    Said Kelly and Burke and Shea.

And Shea, the scholar, with rising joy,
    Said, "We were at Ramillies;
We left our bones at Fontenoy
    And up in the Pyrenees;
Before Dunkirk, on Landen's plain,
    Cremona, Lille, and Ghent,
We 're all over Austria, France, and Spain,
    Wherever they pitched a tent.
We 've died for England from Waterloo
    To Egypt and Dargai;
And still there 's enough for a corps or crew,
    Kelly and Burke and Shea."
"Well, here is to good honest fighting blood!"
    Said Kelly and Burke and Shea.

"Oh, the fighting races don't die out,
    If they seldom die in bed,
For love is first in their hearts, no doubt,"
    Said Burke; then Kelly said:
"When Michael, the Irish Archangel, stands,
    The angel with the sword,
And the battle-dead from a hundred lands
    Are ranged in one big horde,
Our line, that for Gabriel's trumpet waits,
    Will stretch three deep that day,
From Jehoshaphat to the Golden Gates —
    Kelly and Burke and Shea."
"Well, here 's thank God for the race and the sod!"
    Said Kelly and Burke and Shea.

Joseph I. C. Clarke

CLXXVI

The New Memorial Day

"Under the roses the blue ;
  Under the lilies the gray."

Oh, the roses we plucked for the blue,
  And the lilies we twined for the gray,
We have bound in a wreath,
And in silence beneath
  Slumber our heroes to-day.

Over the new-turned sod
  The sons of our fathers stand,
And the fierce old fight
Slips out of sight
  In the clasp of a brother's hand.

For the old blood left a stain
  That the new has washed away,
And the sons of those
That have faced as foes
  Are marching together to-day.

Oh, the blood that our fathers gave!
  Oh, the tide of our mothers' tears!
And the flow of red,
And the tears they shed,
  Embittered a sea of years.

But the roses we plucked for the blue,
  And the lilies we twined for the gray
We have bound in a wreath,
And in glory beneath,
  Slumber our heroes to-day!

Albert Bigelow Paine

CLXXVII

The Flag Goes By

>   Hats off!
> Along the street there comes
> A biare of bugles, a ruffle of drums,
> A flash of color beneath the sky:
>   Hats off!
> The flag is passing by!

> Blue and crimson and white it shines,
> Over the steel-tipped, ordered lines.
>   Hats off!
> The colors before us fly;
> But more than the flag is passing by.

> Sea-fights and land-fights, grim and great,
> Fought to make and save the State:
> Weary marches and sinking ships;
> Cheers of victory on dying lips;

> Days of plenty and years of peace;
> March of a strong land's swift increase;
> Equal justice, right, and law,
> Stately honor and reverend awe;

> Sign of a nation, great and strong
> To ward her people from foreign wrong:
> Pride and glory and honor, — all
> Live in the colors to stand or fall.

>   Hats off!
> Along the street there comes
> A blare of bugles, a ruffle of drums;
> And loyal hearts are beating high:
>   Hats off!
> The flag is passing by!
>
> Henry Holcomb Bennett

CLXXVIII

When the Great Gray Ships Come In

NEW YORK HARBOR, AUGUST 20, 1898

To eastward ringing, to westward winging, o'er mapless miles of sea,
On winds and tides the gospel rides that the furthermost isles are free,
And the furthermost isles make answer, harbor, and height, and hill,
Breaker and beach cry, each to each, "'T is the Mother who calls! Be still!"
Mother! new-found, belovèd, and strong to hold from harm,
Stretching to these across the seas the shield of her sovereign arm,
Who summoned the guns of her sailor sons, who bade her navies roam,
Who calls again to the leagues of main, and who calls them this time home!

And the great gray ships are silent, and the weary watchers rest,
The black cloud dies in the August skies, and deep in the golden west

Invisible hands are limning a glory of crimson bars,
And far above is the wonder of a myriad wakened stars!
Peace! As the tidings silence the strenuous cannonade,
Peace at last! is the bugle blast the length of the long blockade,
And eyes of vigil weary are lit with the glad release,
From ship to ship and from lip to lip it is "Peace! Thank God for peace."

Ah, in the sweet hereafter Columbia still shall show
The sons of these who swept the seas how she bade them rise and go, —
How, when the stirring summons smote on her children's ear,
South and North at the call stood forth, and the whole land answered, "Here!"
For the soul of the soldier's story and the heart of the sailor's song
Are all of those who meet their foes as right should meet with wrong,
Who fight their guns till the foeman runs, and then, on the decks they trod,
Brave faces raise, and give the praise to the grace of their country's God!

Yes, it is good to battle, and good to be strong and free,
To carry the hearts of a people to the uttermost ends of sea,
To see the day steal up the bay where the enemy lies in wait,
To run your ship to the harbor's lip and sink her across the strait: —
But better the golden evening when the ships round heads for home,

And the long gray miles slip swiftly past in a swirl of seeth-
    ing foam,
And the people wait at the haven's gate to greet the men
    who win!
Thank God for peace! Thank God for peace, when the
    great gray ships come in!

Guy Wetmore Carryl

CLXXIX

The Parting of the Ways

Untrammelled Giant of the West,
   With all of Nature's gifts endowed,
With all of Heaven's mercies blessed,
   Nor of thy power unduly proud —
Peerless in courage, force, and skill,
And godlike in thy strength of will, —

Before thy feet the ways divide :
   One path leads up to heights sublime ;
Downward the other slopes, where bide
   The refuse and the wrecks of Time.
Choose then, nor falter at the start,
O choose the nobler path and part!

Be thou the guardian of the weak,
   Of the unfriended, thou the friend ;
No guerdon for thy valor seek,
   No end beyond the avowèd end.
Wouldst thou thy godlike power preserve,
Be godlike in the will to serve!

Joseph B. Gilder

MISCELLANEOUS SONGS AND BALLADS

CLXXX

Yankee Doodle

Father and I went down to camp,
    Along with Cap'n Goodin',
And there we saw the men and boys
    As thick as hasty pudding.

    Yankee Doodle, keep it up,
        Yankee Doodle dandy,
    Mind the music and the step,
        And with the girls be handy.

And there we see a thousand men,
    As rich as Squire David;
And what they wasted ev'ry day,
    I wish it could be saved.

The 'lasses they eat ev'ry day,
    Would keep a house a winter;
They have so much that, I'll be bound,
    They eat it when they've mind ter.

And there I see a swamping gun,
    Large as a log of maple,
Upon a deuced little cart,
    A load for father's cattle.

And every time they shoot it off,
    It takes a horn of powder,
And makes a noise like father's gun,
    Only a nation louder.

Yankee Doodle

I went as nigh to one myself
 As 'Siah's underpinning;
And father went as nigh agin,
 I thought the deuce was in him.

Cousin Simon grew so bold,
 I thought he would have cocked it;
It scared me so I shrinked it off
 And hung by father's pocket.

And Cap'n Davis had a gun,
 He kind of clapt his hand on 't,
And stuck a crooked stabbing iron
 Upon the little end on 't.

And there I see a pumpkin shell
 As big as mother's basin;
And every time they touched it off
 They scampered like the nation.

I see a little barrel too,
 The heads were made of leather;
They knocked upon 't with little clubs
 And called the folks together.

And there was Cap'n Washington,
 And gentlefolks about him;
They say he's grown so 'tarnal proud,
 He will not ride without 'em.

He got him on his meeting clothes
 Upon a slapping stallion,
He set the world along in rows,
 In hundreds and in millions.

         The flaming ribbons in his hat,
            They looked so taring fine, ah,
         I wanted dreadfully to get
            To give to my Jemima.

         I see another snarl of men
            A digging graves, they told me,
         So 'tarnal long, so 'tarnal deep,
            They 'tended they should hold me.

         It scared me so I hooked it off,
            Nor stopped, as I remember,
         Nor turned about till I got home,
            Locked up in mother's chamber.

                              Richard Shuckburg

CLXXXI

Nathan Hale

1776

The breezes went steadily thro' the tall pines,
   A saying "oh! hu-ush!" a saying "oh! hu-ush!"
As stilly stole by a bold legion of horse,
   For Hale in the bush, for Hale in the bush.

"Keep still!" said the thrush as she nestled her young,
   In a nest by the road; in a nest by the road.
"For the tyrants are near, and with them appear,
   What bodes us no good, what bodes us no good."

The brave captain heard it, and thought of his home,
   In a cot by the brook; in a cot by the brook.

With mother and sister and memories dear,
   He so gaily forsook; he so gaily forsook.

Cooling shades of the night were coming apace,
   The tattoo had beat; the tattoo had beat.
The noble one sprang from his dark lurking place,
   To make his retreat; to make his retreat.

He warily trod on the dry rustling leaves,
   As he pass'd thro' the wood; as he pass'd thro' the wood;
And silently gain'd his rude launch on the shore,
   As she play'd with the flood; as she play'd with the flood.

The guards of the camp, on that dark, dreary night,
   Had a murderous will; had a murderous will.
They took him and bore him afar from the shore,
   To a hut on the hill; to a hut on the hill.

No mother was there, nor a friend who could cheer,
   In that little stone cell; in that little stone cell.
But he trusted in love, from his father above.
   In his heart all was well; in his heart all was well.

An ominous owl with his solemn base voice,
   Sat moaning hard by; sat moaning hard by.
"The tyrant's proud minions most gladly rejoice,
   For he must soon die; for he must soon die."

The brave fellow told them, no thing he restrain'd,
   The cruel gen'ral; the cruel gen'ral.
His errand from camp, of the ends to be gain'd,
   And said that was all; and said that was all.

They took him and bound him and bore him away,
   Down the hill's grassy side; down the hill's grassy side.

'T was there the base hirelings, in royal array,
　　His cause did deride ; his cause did deride.

Five minutes were given, short moments, no more,
　　For him to repent ; for him to repent ;
He pray'd for his mother, he ask'd not another,
　　To Heaven he went ; to Heaven he went.

The faith of a martyr, the tragedy shew'd,
　　As he trod the last stage ; as he trod the last stage.
And Britons will shudder at gallant Hale's blood,
　　As his words do presage, as his words do presage.

" Thou pale king of terrors, thou life's gloomy foe,
　　Go frighten the slave, go frighten the slave ;
Tell tyrants, to you, their allegiance they owe.
　　No fears for the brave ; no fears for the brave."

Anonymous

CLXXXII

All Quiet along the Potomac

" All quiet along the Potomac," they say,
　　" Except now and then a stray picket
Is shot, as he walks on his beat to and fro,
　　By a rifleman hid in the thicket.
'T is nothing : a private or two now and then
　　Will not count in the news of the battle ;
Not an officer lost, only one of the men
　　Moaning out all alone the death rattle."

All quiet along the Potomac to-night,
　　Where the soldiers lie peacefully dreaming ;

All Quiet along the Potomac

Their tents, in the rays of the clear autumn moon,
    Or the light of the watch-fires are gleaming.
A tremulous sigh, as the gentle night-wind
    Through the forest leaves softly is creeping;
While stars up above, with their glittering eyes,
    Keep guard, — for the army is sleeping.

There's only the sound of the lone sentry's tread,
    As he tramps from the rock to the fountain,
And thinks of the two in the low trundle-bed,
    Far away in the cot on the mountain.
His musket falls slack, his face dark and grim,
    Grows gentle with memories tender,
As he mutters a prayer for the children asleep;
    For their mother — may Heaven defend her!

The moon seems to shine just as brightly as then,
    That night, when the love yet unspoken
Leaped up to his lips, when low, murmured vows
    Were pledged to be ever unbroken;
Then drawing his sleeve roughly over his eyes,
    He dashes off tears that are welling,
And gathers his gun closer up to its place.
    As if to keep down the heart-swelling.

He passes the fountain, the blasted pine-tree,
    The footstep is lagging and weary;
Yet onward he goes through the broad belt of light?
    Toward the shade of the forest so dreary.
Hark! was it the night-wind that rustled the leaves,
    Was it moonlight so wondrously flashing?
It looked like a rifle . . . "Ha! Mary, good-bye!"
    The red life-blood is ebbing and plashing.

All quiet along the Potomac to-night;
  No sound save the rush of the river;
While soft falls the dew on the face of the dead —
  The picket's off duty forever.

Ethelinda Eliot Beers

CLXXXIII

Tenting on the Old Camp Ground

We're tenting to-night on the old camp ground,
  Give us a song to cheer
Our weary hearts, a song of home,
  And friends we love so dear.

Chorus

Many are the hearts that are weary to-night,
  Wishing for the war to cease,
Many are the hearts looking for the right,
  To see the dawn of peace.
    Tenting to-night,
    Tenting to-night,
  Tenting on the old camp ground.

We've been tenting to-night on the old camp ground,
  Thinking of days gone by,
Of the lov'd ones at home that gave us the hand,
  And the tear that said "good bye!" — *Cho.*

We are tired of war on the old camp ground,
  Many are dead and gone,
Of the brave and true who've left their homes; —
  Others have been wounded long. — *Cho.*

We 've been fighting to-day on the old camp ground.
   Many are lying near;
Some are dead, and some are dying,
   Many are in tears.

Chorus

Many are the hearts that are weary to-night,
   Wishing for the war to cease,
Many are the hearts looking for the right,
   To see the dawn of peace.
         Dying to-night,
      Dying to-night,
   Dying on the old camp ground.

Walter Kittredge

CLXXXIV

Home, Sweet Home

Mid pleasures and palaces though we may roam,
Be it ever so humble, there 's no place like home;
A charm from the sky seems to hallow us there,
Which, seek through the world, is ne'er met with elsewhere.
   Home, Home, sweet, sweet Home!
There 's no place like Home! there 's no place like Home!

An exile from home, splendor dazzles in vain;
O, give me my lowly thatched cottage again!
The birds singing gayly, that came at my call, —
Give me them, — and the peace of mind, dearer than all!
   Home, Home, sweet, sweet Home!
There 's no place like Home! there 's no place like Home!

How sweet 't is to sit 'neath a fond father's smile,
And the cares of a mother to soothe and beguile!
Let others delight mid new pleasures to roam,
But give me, oh, give me, the pleasures of home!
    Home! Home! sweet, sweet Home!
There's no place like Home! there's no place like Home!

To thee I'll return, overburdened with care;
The heart's dearest solace will smile on me there;
No more from that cottage again will I roam;
Be it ever so humble, there's no place like home.
    Home! Home! sweet, sweet Home!
There's no place like Home! there's no place like Home!

John Howard Payne

CLXXXV

A Life on the Ocean Wave

A life on the ocean wave!
    A home on the rolling deep,
Where the scatter'd waters rave,
    And the winds their revels keep:
Like an eagle cag'd I pine
    On this dull, unchanging shore:
Oh, give me the flashing brine,
    The spray and the tempest-roar!

Once more on the deck I stand. . . .
    Of my own swift-gliding craft: . . .
Set sail! farewell to the land!
    The gale follows fair abaft.

We shoot thro' the sparkling foam,
    Like an ocean-bird set free; —
Like the ocean-bird, our home
    We 'll find far out on the sea!

The land is no longer in view,
    The clouds have begun to frown;
But with a stout vessel and crew,
    We 'll say, Let the storm come down!
And the song of our hearts shall be,
    While the winds and the waters rave,
A home on the rolling sea!
    A life on the ocean wave!

Epes Sargent

CLXXXVI

Ben Bolt

Don't you remember sweet Alice, Ben Bolt, —
    Sweet Alice, whose hair was so brown,
Who wept with delight when you gave her a smile,
    And trembled with fear at your frown?
In the old church-yard in the valley, Ben Bolt,
    In a corner obscure and alone,
They have fitted a slab of the granite so gray,
    And Alice lies under the stone.

Under the hickory tree, Ben Bolt,
    Which stood at the foot of the hill,
Together we 've lain in the noonday shade,
    And listened to Appleton's mill.
The mill-wheel has fallen to pieces, Ben Bolt,
    The rafters have tumbled in,

And a quiet that crawls round the walls as you gaze
   Has followed the olden din.

Do you mind of the cabin of logs, Ben Bolt,
   At the edge of the pathless wood,
And the button-ball tree with its motley limbs,
   Which nigh by the doorstep stood?
The cabin to ruin has gone, Ben Bolt,
   The tree you would seek for in vain;
And where once the lords of the forest waved
   Are grass and the golden grain.

And don't you remember the school, Ben Bolt,
   With the master so cruel and grim,
And the shaded nook in the running brook
   Where the children went to swim?
Grass grows on the master's grave, Ben Bolt,
   The spring of the brook is dry,
And of all the boys who were schoolmates then
   There are only you and I.

There is change in the things I loved, Ben Bolt,
   They have changed from the old to the new;
But I feel in the deeps of my spirit the truth,
   There never was change in you.
Twelvemonths twenty have past, Ben Bolt,
   Since first we were friends — yet I hail
Your presence a blessing, your friendship a truth,
   Ben Bolt, of the salt-sea gale!

Thomas Dunn English

CLXXXVII

My Old Kentucky Home, Good-Night

The sun shines bright in the old Kentucky home;
   'T is summer, the darkeys are gay;
The corn-top 's ripe, and the meadow 's in the bloom,
   While the birds make music all the day.
The young folks roll on the little cabin floor,
   All merry, all happy and bright;
By'm by, hard times comes a-knocking at the door: —
   Then my old Kentucky home, good night!

     Weep no more, my lady,
       O, weep no more to-day!
We will sing one song for the old Kentucky home,
     For the old Kentucky home, far away.

They hunt no more for the possum and the coon,
   On the meadow, the hill, and the shore;
They sing no more by the glimmer of the moon,
   On the bench by the old cabin door.
The day goes by like a shadow o'er the heart,
   With sorrow where all was delight;
The time has come when the darkeys have to part: —
   Then my old Kentucky home, good-night!

The head must bow and the back will have to bend,
   Wherever the darkey may go;
A few more days, and the trouble all will end,
   In the field where the sugar-canes grow:
A few more days for to tote the weary load, —
   No matter, 't will never be light;
A few more days till we totter on the road: —
   Then my old Kentucky home, good-night!

Weep no more, my lady,
O, weep no more to-day!
We will sing one song for the old Kentucky home,
For the old Kentucky home, far away.

Stephen C. Foster

CLXXXVIII

Massa's in de Cold Ground

Round de meadows am a-ringing
　De darkeys' mournful song,
While de mocking-bird am singing,
　Happy as de day am long.
Where de ivy am a-creeping
　O'er de grassy mound,
Dere old massa am a-sleeping,
　Sleeping in de cold, cold ground.

　　Down in de corn-field
　　　Hear dat mournful sound:
　　All de darkeys am a-weeping, —
　　　Massa's in de cold, cold ground.

When de autumn leaves were falling,
　When de days were cold,
'T was hard to hear old massa calling,
　Cayse he was so weak and old.
Now de orange tree am blooming
　On de sandy shore,
Now de summer days am coming, —
　Massa nebber calls no more.

Massa make de darkeys love him,
  Cayse he was so kind;
Now dey sadly weep above him,
  Mourning cayse he leave dem behind.
I cannot work before to-morrow,
  Cayse de tear-drop flow;
I try to drive away my sorrow,
  Pickin' on de old banjo.

  Down in de corn-field
    Hear dat mournful sound:
  All de darkeys am a-weeping, —
    Massa 's in de cold, cold ground.

Stephen C. Foster

CLXXXIX

Old Folks at Home

Way down upon de Swanee Ribber,
  Far, far away,
Dere 's wha my heart is turning ebber,
  Dere 's wha de old folks stay.
All up and down de whole creation
  Sadly I roam,
Still longing for de old plantation,
  And for de old folks at home.

  All de world am sad and dreary,
    Eberywhere I roam;
  Oh! darkeys, how my heart grows weary,
    Far from de old folks at home!

All round de little farm I wandered
    When I was young,
Den many happy days I squandered,
    Many de songs I sung.
When I was playing wid my brudder,
    Happy was I ;
Oh, take me to my kind old mudder!
    Dere let me live and die.

One little hut among de bushes,
    One dat I love,
Still sadly to my memory rushes,
    No matter where I rove.
When will I see de bees a-humming
    All round de comb?
When will I hear de banjo tumming
    Down in my good old home?

All de world am sad and dreary,
    Eberywhere I roam ;
Oh! darkeys, how my heart grows weary,
    Far from de old folks at home!

Stephen C. Foster

CXC

Dixie's Land

I wish I wuz in de land ob cotton ;
Ole times dar am not forgotten ;
    Look away! look away! look away!
        Dixie land.
In Dixie land, whar I wuz born in,
Early on one frosty mornin',
    Look away! look away! look away!
        Dixie land.

Chorus

Den I wish I wuz in Dixie,
    Hooray! hooray!
In Dixie land I'll took my stand
    To lib an' die in Dixie.
        Away, away, away down South in Dixie.
        Away, away, away down South in Dixie.

Ole Missus marry "Will-de-weaber,"
William wuz a gay deceaber;
    Look away! etc.
But when he put his arm around 'er,
He look as fierce as a forty pounder.
    Look away! etc. — *Cho.*

His face wuz sharp as a butcher's cleaber,
But dat did n't seem to greab 'er;
    Look away! etc.
Ole Missus acted de foolish part,
And died for a man dat broke her heart.
    Look away! etc. — *Cho.*

Now here's a health to de next ole Missus,
And all de gals dat wants to kiss us;
    Look away! etc.
But if you want to dribe away sorrow,
Come and hear dis song to-morrow,
    Look away! etc. — *Cho.*

Dar's buckwheat cakes an' Ingen batter,
Makes you fat or a little fatter;
    Look away! etc.
Den hoe it down an' scratch your grabble,
To Dixie's land, I'm bound to trabble,
    Look away! etc. — *Cho.*

                            Daniel Decatur Emmett

SONS OF THE SELF-SAME RACE

1898

What is the Voice I hear
On the wind of the Western Sea?
Sentinel! Listen from out Cape Clear,
And say what the voice may be.
"'T is a proud free People calling loud to a People proud and free.

"And it says to them, 'Kinsmen, hail!
We severed have been too long;
Now let us have done with a worn-out tale,
The tale of an ancient wrong,
And our friendship last long as Love doth last, and be stronger than Death
  is strong.'"

Answer them, Sons of the self-same race,
And blood of the self-same clan,
Let us speak with each other, face to face,
And answer, as man to man,
And loyally love and trust each other, as none but free men can.

Now, fling them out to the breeze,
Shamrock, Thistle, and Rose!
And the Star-Spangled Banner unfurl with these,
A message to friends and foes,
Wherever the sails of Peace are seen, and wherever the War-wind blows.

A message to bond and thrall to wake,
For, whenever we come, we twain,
The throne of the Tyrant shall rock and quake,
And his menace be void and vain:
For you are lords of a strong young land, and we are lords of the main.

Yes, this is the Voice on the bluff March gale,
"We severed have been too long:
But now we have done with a worn-out tale,
The tale of an ancient wrong,
And our friendship shall last as Love doth last, and be stronger than Death
  is strong."

            ALFRED AUSTIN

NOTES

BOOK FIRST — THE OLDER BALLADS

Page 1, I. SIR PATRICK SPENS. — "This admired and most admirable ballad," says Professor Child in his *English and Scottish Popular Ballads*, "is one of many which were first made known to the world through Percy's Reliques, 1765. Percy's Version" (which is here given) "remains, poetically the best. . . . It would be hard to point out in ballad poetry, or other, happier and more refined touches than the two stanzas which portray the bootless waiting of the ladies for the return of the sea-farers." Whether the story is based upon the voyage of Margaret of Scotland to Norway in 1281, to be married to King Eric, and the shipwreck of her attendants on their return journey; or on the death of her daughter Princess Margaret during a voyage to Scotland in 1290, matters little. As Professor Child well says, "a strict accordance with history should not be expected, and indeed would be almost a ground of suspicion. Ballad singers and their hearers would be as indifferent to the facts as the readers of ballads are now; it is only editors who feel bound to look closely into such matters."

Page 3, II. THE BATTLE OF OTTERBOURNE. — The Scots and English, north and south of the Border between their respective countries, were, during the reigns of Richard II and Henry IV of England, in a state of petty warfare even more keen perhaps than at other periods of history. The battle of which this ballad tells was provoked by a raid on a large scale into Northumberland under the command of James, Earl of Douglas, and others. At Newcastle Douglas met Percy in single combat and succeeded in carrying off the Englishman's pennon (spear or sword, as the versions say). Percy caught up with the Scots at Otterbourne, and the sequel, as recounted in the poem, is substantially historical. The version printed in the text is from Scott's *Minstrelsy of the Scottish Border*. It is of Scottish sympathies and composition, and is thought by Motherwell to be the original of two English versions in the British Museum. But Professor Child (*English and Scottish Ballads*, Pt. VI, 289, etc.) thinks that this Scottish version had its own predecessor in Scotland, and that this in turn may have been derived from the English version. The parent ballad, whatever its nationality, may date back to about 1400; but the forms that we now possess are of much later composition.

Page 8, III. THE HUNTING OF THE CHEVIOT. — The version here given of this Border ballad is that of an Ashmolean manuscript (not earlier than 1550) in the Bodleian Library. The song was already old and popular in the middle of the sixteenth century; the stanza mentioning James of Scotland cannot, however, have been composed before 1424, when the first of that name ascended the throne. The history and geography are so freely poetized as to render impossible any attempt to fix the circumstances related. The historical basis may be the same as that of the *Ballad of Otterbourne*, but that place is not in the Cheviot region, and the battle, which was fought in 1388, cannot have taken place in Henry IV's reign (1399–1413), nor have been *immediately* followed by the fight at Homildon (1402), nor have been reported to James I of Scotland. The Douglas, Percy, James, and Harry may indeed all have been of even later date than 1424. But why bother about dates when reading that of which Sir Philip Sidney wrote, "I never heard the old song of Percy and Douglas that I found not my heart moved more than with a trumpet; and yet is it sung by some blind crowder with no rougher voice than rude style." Ben Jonson used to say that he had rather have been the author of *Chevy Chase* than of all his works; and Addison, who knew only the more modern and inferior version of the seventeenth and eighteenth centuries, says that it was in his day the most popular ballad of the common people of England. (See Child's *Ballads*, Pt. VI.) — *And a vowe*, a vow. — *In the magger*, in spite of. — *Dogles*, Douglas. — *Meany*, company; suite. — *So he*, so high. — *The hyls abone*, above the hills. — *Yerly*, early. — *Be that*, by the time that, when. — *Blewe a morte*, blew a blast to celebrate the death (*mort*) of the deer. — *The*, they. — *The semblyde on sydis shear*, they gathered together from all sides. — *Lokyde at his hand full ny*, observed near at hand (Gummere). — *The wear*, they were. — *Yth*, in the. — *Tividale*, Teviotdale. — *Boys*, bows. — *Chyviat chays*, hunting ground upon the Cheviot hills. — *Cast*, intend. — *The ton*, the one, one. — *Yerle*, earl. — *Uppone a parti stande*, stand aside. — *Do*, let us do. — *Cristes cors on his crowne*, the curse of Christ on his head. — *On man for on*, man for man. — *Sothe*, south. — *The first fit here I fynde*, here I end the first division of the ballad. — *Hom*, them. — *Gave*, i.e., they gave. — *Many a doughetë the garde to dy*, many a doughty (knight) they caused to die. — *Many sterne*, etc., many brave ones they struck down straight. — *Heal or rayn*, hail or rain. — *Say slean was*, etc., saw (that) slain was, etc. — *Stele*, steel head. — *Halyde*, pulled. — *Evensonge*, vespers. — *The tocke*, they took; words are here missing in the MS. — *Carpe off care*, tell of sorrow. — *Jamy*, James I. — *Ye-feth*, in faith. — *Hombyll-down*, there was a battle of Homildon in 1402, though the Percy of *Otterbourne* and *Cheviot* fought in it (*Gummere*). — *Ther was never a tym*, etc., 'There was never a time, on the Border-land, since the Douglas and Percy thus met, but it is a marvel if the red blood ran not as rain does in the street.' — *Balys bete*, remedy our evils.

Page 18, IV. EDOM O' GORDON. — This thrilling recital is both domestic and historical. Professor Gummere (*Old English Ballads*) sums up the accounts of its source, from Child's edition, thus: "Adam Gordon, a deputy of the Scottish Queen Mary, in November, 1571, sent one Captain Ker to the house of one of the Forbeses, a family attached to the Protestant or regent's party. Captain Ker demanded surrender; the lady of the house refused; and thereupon he burned down the house, to the destruction of the inmates. In some of the versions Gordon is treated as the principal actor." The text here given is from a MS. of the last quarter of the sixteenth century (in the British Museum), slightly emended from other versions by Professor Gummere.

Page 24, V-IX. OF ROBIN HOOD. — Rhymes of Robin Hood are spoken of as early as 1377 in *Piers Plowman*. The hero himself has been variously assigned to the reigns of Henry II (1154–1189), Richard I (1189–1199), Henry III (1216–1272), Edward I (1272–1307), Edward II (1307–1327), and Edward III (1327–1377). There were indeed no less than six English Robin Hoods in the flesh during the forty years preceding 1337, each earning his living in some unimportant but honest fashion. None of these can be identified with the ballad-hero, who is, as Professor Child has said, "absolutely a creation of the ballad-muse." He is no more a political character than a historical entity. "In the *Gest of Robin Hood* (the ballads composing which were probably put together, says Professor Child, as early as 1400, or before) he is a yeoman, outlawed for reasons not given but easily surmised, 'courteous and free,' religious in sentiment, and above all reverent of the Virgin, for the love of whom he is respectful to all women." He shoots the king's deer but professes loyalty to the king. He is the champion of the common people against such representatives of the law, civil or ecclesiastical, as show themselves unjust, overbearing, avaricious, or hypocritical; he is friendly to the simple and the poor. "The late ballads debase this primary conception in various ways and degrees." Of the various fyttes, or divisions of this *Gest of Robin Hood*, we have given, in the text, the seventh under the title "Robin Hood and the King." Some of the ballads make Barnsdale in Yorkshire the basis of Robin's operations; some of another cycle, the Sherwood, center about Nottingham.

Page 24, V. ROBIN HOOD AND LITTLE JOHN. — Recorded as early as 1689. The version which we now have is probably not the original, and still ours may have been composed before 1700.

Page 29, VI. ROBIN HOOD RESCUING THREE SQUIRES, or THE WIDOW'S THREE SONS, was printed by Ritson in 1795 from the York edition of a Robin Hood garland of which the earliest date known is 1670. Ritson thinks that this is one of the oldest Robin Hood ballads.

Page 34, VII. The adventure of ALLIN A DALE is told as happening to Scarlock (one of Robin's men) in a life of Robin Hood of the end of the sixteenth century. The earliest broadsides of the ballad are of the latter half of the seventeenth. — *Child*.

Page 38, VIII. ROBIN HOOD AND THE KING. — The seventh fytte of the old *Gest*, composed, as stated above, before the end of the fourteenth century. The text is from Gummere, as based upon Child's copy from an early sixteenth-century version in the Advocates' Library, Edinburgh. — The *gentyll knight* here spoken of has been, in earlier fyttes, befriended by Robin. Here he is identified with a certain Rycharde of the Lee. — The *kynge* is said by some, but on insufficient evidence, to be Edward II, and the year, 1323. — *Passe*, bounds. — *Faylyd of*, missed. — *Gone*, go, walk. — *That he ne shall lese*, without losing. — *Halke*, corner. — *Welt*, managed. — *Full moche good*, full many goods. — *Departed it*, divided it. — *Targe* (doubtful reading but may be), seal. — *In Robyn's lote*, to Robin's lot. — *Frendës fare*, in spite of his friend's experience (*Gummere*). — *For God*, fore God. — *Sent I me*, I assent. — *With that thou*, if thou. — *But me lyke*, unless I like.

Page 47, IX. ROBIN HOOD'S DEATH AND BURIAL. — One of the most affecting and unaffected of the ballads. Printed by Ritson in 1795 from a collation of two copies of a York garland. The ballad was evidently composed much earlier.

Page 50, X. THE DOUGLAS TRAGEDY. — Put together by Sir Walter Scott from two different copies and from oral tradition. It is also known as Earl Brand, Lord Douglas, Lady Margaret, and the Child of Ell. The theme is also treated in north European ballads of considerably earlier date.

Page 53, XI. LORD RANDAL. — Version from Scott's *Minstrelsy*, 1803. The story in various forms is widely distributed through Europe; in Italy it goes back two hundred and fifty years.

Page 54, XII. BONNIE GEORGE CAMPBELL. — As in Gummere, *Old English Ballads*, from Motherwell's *Minstrelsy*. The event may be of the end of the sixteenth century, but no one knows.

Page 55, XIII. BESSIE BELL AND MARY GRAY. — Well-known ballad before the end of the seventeenth century. According to tradition Bessie Bell and Mary Gray, daughters of country gentlemen near Perth, went into seclusion in a bower or summerhouse of some kind at a place called Burnbraes to escape the plague in the city, 1645, but caught the sickness from a young man who visited them. They were said to have been buried at Dranoch Haugh.

Page 56, XIV. THE TWA CORBIES. — From Scott's *Minstrelsy*.

Page 57, XV. HELEN OF KIRCONNELL. — From the same.

Page 58, XVI. THE WIFE OF USHER'S WELL. — From the same.

Page 60, XVII. THE DEMON LOVER. — From the same.

BOOK SECOND — POEMS OF ENGLAND

Page 65, XVIII. GOD SAVE THE KING. — The English national anthem has been ordinarily but without proof attributed to Dr. John Bull (1563-1628), an English composer and organist, and chamber musician to James I; but not, as is commonly supposed, professor of music at Oxford. It is more likely that the song was written by Henry Carey, who died in 1743 at the age of fifty or thereabout. He was both poet and musical composer; and to him we owe *Sally in our Alley* and many other popular songs of far greater merit than *God Save the King*. It is said, however, that the germ of this anthem is found in one which Sir

Peter Carew used to sing before Henry VIII (1509-1547), of which the chorus ran,

> And I said, Good Lord defend
> England with thy most holy hand
> And save noble Henry our King.

Page 66, XIX. ENGLAND. — From *King Richard II*, Act II, Sc. 1. John of Gaunt upon his deathbed resolves to rebuke his nephew Richard II for the selfish and riotous policy with which he is ruining England. — *Feared by their breed*, by reason of their breed.

Page 67, XX. BEFORE HARFLEUR. — From *King Henry the Fifth*, Act III, Sc. 1. In his invasion of France, 1415, Henry took Harfleur, the key of Normandy, after a siege of thirty-eight days. — *Portage*, loop-holes. — *Jutty*, jut over. — *Swilled*, surrounded by. — *Confounded*, troubled. — *Fet*, fetched. — *Copy*, example.

Page 68, XXI. BEFORE AGINCOURT. — From *King Henry the Fifth*, Act IV, Sc. 3. (See next note.) The 25th of October is called the day of St. Crispin and St. Crispian after two brothers, early Christians and martyrs of the beginning of the fourth century. They are the patron saints of shoemakers. — *To gentle his condition* means to elevate to the status of gentleman.

Page 70, XXII. THE BALLAD OF AGINCOURT. — Dedicated to the Cambrio-Britons, or the Welsh, because Henry was born at Monmouth in Wales. — Stanza 3. *Which*, for who. The French general derides Henry by ordering him to provide for his ransom even before the battle is begun. — Stanza 6. *At Crecy* (1346) and *Poitiers* (1356) Edward III, the great-grandsire of Henry V, had, with his son Edward, the Black Prince, routed the French. *Lilies*, the *fleurs-de-lis* on the French coat of arms. — Stanzas 7-14. *Sir Thomas Erpingham* led the archery. The Dukes of *Gloucester* and *Clarence* were younger brothers of the king. The other warriors were of the English nobility.

Page 74, XXIII. THE "REVENGE." — For the incidents of this ballad Tennyson has relied mainly upon Sir Walter Raleigh's report of the engagement published in 1591. At the time of the Armada, Grenville, who had already distinguished himself by romantic bravery, pride, and ferocity, had been commissioned by Elizabeth to protect Cornwall and Devon. When, later, the admiral, Lord Thomas Howard, was sent to the Azores with a squadron of sixteen ships, of which but six were of the line, to intercept the Spanish treasure fleet, he took Sir Richard with him. Overtaken at Flores by a fleet of fifty-three Spanish men-of-war, he was forced to retreat; but Sir Richard, as vice admiral, stayed to rescue those of his men who were sick on shore, intending to bring up the rear with his little ship (Drake's ship of the Armada), the *Revenge*.

Stanza 1. Many cruelties have been ascribed, especially by those of differing faith, to the efforts made by the Holy Inquisition in Spain to put down religious movements directed against the Roman Catholic Church.

Page 81, XXV. THE SALLY FROM COVENTRY. — The cavalier, Sir Richard Tyrone, breaking from Coventry Keep during the Civil War (1642-1649) in order to disperse the besieging Roundheads, is surprised from the rear by their allies of Scotland who march into Coventry in his absence.

Page 82, XXVI. THE BATTLE OF NASEBY. — Fought in Northamptonshire (or the "North" of the poem), June 14, 1645. The victory gained by the Parliamentary forces decided the fate of Charles, who took refuge among the Scots and was within a year surrendered by them to the English, who put him to death in 1649. Sir Thomas Fairfax was general of the Parliamentary army; Skippon, major general. Ireton commanded the left wing and Cromwell with his Ironsides stood upon the right. The king — whom the supposed author of this ballad, with his scriptural name after the style of the Puritans, calls the "Man of Blood" and "Accurst" — viewed the rout from a neighboring eminence. The royal cavalry on the right wing was under the immediate charge of Prince Rupert of the Rhine, Charles's nephew and the son of the Elector Palatine of Germany; he was assisted in command by Sir Marmaduke Langdale and Sir Jacob Astley. — The animosity of the Puritan sergeant for the Churches of Rome and England is evident in his objurgation of the 'mitre' of the bishop and the Mammon (riches) of the Pope. — Oxford University sided with the king. Durham with its "stalls" (the seats in the choir) was one of the cathedral-towns that espoused his side. — The invective against the Jesuits and the city of the seven hills (Rome, of course) was provoked by the suspicion of the Puritans that Charles's marriage with Henrietta of France meant the restoration of the Catholic form of religion, and of the Order of Jesus.

Stanza 1. *Wine-press*, see Rev. xiv. 18-20. — Stanza 6. *Alsatia*, that part of London frequented by fugitives from justice, acknowledged criminals, and bullies. *Whitehall*, the palace. — Stanza 10. *Temple*

Bar, one of the gateways or barriers of ancient London, now removed, on the top of which were exposed the heads of traitors. — Stanza 15. The *Houses* of Parliament and the *Word* of God.

Page 87, XXVIII. THE BRITISH GRENADIERS. — The words of this stirring military song date from about 1690, but the music is founded on an air of the sixteenth century.

Page 88, XXIX. RULE, BRITANNIA. — The well-known tune is by Arne.

Page 90, XXXI. BATTLE OF THE BALTIC. — Denmark, by entering into a coalition with Russia and Sweden to prevent England from searching neutral vessels, brought about the bombardment of Copenhagen by Admiral Nelson in 1801. Hence the "Battle of the Baltic" by which the coalition was broken up. — *Elsinore*, the ancient seat of the Danish kings, near Copenhagen. — *Captain Riou* of the English fleet, killed during the engagement.

Page 93, XXXII. YE MARINERS OF ENGLAND. — The first draft of this song (written in 1800) was based upon an ancient melody, "Ye Gentlemen of England," by Martin Parker, about 1630, which has considerable merit. — The English admiral, *Robert Blake*, had defeated De Reuter, De Wit, and Van Tromp on various occasions during the Dutch War of 1652–1653. He died at sea in 1657 after routing the navies of Spain. — *Nelson* was mortally wounded at Trafalgar, 1805, in the moment of victory. — The *meteor flag*, because of its fiery hue.

Page 94, XXXIII. CHARACTER OF THE HAPPY WARRIOR. — Wordsworth had in view both Lord Nelson and his own brother, Captain John Wordsworth. The latter perished in the wreck of his vessel, 1805. From the former the poet has drawn much that was generally acknowledged to be excellent and commendable in his professional career; from the latter the higher qualities of personal and social conduct.

Page 97, XXXIV. THE BURIAL OF SIR JOHN MOORE. — After the capture of Madrid by Napoleon, 1809, Sir John Moore, commanding a portion of Wellington's army, was forced to retreat before the French and was killed at Corunna while striving to embark his troops. He was buried the same night on the ramparts of the city. Of the "Burial" Byron said that it was "the most perfect ode in the language."

Page 98, XXXV. THE FIELD OF WATERLOO. — The third canto of *Childe Harold*, from which these stanzas are taken, was written two years after Waterloo was fought. The ball referred to in the second stanza of the text was given by the Duchess of Richmond on June 15, three days before the battle. — *The Duke of Brunswick*, commanding a German contingent and acting with Blücher and Wellington, fell at the preliminary battle of Quatre Bras, on the 16th. — The *Camerons' gathering* stands, of course, for many a war tune of the Scottish regiments. Byron refers especially to "*Sir Evan Cameron* and his descendant *Donald*, the 'gentle Lochiel' of the 'forty-five' (1745)." In a note on the next stanza Byron says, "The wood of Soignies is supposed to be a remnant of the forest of *Ardennes*, famous in Boiardo's *Orlando*, and immortal in Shakespeare's *As You Like It*."

Page 101, XXXVI. THE LOST LEADER. — From *Dramatic Romances and Lyrics*, 1845. "A great leader of a party has deserted the cause, fallen away from his early ideals, and forsaken the teaching which has inspired disciples who loved and honored him. They are sorrowful not so much for their own loss as for the moral deterioration he has himself suffered." Browning in writing of the poem some thirty years later confesses that in his hasty youth he did use, as a sort of painter's model for this picture, one or two features of the great and venerable personality of Wordsworth, who, though extremely liberal in his political sentiments during his earlier manhood, became, like many a hot-headed revolutionary before him and since, a rigid conservative in his middle and later years. "Had I intended more," he continues, "above all such a boldness as portraying the entire man, I should not have talked about 'handfuls of silver and bits of ribbon.' These never influenced the change of politics in the great poet.... I altogether refuse to have my little poem considered as the 'very effigies' of such a moral and intellectual superiority."

Page 102, XXXVII. ON THE DEATH OF WORDSWORTH. — The three men here celebrated are regarded as the poetic voices of Europe during the early part of the nineteenth century, the period of storm and transition, — a Titanic age in politics and poetry. Goethe had died in 1832; Byron, in 1824, while assisting the Greeks in their war of independence against the Turks. Another excellent appreciation of Wordsworth's contribution to English sentiment and conduct is William Watson's poem entitled *Wordsworth's Grave*.

Page 105, XXXVIII. ON THE DEATH OF WELLINGTON. — September 14, 1852. The lines "Who is he that cometh" to "on my rest" are supposed to be uttered by Lord Nelson, and call forth the recital of

Wellington's feats on land. This poem may profitably be compared with Longfellow's *Warden of the Cinque Ports*, a title borne by Wellington at the time of his death.

Page 114, XXXIX. LOSS OF THE "BIRKENHEAD." — English troopship wrecked off the African coast in 1852. "She had on board her crew, one hundred and thirty-two in number, and about five hundred other persons consisting of soldiers with their wives and children. The women and children were sent off in the boats. The men remained on board to face almost certain death. Many were young soldiers who had been but a short time in the service. All were swept into the sea by the waves, and nearly all were lost" (Montgomery, *Heroic Ballads*; Ginn & Company, Boston). The *clasp* and *cross of bronze* are military decorations. A more recent treatment of this theme is Kipling's *Soldier an' Sailor too*:

Their work was done when it 'ad n't begun; they was younger nor me an' you;
... So they stood an' was still to the Birken'ead drill, soldier an' sailor too!

Page 116, XL. THE CHARGE OF THE LIGHT BRIGADE. — At the battle of Balaklava, 1854, during the Crimean War, a band of English light horsemen, "owing to some fatal misconception of the meaning of an order from the commander-in-chief, rode a mile down a slight slope, exposed to a merciless cross fire, for the purpose of saving a few guns from capture by the Russians. They reached the battery, sabred the gunners, and rode back," less than two hundred of the six hundred and seven who had started. "All the world rang with wonder and admiration," says McCarthy, "of the futile and splendid charge.... Perhaps its best epitaph was contained in the comment of the French general, Bosquet, 'It was magnificent, but it was not war.'"

Page 118, XLI. SANTA FILOMENA. — It has been well said that of all the heroes of the Crimean War Miss Nightingale was the noblest. "She went forth not to slay, but to heal, and she came back with more honors on her brow than any hero of them all." Of the saint whose name our American poet prefixes to these verses, Mrs. Jameson in her *Sacred and Legendary Art*, II, 298, says, "At Pisa, the church of San Francisco contains a chapel dedicated lately to Santa Filomena; over the altar is a picture by Sabatelli, representing the saint as a beautiful, nymph-like figure, floating down from heaven, attended by two angels, bearing the lily, palm, and javelin, and beneath, in the foreground, the sick and maimed, who are healed by her intercession." Longfellow in choosing this title was naturally influenced by the resemblance of the name to Philomela (the nightingale).

Page 119, XLII. THE SONG OF THE CAMP. — The British soldiers — English, Welsh, Scotch, and Irish (from Severn, Clyde, and Shannon) — are besieging Sebastopol during the Crimean War, 1855. — *Redan* and *Malakoff* are Russian forts. The author is the American, Bayard Taylor.

Page 121, XLIII. THE RELIEF OF LUCKNOW. — During the mutiny of the Sepoy, or native, regiments in Hindostan, 1857, a number of English women and children with but a small garrison were besieged in the fort of Lucknow from July 1 till September 25, when General Havelock fighting his way into the town prevented a massacre. The rescue was, however, but temporary; and if Sir Colin Campbell, recently appointed commander in chief, had not reached Lucknow with his plucky force of five thousand on November 14, Havelock's soldiers would merely have swelled the list of victims for whom the Sepoys were preparing a frightful end. The author of the poem was the brother of James Russell Lowell.

Page 124, XLIV. THE MARCH OF THE WORKERS. — In his later years Morris, as is well known, devoted much time and energy to the furtherance of socialistic doctrines. His best prose works upon this subject are *A Dream of John Ball* and *News from Nowhere;* his best verse *The Pilgrims of Hope* and *Chants for Socialists*. From the last, written in 1885, the poem in the text is taken. It is included in this collection as representing the poetic high-water mark of a movement whose importance in history no impartial observer can underrate. Other poems of the same kind are his *Death Song*, 1887; Ebenezer Elliott's *Corn Law Rhymes* of 1827; Eliza Cook's *The People of England;* Ernest Charles Jones's *Songs of Democracy;* Gerald Massey's *Cries of Forty-Eight;* Brough's *Songs of the Governing Classes*, 1855; and some of Swinburne's *Songs before Sunrise*.

Page 126, XLV. RECESSIONAL. — Written to celebrate the close of Queen Victoria's Diamond Jubilee, 1897.

Page 138, LV. VICAR OF BRAY. — Attributed to an officer in the English army during the reign of George I (1714–1727). A certain Vicar of Bray called "Simon Alleyn was twice a Papist and twice a

Protestant in the reign of Henry VIII, Edward VI, Mary, and Elizabeth. Hence the modern application of the title."

Page 142, LVIII. TOM BOWLING. — From a musical dramatic composition called *The Oddities.* Dibdin's sea songs are not only numerous but probably the best that England has produced. — *Broached him to;* not "too," as some editors print it, conceiving that Death has tapped him like a cask. *To broach to* is a nautical term meaning to bring up or come, by mistake of steering, to the wind. Hence the wreck of Tom Bowling.

BOOK THIRD — POEMS OF SCOTLAND

Page 143, LIX. MY NATIVE LAND. — The Song of the Aged Harper, which opens the sixth canto of *The Lay of the Last Minstrel.* — *Yarrow* and *Ettrick*, rivers in the south of Scotland.

Page 144, LX. BANNOCKBURN. — Sir William Wallace, attempting to cast off the yoke of suzerainty recently imposed upon Scotland by Edward I of England, was at first victorious, 1296–1297; but, overthrown in the battle of Falkirk, 1298, he was later taken prisoner by the English and in 1305 put to death as a traitor. Robert Bruce, who arose to fill his place, was crowned king of Scotland in 1306. In 1314 he met and routed the forces of England under Edward II at Bannockburn, thus regaining for his country its independence.

Page 145, LXI. GATHERING SONG. — "This," says Sir Walter Scott, "is a very ancient pibroch belonging to Clan MacDonald, and supposed to refer to the expedition of Donald Balloch, who in 1431 launched from the Isles with a considerable force, invaded Lochaber, and at Inverlochy defeated and put to flight the Earls of Mar and Caithness, though at the head of an army superior to his own."

Page 146, LXII. THE FLOWERS OF THE FOREST, ETC. — The Forest here is a district of Scotland "which boasted the best archers and perhaps the finest men in the kingdom. It comprehended Selkirkshire, part of Peeblesshire and of Clydesdale." The battle of Flodden (1513) was one of the most awful disasters that have ever befallen Scotland. James IV, who had invaded England at the head of thirty thousand men, was utterly crushed by the English commander, the Earl of Surrey, and, in company with the flower of Scottish chivalry and yeomen, lost his life. The last part of the poem as here given, beginning with stanza 4, was written by Alison Rutherford (afterward Mrs. Cockburn) as a complete song several years before her younger contemporary, Jean Elliott, wrote the first three stanzas.

Page 149, LXIII. BLUE BONNETS OVER THE BORDER. — From *The Monastery*, Chapter XXV. Mary, Queen of Scots, was born 1542, crowned 1543. She fled to England, 1568, and was beheaded on charge of conspiring against the life of Elizabeth, 1587. Sir Walter founded this song, however, on a later production of popular origin composed to celebrate General Lesley's (the Earl of Leven's) march over the Border to Longmarston Moor, where in 1644 he helped to overcome the forces of Charles I.

Page 150, LXIV. THE EXECUTION OF MONTROSE. — Having headed a fruitless rising in favor of Charles, afterward the Second, in 1650, the Marquis of Montrose (James Graham, or Graeme) "was taken prisoner and executed in Edinburgh (Dunedin) with all the vindictive insult that his hereditary enemy, the Marquis of Argyle (Archibald Campbell), himself suspected of having previously plotted the execution of Charles I, could heap upon him." According to Professor Aytoun, "The most poetical chronicler would find it impossible to render the incidents of Montrose's brilliant career more picturesque than the reality. Among the devoted champions, who, during the wildest and most stormy period of our history, maintained the cause of Church and King 'the great Marquis' undoubtedly is entitled to the foremost place. Cardinal Retz has said of him 'he is the only man in the world that has ever realized to me the ideas of certain heroes whom we now discover nowhere but in the lives of Plutarch.' . . . There is no ingredient of fiction in the historical incidents recorded in the following ballad. . . . It may be considered as a narrative of the transactions related by an aged Highlander, who had followed Montrose through his campaigns, to his grandson — Evan Cameron." *Macleod of Assynt* betrayed Montrose to his enemies. — The *Watergate*, in Edinburgh. — The *Solemn League and Covenant* between the Scottish church and the English Parliament, 1643, aimed to establish Presbyterianism throughout Great Britain and Ireland. — The flag bore *the cross of Saint Andrew*, the patron of Scotland. The Presbyterian ministers had been largely trained under John Calvin at *Geneva*.

Page 157, LXV. THE BONNETS O' BONNIE DUNDEE. — After James II had fled from England before the invading army of William of

Orange (William III), his cause was maintained in Scotland by Viscount Dundee (John Graham of Claverhouse), the Duke of Gordon, and others. The Lords of Convention, or Scottish Parliament, in spite of the threats of Claverhouse (Claver'se), swore allegiance to William and Mary; and the Whig, or Puritan, element of the city of Edinburgh approved their decision. The Viscount galloped away to raise an army of Highland chieftains and their clans, "wild Duniewassals" in the North, for the Lowland lords also had thrown their influence to King William. — The *Westport*, the western gate. — The *Bow*, a famous street whose "bends" had been "sanctified" by the assembling there of the Scottish Church. — The *Grass-Market*, a central square. — The Covenanting Protestants from Kilmarnock are sneeringly called "cowls" because of their austere appearance. — *Mons Meg* and her marrows (companions) are the cannon in the castle. — *Viscount Dundee* boasts that not all the power of Scotland is confined within the environment of Edinburgh bounded by the *Pentland Hills* and the *Firth of Forth*. — *Ravelston* and *Clermiston* are near Edinburgh. — For *Montrose*, see the preceding poem. — A good characterization of Claverhouse may be found in Scott's *Old Mortality* and in Aytoun's *Burial March of Dundee*. The poem is in the *Doom of Devorgoil*.

Page 159, LXVI. THE OLD SCOTTISH CAVALIER. — William Edmonstoune Aytoun, the author of the stirring *Lays of the Scottish Cavaliers*, 1849, was a professor in the University of Edinburgh. He says in his preface to this poem that the subject of it is Alexander Forbes, Lord Pitsligo, a nobleman whose conscientious views impelled him to follow the fortunes of the exiled house of Stuart. His *castle by the Spey* was in Aberdeenshire. Of the cavalier of the lay it is said that his father had died for James II in 1689, at Killiecrankie Pass, with that Graeme of Claverhouse celebrated in *The Bonnets of Bonnie Dundee;* and that he himself was with Prince Charles Edward in the Jacobite victory at Prestonpans, and fell in the battle that decided the fate of the Jacobite cause, — Culloden Moor, 1746. — The White Rose and the White Cockade are, of course, emblems of the Stuarts.

Page 162, LXVII. THE LAMENT OF FLORA MACDONALD. — After his flight from Culloden, Charles Edward Stuart was saved from the pursuit of some two thousand men by Flora Macdonald, who took him over the Skye in disguise. After numerous hardships, he reëmbarked for France some five months later. In the *Jacobite Relics*, James Hogg says that he versified anew the original of this song which he had obtained in a rude translation from the Gaelic.

Page 163, LXVIII. WAE'S ME FOR PRINCE CHARLIE. — James Hogg attributes this song to William Glen of Glasgow, author of a few other popular songs. The Young Pretender's ill-starred invasion of Great Britain was brought to a close at Culloden, April 16, 1746.

Page 165, LXX. THE BLUE BELL OF SCOTLAND. — This version is from Chappell's *Popular Music of the Olden Time* and Ritson's *North Country Chorister*. The well-known air was composed by Mrs. Jordan, perhaps as early as 1786; she sang it first in London in 1786, and again in 1800, when it acquired general popularity. Chappell describes it as an "old English Border song," and the version given by him is far older and simpler than others (like that attributed to Mrs. Grant of Laggan, 1799, which has nothing about the Blue Bell, and need not be here retailed). Miss Stirling Graham's still more recent version has "where blooms the sweet blue bell," which may be poetic but is less naïve than the commemoration of the tavern sign which is found in the original.

Page 166, LXXI. ANNIE LAURIE. — The heroine of this the sweetest of Scottish love songs was born on December 16, 1682, — one of four daughters of Sir Robert Laurie of Maxwelton House, Scotland. We may conjecture that it was about 1700 that she "made up the bargain" with the lover who immortalized her, William Douglas of Finland, or Fingland. But "he didna get her after a'," said his own granddaughter, Clark Douglas, an old lady who was still living in 1854. According to her, the words as sung at that date were not as they first were written. "Oh, I mind them fine," she said, "I have remembered them a' my life. My father often repeated them to me." She then recited:

> Maxwelton's banks are bonnie,
>   They're a' clad owre wi' dew,
> Where I an' Annie Laurie
>   Made up the bargain true.
> Made up the bargain true,
>   Which ne'er forgot s'all be,
> An' for bonnie Annie Laurie
>   I'd lay me doun an' dee, —

but remembered "nae mair." And probably that was all that Douglas of Fingland had composed. The second stanza of the song, as it was said to have been written by him, might have been put together by anybody; for there is only one line that evinces any effort of composition. The first five were borrowed, says Fitzgerald, from an old ballad of *John Anderson, my Jo*, and the last two are simply the refrain. The following is the old second stanza, as attributed to Douglas:

> She's backit like the peacock,
>   She's bristit like the swan,
> She's jimp around the middle,
>   Her waist ye weel micht span — .
>   Her waist ye weel micht span —
> An' she has a rolling ee,
> An' for bonnie Annie Laurie
>   I'd lay me doun an' dee.

The first stanza was altered by Lady John Scott to the form given in the text. She substituted the second as there given; and added the third. The third line of her third stanza has been changed by some one, but without advantage, to "Like the winds in summer sighing." Fitzgerald (in whose *Famous Songs* the poem is discussed) says that the melody now sung was composed by this lady, though it is attributed by some to a Scotchman named R. Findlater.

Page 167, LXXII. LOCHABER. — "A lady, in whose father's house at Edinburgh Burns was a frequent and honored guest, one evening played the tune of *Lochaber* on the harpsichord to Burns. He listened to it attentively, and then exclaimed, with tears in his eyes, 'Oh, that's a fine tune for a broken heart.' It is said that the tune is derived from a seventeenth-century air of Irish composition entitled *King James's March to Ireland*." — Wood's *Scottish Songs*.

Page 168, LXXIII. NAE LUCK ABOUT THE HOUSE. — This Burns used to call "the finest love-ballad of the kind in the Scottish or perhaps any other language." While it is said to have been written by William Mickle, we know that the fifth and most poetic stanza was added by Dr. James Beattie.

Page 171, LXXIV. A RED, RED ROSE. — Burns's contribution to this song would seem to be limited to the exquisite first stanza. The rest constitute a very old ditty, said to have been written by a Lieutenant Hinches as a farewell to his sweetheart. It is one of the songs that Burns picked up from the old wives of the countryside.

Page 171, LXXV. FOR A' THAT. — Written about January, 1795. "Is there any one that, because of honest poverty, hangs, etc."

Page 173, LXXVI. JOHN ANDERSON, MY JO.—Burns took the opening phrase from a very old and worthless song of the sixteenth century. The sentiment and poetry are his own.

Page 174, LXXVII. AFTON WATER.—Afton is an Ayrshire stream. It is reported that Burns wrote the verses as a tribute of gratitude to Mrs. Stewart of Afton Lodge, "for the notice she had taken of him — the first he had received from one in her rank of life."

Page 176, LXXIX. MY HEART'S IN THE HIGHLANDS. — Burns said that the first half stanza was from an old song, the rest was by himself.

Page 176, LXXX. JOCK OF HAZELDEAN. — The first stanza comes from an old ballad, the others were added by Scott.

Page 178, LXXXI. LOCHINVAR. — Lady Heron's song in the fifth canto of *Marmion*. — The *Eske* flows into Solway. — *Netherby* is in Cumberland.

Page 185, LXXXVI. AULD LANG SYNE. — Burns himself said that this song was old. To his friend Mrs. Dunlop he wrote: " Is not the Scots phrase 'Auld Lang Syne' exceedingly expressive? There is an old song and tune which has often thrilled through my soul. You know I am an enthusiast on old Scot songs. I shall give you the verses." He enclosed the words of the song as we know it, and continued, "Light lie the turf on the breast of the heaven-inspired poet who composed this glorious fragment." To Thomson, his publisher, he wrote: " One song more, and I am done — *Auld Lang Syne*. The air is but mediocre; but the following song, the old song of the olden times, and which has never been in print, nor even in manuscript, until I took it down from an old man's singing, is enough to recommend any air." Fitzgerald (in his *Stories of Famous Songs*) adds to this information the following, that Sir Robert Ayton (1570–1638), "a friend of Ben Jonson and other Elizabethan writers," wrote a poem in which occurs this stanza:

> Should auld acquaintance be forgot,
>   And never thought upon,
> The flame of love extinguished
>   And fairly passed and gone?
> Is thy kind heart now grown so cold,
>   In that loving breast of thine,
> That thou canst never once reflect
>   On old long syne?

In 1724 the poet Allan Ramsay tried his hand at the song. In an old collection of 1775, called the *Caledoniad*, this Ayton stanza appears as the first of ten in an *Old-Long-Syne*—a love song of no particular merit. And it is interesting to note that this poem is preceded in the *Caledoniad* by one entitled "*Auld Kyndness quite forget*," the refrain of which would seem to have suggested "We'll tak a cup of kindness yet" in the song as we now have it. Burns reshaped and vastly improved the first stanza of the Ayton song, and probably added the stanzas which now stand second and third. The old tune has been abandoned since 1795. That now in use was composed by William Shield, an Englishman.

BOOK FOURTH — POEMS OF IRELAND

Page 188, LXXXVIII. THE IRISH WIFE. — "In 1376 the Statute of Kilkenny forbade the English settlers in Ireland to intermarry with the Irish under pain of outlawry. James, Earl of Desmond, was one of the first to violate this law. He was an accomplished poet." He is therefore well represented as the author of these thrilling lines. Thomas D'Arcy McGee, who wrote the poem, was one of the Irish patriots of 1848.

Page 190, LXXXIX. DARK ROSALEEN. — The Róisín Dubh (Roseen dhu), or little black rose, symbolizes Ireland. The original of this song is in the Irish tongue and was composed during the reign of Elizabeth, about 1601. "It purports to be an allegorical address from the chieftain, Hugh the Red O'Donnell, to Ireland on the subject of his love and struggles for her, and his resolve to free her from the English yoke." The date of this address would be about 1601, when the Spaniards landed at Kinsale to help the Irish. It has been translated by Thomas Furlong and by Aubrey De Vere. Mangan has given it all the passion of a love song. This poet, the most original song writer of Ireland, lived most of his life in Dublin. He was for a time associated with the staff of Trinity College Library.

Page 193, XC. THE BATTLE OF THE BOYNE. — With an army of Stuart loyalists and Frenchmen James II of England had landed in Ireland, in 1689, to regain his throne. That year he was defeated in an attempt to take the Protestant town of Derry in the north. During the next year, William of Orange and his marshal, the Duke of Schomberg, drove him down from Dundalk, fifty miles from Dublin, to the southern banks of the river Boyne, which flows into Drogheda Bay about twenty miles north of Dublin. William III crossed to the attack at Old Bridge. Schomberg fell as recounted in the ballad; but the Orange forces swept clean the entrenchments of James and sent him flying by the Pass of Duleek for Dublin. — *Faith's defender*, *Fidei Defensor*, a title bestowed by Pope Leo X upon Henry VIII, in 1521, and retained by him as a Protestant, and by his successors. Fragments of the original ballad of the Boyne Water composed soon after the battle may still be heard in the north of Ireland, but the version here given, attributed to a certain Captain Blacker, is that used by the Orangemen in their meetings at the present day. Neither version has any literary merit; but the battle was one of the turning points of British history. The society of Irish Protestants called "Orangemen," which commemorates the event, is as keenly interested in political and religious affairs to-day as in 1795, when it was organized in order to oppose the spread of Roman Catholicism.

Page 195, XCI. AFTER AUGHRIM. — Ginckel, a Dutchman, being left in command of the English forces by William III after the battle of the Boyne, drove Sarsfield, King James's general, out of Athlone and back to the bogs of Aughrim, and defeated him there on July 12, 1691. Soon after, Ginckel and the Irish leader Sarsfield met again at Limerick, where the cause of the Stuarts was finally lost by Sarsfield's defeat.

Page 196, XCII. SHAN VAN VOCHT, or Poor Old Woman, is one of the many names under which Ireland has been personified by those of her sons who would sever the connection with England. This ballad is an anonymous composition of the year 1797 when the French fleet arrived in Bantry Bay to support the uprising of the United Irishmen. The movement was chiefly for Catholic emancipation, and one of its leaders was the well-known Lord Edward Fitzgerald. The rebellion failed and Lord Edward died in prison.

Page 198, XCIII. THE WEARING OF THE GREEN. — Numerous versions of this street ballad exist. That of the text, however, is best known. It was introduced by Dion Boucicault (born in Dublin, 1822) into one of his plays about 1870. — *Napper Tandy*, a patriot of 1798.

Page 200, XCIV. THE MEMORY OF THE DEAD. — The author of this stirring song, often called *Ninety-Eight*, was for many years a Fellow, and librarian, of Trinity College, Dublin.

Page 202, XCV. THE GERALDINES. — The author, Davis, was one of the most brilliant poets and political agitators of his day in Ireland. He was educated at Trinity College, Dublin, and became a member of the Irish bar. "There were two distinct families known in Irish history as 'the Geraldines,' and both were descended from Maurice Fitzgerald, one of the Anglo-Normans who invaded Ireland under 'Strongbow,' the Earl of Pembroke, during 1169-1170 — (1) the Fitzgeralds of Desmond, or South Munster; (2) the Fitzgeralds of Kildare, to whom the Duke of Leinster belongs." The descendants of these and other Anglo-Norman conquerors became in time more Irish than the Irish themselves — largely because they adopted the Irish practice of fosterage, by which the children of the lord of an estate were sent out to nurse with the family of his native retainer. Children thus brought up naturally took to the Irish customs of dress, of native or *Brehon* law, of bardic festivals, of keeping great retinues of mercenaries or *kerns*. — *Crom abú*, the war cry and motto of the Geraldines. — *Maynooth Castle*, the Geraldine stronghold. — *Silken Thomas*, tenth Earl of Kildare, who, when he heard that Henry VIII had beheaded his father, the ninth Earl, flung the sword of state on the council table in contemptuous defiance of the king. Thomas was himself beheaded in 1537. — The sixteenth Earl of *Desmond* lost his estates and life by an unsuccessful rebellion against Elizabeth in 1580. — *Lord Edward*, or the *Sainted Edward*, the son of the first Duke of Leinster referred to in *The Shan Van Vocht*. — For Ginckel and Limerick, see note to *After Aughrim*.

Page 205, XCVI. SOGGARTH AROON. — *Aroon* (arún), Irish for "beloved" — *Soggarth*, priest. — Banim was an Irish novelist and dramatist.

Page 207, XCVII. THE GIRL I LEFT BEHIND ME is an air perhaps of the seventeenth century. It came into general use as the soldier's tune of departure about 1750. The words and music are both of Irish composition. An English version of later date exists, but it lacks the ballad ring of the Irish original.

Page 209, XCVIII. THE HARP THAT ONCE. — *Tara*, in County Meath, near Dublin, is famous as a royal castle in the early history of Ireland. Moore's *Irish Melodies* were written between 1807 and 1834.

Page 213, CIII. THE COOLUN. — *Coolun*, the flowing love-locks of the native Irish of earlier days, used here as a term of fondness. — *Colleen*, lass; *oge*, young; *bawn*, fair. The author is perhaps the most thoroughly

Irish of the poets of his country. He has hardly the originality, however, of Mangan.

Page 214, CIV. THE BELLS OF SHANDON. — The bells here celebrated are in the steeple of the church of St. Anne, or Upper Shandon, in Cork. The lyric was published in 1834. The Reverend Francis Mahony is better known under the pen name of Father Prout.

Page 215, CV. KATHLEEN MAVOURNEEN. — The words by (Mrs.) Julia Crawford, a native of County Cavan. They were first published between 1830 and 1840, in the *Metropolitan Magazine;* and were soon afterwards set to music by Frederick Nicholls Crouch.

Page 216, CVI. THE LAMENT OF THE IRISH EMIGRANT. — Helena Selina Blackwood, Lady Dufferin, was one of the three brilliant granddaughters of Richard Brinsley Sheridan. She was the mother of the famous Marquis of Dufferin, recently deceased. This tender idyllic ballad was published about 1838.

Page 218, CVII. DEAR LAND. — The rousing songs which appeared in *The Nation*, an Irish newspaper, over the name of Sliabh Cuilinn, have with some degree of probability been attributed to John O'Hagan, a distinguished Irish jurist, who was born in 1822.

Page 223, CX. — SONG FROM THE BACKWOODS. — Written in 1857. The author has been for years editor and proprietor of the Irish newspaper, *The Nation*.

BOOK FIFTH — POEMS OF AMERICA

Page 236, CXVII. CONCORD HYMN. — On the night of April 18, 1775, eight hundred British regulars were secretly dispatched from Boston to arrest Samuel Adams and John Hancock at Lexington, and to seize the military stores collected at Concord. The vigilant patriots, however, had discovered the secret and were on the alert, and when the expedition moved to cross the Charles River, Paul Revere, one of the most active of the Sons of Liberty in Boston, had preceded them and was on his way toward Concord to arouse the inhabitants and the minute-men. Soon after church bells, musketry, and cannon spread the news over the country; and when, at dawn, April 19, the British arrived at Lexington they found seventy minute-men drawn up on the village green to oppose them. The advance guard under Major Pitcairn fired upon them, but they held their ground until the main body of the British appeared. Then they gave way and the regulars pushed forward to Concord. Here they were unable to discover any military stores, and while they were committing some depredations affairs took a sudden turn. Two hundred regulars who guarded the Concord bridge were routed by some four hundred minute-men who had hastily collected from neighboring towns. The position of the British thus became perilous. About noon they started for Boston, subjected to a galling fire from all sides. Exhausted by their long march they fell into a disorderly flight and were saved only by the timely assistance of Lord Percy, who came from Boston with reënforcements. Seven miles from Boston their passage was again disputed by a force of militia. The whole countryside was out against them; once more their retreat became a rout, and at sunset they entered Charlestown under the welcome protection of the fleet, on the full run, just in time to avoid an encounter with Colonel Pickering and seven hundred Essex militia. The loss of the British was two hundred and seventy-three; that of the Americans about one-third that number. The battle showed that the colonists could not be frightened into submission. — *From Jameson.* This hymn was sung at the completion of the Battle Monument, April 19, 1836, on the occasion of the anniversary of the battle of Lexington.

Page 238, CXIX. THE MARYLAND BATTALION. — This poem has reference to the battle of Long Island, August 27, 1776, won by the British, under Howe, Clinton, Percy, Cornwallis, and Grant, with the Hessians under von Heister, over the Americans commanded by William Alexander (known as Lord Stirling), Sullivan, and Putnam. See Fiske's *American Revolution*, 1: 207. — *Macaroni* was used for an exquisitely dressed person a century and more before the Revolution.

Page 240, CXX. COLUMBIA, ETC. — The author, who was later President of Yale College, was a chaplain in the Revolutionary army when he wrote this prophetic poem.

Page 241, CXXI. MARION'S MEN. — A brigade organized by Francis Marion (b. 1732, d. 1795), an American Revolutionary general. It was noted for the celerity of its movements and the sudden fierceness of its attacks. Marion operated from his swamp fastnesses on the Pedee and Santee rivers, whence he led or sent out expeditions against the British which accomplished marvelous results.

Page 244, CXXII. EUTAW SPRINGS.— On September 8, 1781, General Greene commanding the American forces attacked the British under Colonel Stuart at Eutaw Springs, a place about fifty miles from Charleston, South Carolina, on the Santee. There were two brief actions. In the first the British line was broken and driven from the field. In the second Stuart succeeded in forming a new line, supported by a brick house, and from this position Greene was unable to drive him. The total American loss was five hundred and fifty-four; that of the British about one thousand.

Page 245, CXXIII. CARMEN BELLICOSUM.— *Old Continentals*, the American Revolutionary soldiers.— *Grenadiers*, the English forces.— *Unicorn*, the sinister supporter of the arms of England.

Page 249, CXXVI. HAIL, COLUMBIA. — Written in 1798 to the tune of "The President's March." Intense feeling was rife in America at that time with respect to the war then raging between France and England. The famous ode, sung first at the benefit performance of a Philadelphia actor, was composed with the object of inspiring in the hostile factions a patriotism which should transcend the bitterness of party feeling.— *Stedman*.

Page 254, CXXVIII. "OLD IRONSIDES."— The popular name of the frigate *Constitution*, the most celebrated vessel in the United States navy. She was built in Boston in 1797, and during the War of 1812 rendered glorious service to the nation. Her victory over the English frigate *Guerrière* "raised the United States in one half hour to the rank of a first-class naval power." In 1830 the Navy Department deeming the *Constitution* no longer useful ordered her broken up and sold. This order met with so much popular opposition that it was abandoned. Dr. Holmes's poetic protest did much to create and call forth the public sentiment against it.

Page 256, CXXX. THE STAR-SPANGLED BANNER. — Written during the bombardment of Fort McHenry by the British fleet, the author being at the time detained on board one of the British ships.

Page 259, CXXXII. THE AMERICAN FLAG.— To this poem of Drake's, which has become a national classic, Halleck is said to have added the closing quatrain.

Page 262, CXXXIV. THE DEFENCE OF THE ALAMO. — The Alamo was a fort at San Antonio, Texas, made memorable by the heroic defense of its little garrison in 1836, during the war of Texan Independence. A force of one hundred and forty Texans withstood for two weeks an army of nearly four thousand Mexicans under Santa Ana. Finally, after a desperate defense, the fort was taken by assault, March 6. Of its defenders only six remained alive, and these, including the famous Davy Crockett, were immediately butchered by order of the Mexican general.

Page 263, CXXXV. THE BIVOUAC OF THE DEAD. — This poem commemorates the Kentuckians who fell at Buena Vista, February 22–23, 1847.

Page 268, CXXXVII. BATTLE-HYMN OF THE REPUBLIC. — This hymn " will last as long as the Civil War is remembered in history. It was written in 1861, after the author's observing, in the camps near Washington, the marching of the enthusiastic young soldiers to the song *John Brown's Body*. Mrs. Howe's words were at once adopted and sung throughout the North." — *Stedman*.

Page 271, CXL. THE "CUMBERLAND." — A Federal sloop of war (Lieutenant George U. Morris commander) sunk by the Confederate ram *Merrimac* in Hampton Roads, March 8, 1862, after making a most heroic defense in an unequal contest. She went down with all on board, and colors flying.

Page 277, CXLIII. VICKSBURG. A position most important for the Confederacy to hold. It was unsuccessfully attacked by Sherman in 1862. Grant began to advance upon it in April of the next year, and took it after desperate assaults on July 4.

Page 279, CXLIV. KEENAN'S CHARGE. In the battle of Chancellorsville, where Lee defeated the Union forces under Hooker, May 2–4, 1863.

Page 294, CL. SHERIDAN'S RIDE. — "A famous incident of the battle of Cedar Creek, Virginia, October 19, 1864. Sheridan's army, which was encamped on Cedar Creek in the Shenandoah Valley, was surprised before daybreak and defeated by the Confederates under General Early. Sheridan, who was at Winchester, twenty miles from the field, on his return from a visit to Washington, heard the sound of battle and rode rapidly to the scene of action. As he galloped past the retreating soldiers, he shouted, 'Face the other way, boys! We are going back!' He re-formed his corps, and before the close of the day had gained a decisive victory." — *Century Cyclopedia*.

Page 300, CLIII. DIXIE.— The most famous Southern war song. There is another and more popular Civil War ballad called *Dixie*, beginning

> I wish I was in de land of cotton, old times dar are not forgotten,

which was composed in 1859 by D. D. Emmett.— *Dixie*, a collective designation for the Southern states.

Page 302, CLIV. MY MARYLAND.— One of the most popular Southern war songs. It has been called the Marseillaise of the Confederate cause.

Page 305, CLV. THE BONNIE BLUE FLAG.— Assigned variously, to H. McCarthy, to (Mrs.) Annie Chambers Ketchum, and to Alexander White of Birmingham, Alabama Definite information will be welcomed by the editors.

Page 310, CLVIII. THE CONQUERED BANNER.— Written soon after the surrender of Lee.

Page 318, CLXIV. THE BLUE AND THE GRAY.— This poem, which has now become a national classic, was inspired by the fact that the women of Columbus, Mississippi, on their Decoration Day placed flowers on the graves of Northern and Southern soldiers alike.

Page 340, CLXXX. YANKEE DOODLE.— We find the following in *Our Familiar Songs*. "The air of 'Yankee Doodle' is claimed by several nations. It is said to be an old vintage song in the south of France. In Holland, when the laborers received for wages 'as much buttermilk as they could drink and a tenth of the grain,' they used to sing as they reaped, to the tune of 'Yankee Doodle,' the words:

> Yanker dudel, doodle down, etc.

The tune was sung in England in the reign of Charles I to a rhyme which is still alive in our nurseries:

> Lucy Locket lost her pocket,
>   Kitty Fisher found it —
> Nothing in it, nothing on it,
>   But the binding round it.

The words, supposed to be said by a green New Englander, would naturally catch the fancy of the British soldiers. Later on, the revolutionists adopted the tune in derision of their deriders. The tune first appeared in this country in June, 1775. The words are ascribed to Dr. Richard

Shuckburg, a British regimental surgeon. He was 'mightily amused' at the uncouth appearance of the Colonial troops in their tattered uniforms and with their antique equipments. He planned a joke upon the instant. He set down the notes of 'Yankee Doodle,' wrote underneath them this lively adaptation of a Cromwellian verse, and gave it to the band. For during the English Civil War a similar song had been sung by the Cavaliers in ridicule of Cromwell, who was said to have ridden into Oxford on a small horse, with his single plume fastened into a sort of knot, which was derisively called a 'macaroni.' The words were:

> Yankee doodle came to town,
> Upon a Kentish pony;
> He stuck a feather in his cap,
> Upon a macaroni."

This use of "macaroni" might have been suggested by the resemblance of the cap-knot to a macaroon, for that word was used to mean a small sweet cake as early as 1610. It is, however, possible that the original line ran "And called it macaroni," for the poet Donne uses the word "macaroon" or "macaroni" for a foppishly dressed person in 1650.

Page 342, CLXXXI. NATHAN HALE.— The hero was a school teacher. At Washington's request he undertook to act as a spy. His heroic death was a spiritual assistance to the revolutionists. See Tyler's *Literary History of the Revolution*.

Page 354, CXC. DIXIE'S LAND.— A version of the original ballad as composed to his own inspiring music by Daniel Decatur Emmett in 1859. Variations are, however, handed down; as, for instance, for the second line of the first stanza,

> Cimmon seed and sandy bottom;

and after "Look away!" in the fourth stanza,

> Will run away.— Missus took a decline, oh,
> Her face was de color ob bacon-rine— oh;

and instead of "Ole Missus acted de foolish part," etc.,

> How could she act such a foolish part,
> As marry a man dat break her heart?

and at the opening of the sixth stanza,

> Sugar in de gourd and stonny batter,
> De whites grow fat and de niggers fatter.

GLOSSARY

a, a', all.
abone, aboon, above.
aften, often.
ain, own.
ane, one.
anither, another.
aros, arrows.
awa', away.
ayont, beyond.

backit, backed, dressed.
baith, both.
balys bete, remedy our evils.
bandsters, binders.
bannet, bonnet, cap.
bar, bore, carried.
barkened, hardened.
barne, berne, a man.
basnites, helmets.
bauk, crossbeam.
beld, bald.
bent, open grassy place, field.
bi (be), by.
biek, to bask; *to biek forenent the sin*, to bake against (in the rays of) the sun (*Gummere*).
bigget, builded.
bigonet, a cap of silk or other cloth stuff, a mutch.
bigs, builds.
bilbows, swords, the best of which were made in Bilboa in Spain.

birk, birch.
birkie, a smart-appearing, conceited youth.
blane, halted.
blawn, blown.
bluart, bilberry.
blyve, quickly.
bogles, ghosts.
bomen, bowmen.
bonnets, in the Scotch, caps.
bow, bow window, bay window (*Montrose*).
boÿs, bowys, bows.
bracken, fern.
brae, slopes.
braid, broad.
braid letter, an open or patent letter, a public document.
brande, sword.
branking, prancing.
braw, handsome.
brent, brente, burnt.
brent, smooth, unwrinkled.
bristit, breasted.
broad pieces, gold coins.
broo, broth.
brook, enjoy, tolerate.
bryttlynge, the cutting, or, literally, the breaking up.
bugelet, a small bugle.
bughts, a place for milking ewes.
burd, young woman, lady.

burn, brook, stream.
burn-brae, "the acclivity at the bottom of which a rivulet runs."
burrows-town, borough town, corporate town.
buskit, make ready; *busk and boun*, up and away.
but an, unless.
but and, and also.
byckarte, skirmished.
byddys, abides, remains.
byears, biers.
bylle, bill, a battle-ax.
byre, cow house, stable.

caller, fresh.
cam, came.
canty, jolly.
carles, churls, low fellows.
carline wife, old peasant woman.
cast, intend.
catches, songs.
caubeen, hat (Irish).
cauld, cold.
channerin, fretting.
chays, chase, hunting ground.
clamb, climbed.
close-heads, to, together.
cloth-yard, an old measure of twenty-seven inches.
cole, cowl.
coof, fool.
corbies, ravens.
cors, curse.
coud, knew.
cowthie, kindly.
curragh, a plain (Irish).

daffing, joking.
daw, to dawn.

dee, die.
deid, deed; dead.
departed it, divided it.
dight, handle (Otterbourne).
dighted, dressed.
dine, dinner time.
ding, beat.
Don, the Spanish for Mr.
donne, dun.
dool, dole, grief.
doops, drops.
doun, down.
dowie, sad.
downa, cannot
dre, endure.
dree, suffer.
drumly, dark, gloomy.
dule, pain.
dyghtande, made ready.
dynte, a blow.

ee, eye; *een*, eyes.
eldern, elderly.
everych, every.

fa', fall.
fa' (in Burns's *For a' that*), claim, try
fail, turf.
fare, doings.
fashes, troubles, storms.
fauld, fauldit, fold, folded.
fause, false.
fay, oath, loyalty.
faylyd of, missed.
feale, fail.
fee, pay, money, property.
fend, sustain.
feth, faith.
fiere, friend, comrade.
fit, foot.
fit, fytte, division of a ballad.

flecking, shadow with flecks of sunshine.
fleeching, coaxing, flattering.
flyting, jeering.
forenent, in the face of.
fostere, forester.
frae, from.
freits, ill omens.
frere, friar.
freyke, man, warrior.
fu, full.

ga, gae, to go.
galleon, a large ship.
galliard, a merry dance.
gang, go.
gar, make.
gie, gi'ed, give, gave.
gin, if.
glacis, a sloping bank used in fortification.
glede, a glowing coal.
glent, flashed.
goun, gown.
gowan, the daisy.
gowd, gold.
gramercy, thanks.
gree, prize.
greet, weep.
grevis, groves.
guid, gude, good.
gullies, knives.

hae, have.
halfendell, in two parts.
Halidom, all that is holy; sacred honor.
halke, corner.
halyde, pulled, hauled.
hame, home.
hamely, homely.
harried, plundered.
haud, hold.
haugh, flat ground on the border of a river.
hauld, shelter, stronghold.
hause, neck.
heal, hail.
hede, heed.
hewmont, helmet.
Hielanders, Highlanders.
hight, promise.
hillys, hills.
hinde, gentle.
hirsels, flocks of sheep.
hodden, wool "holden" in its natural gray color.
hom, them.

idyght, prepared.
ilka, every.
iwys, surely.

jauds, jades.
jimp, slender, neat.
jo, sweetheart.

kale, broth.
kems, combs.
ken, know.
kye, cows (the herd of cows).

laith, loath.
Lammas-tide, the first of August.
lane (*her lane*), alone.
lanely, lonely.
lang, long.
lauch, laugh.
lave, rest.
laverock, lark.

lede, train.
ledesman, guide.
leglin, milk-pail.
lemans, sweethearts.
lende, tarry.
lese, lose.
let, prevent.
levin, lightning.
lieard (liard), gray.
lift, heavens.
light, alighted.
lilt, tune.
lin, pause.
list, inclination, desire.
loaning, a broad lane for milking.
lock, look.
long hafted, long shafted.
loot, let.
lowe, blaze.
lyff-tenant, lieutenant.
lyndes, lindens, trees in general.

magger, mauger; *in the magger of*, in spite of.
maiden knight, i.e., in his first battle.
main, the sea (*Agin.*, st. 1, *Revenge*, st. 14); the main division (*Agin.*, st. 7).
mair, more.
maist, most; almost (*Wae's Me for Prince Charlie*).
makys, mates.
male, mail, armor.
male-horse, pack horse.
march-parti, border side.
mare, more.
Martinmas, the eleventh of November.
maun, must.
mauna, must not.

mavis, thrush.
meany, company.
measure, sometimes a dance.
meikle, mickle, muckle, great.
merkes, targets.
mo, more.
monie, many.
morne, morrow.
mote, may.
muirmen, moormen.
myllan, Milan steel.
myneyeple, a gauntlet covering hand and forearm.

na, not.
nane, none.
neist, next.
noo, now.
nourice, nurse.

o', of, on.
o'ercome, refrain.
on, of, in.
on, one.
Orange, see notes on *Battle of the Boyne*.
oware off none, hour of noon.
owre, or, before.
owre, over.

paidl't, paddled.
pallions, tents.
parti, side; *uppone a parti*, on one side.
passe, limits.
pat, pot.
pawkie, sly, artful.
pelting, paltry, petty.
pibroch, a kind of martial music performed upon the bagpipe.

pike, a kind of spear.
pint-stowp, pint vessel.
plat, intertwined.
pleugh, plough.
pow, poll, head.
protocol, a first draft of a treaty or other such dispatch.
pu', pull.
pyke, pick.
pyne, pains.

quyrry, quarry, slaughtered game.
quyte, avenged.

rade, rode.
rashes, rushes.
rax, reach.
reas, rouse.
red, read.
reek, smoke.
richt, right.
riving, tearing.
row, roll.
runkled, wrinkled.

sae, so.
saft, soft.
s'all, shall.
sare, sair, sore.
sang, song.
scaur, a rocky steep.
se, sea.
se, see, saw.
seased, seized.
semblyde, assembled
sent I me, I assent.
set, struck upon, hit.
shard, used by Kipling for the armor of a battle ship.

shear, several, separate.
shente, injured.
shete, shoot.
sheugh, ditch, furrow.
shyars, shires.
sic, such.
simmer, summer.
sin, sun.
sin', since.
sithe, sith, since.
slaes, sloes.
slee, sly, or shy.
slogan, war cry.
sloughe, slew.
sma', small.
snaw, snow.
somers, sumpters.
span, rope (*Montrose*).
spendyd, grasped.
sprente, sprang, spouted.
spurne, trouble.
starn, star.
staw, stole.
stede, place.
sterne, bold ones.
sterte, started.
stour, conflict, press of battle.
strath, a valley with a river in it.
stynttyde, stopped.
suar, sure.
suner, sooner.
swakkit, smote.
swankie, a gay lad.
swapte, smote, slashed.
syke, marsh.
syne, since.

takyll, arrow, tackle.
tane, one.

targe, shield, buckler (in *Robin Hood and the King*, probably coat of arms, seal).
target, often a shield.
tartan, a Scotch plaid.
teenfu, sorrowful.
thae, those.
the, they.
theekit, thatched.
thegither, together.
thirled, pierced.
thorowe, through.
thraw, wring.
thyder, thither.
till, to.
tocke, took.
ton, one.
tothar, *tother*, other.
toun, *toune*, *towne*, often means simply an enclosed or fortified place.
trystell-tre, trysting tree, meeting place.
twa, two.
tydynge, news.
tyne, forfeit.

unneth, scarcely.
untyll, unto.

vaward, vanguard.
verament, truly.

wa', wall.
wade, gone, passed.
wae, woe; *wae worth ye*, woe be to you.
wane, a great number, multitude.
ware, aware.

wargangs, wagons.
wark, work.
wat, *wot*, know.
waught, draught.
wauken, waken.
waur, worse.
weal, clench, clasp.
weather, the withers.
wede, array, garb.
wede, weeded (*Flowers of the Forest*).
weel, well.
weir', weird, fate.
welt, controlled.
wende, go.
wende, thought.
wha, who.
wham, whom.
whaur, where.
wi', with.
wichty, sturdy.
willie, willing.
wouche, damage, injury.
wroken, avenged.
wude, mad.
wyght, active.
wyld, wild deer (*Cheviot*, 6-1).
wyste, knew.
wystly, carefully

yede, went.
ye-feth, in faith.
yemen, yeomen.
yenough, enough.
yerle, earl.
yew, the Spanish wood best fitted for bows.
ylke, same.
yowes, ewes.
yth, in the.

INDEX OF AUTHORS AND POEMS

	PAGE
Albee, John (1833–)	
A Soldier's Grave	314
Arnold, Matthew (1822–1888)	
Memorial Verses on the Death of Wordsworth	102
Austin, Alfred (1835–)	
Sons of the Self-Same Race	356
Aytoun, William Edmonstoune (1813–1865)	
The Execution of Montrose	150
The Old Scottish Cavalier	159
Anonymous, or of uncertain authorship	
Barbara Allen	128
God Save the King	65
John Brown's Body	267
Marching through Georgia	293
Nathan Hale	342
Older Ballads (see *Table of Contents*)	
The Bailiff's Daughter of Islington	129
The Battle of the Boyne (perhaps by Blacker)	193
The Blue Bell of Scotland	165
The Bonnie Banks o' Loch Lomond	183
The British Grenadiers	87
The Campbells are Comin'	164
The Girl I Left behind Me	207
The Shan Van Vocht	196
The Vicar of Bray	138
The Warship of 1812	255
The Wearing of the Green (Boucicault's version)	198
Yankee Doodle	340
You Gentlemen of England	134
Banim, John (1798–1842)	
Soggarth Aroon	205

389

	PAGE
Beattie, James (see under Mickle)	
Beers, Ethelinda (1827–1879)	
All Quiet along the Potomac	344
Bell, Robert Mowry (1860–)	
For Cuba	328
Bennett, Henry Holcomb (1863–)	
The Flag Goes By	336
Boker, George Henry (1823–1890)	
Dirge for a Soldier	313
Brooks, Charles Timothy (1813–1883), and J. S. Dwight (1813–1893)	
God Bless our Native Land	261
Browning, Robert (1812–1889)	
Give a Rouse	80
The Lost Leader	101
Bryant, William Cullen (1794–1878)	
Song of Marion's Men	241
Abraham Lincoln	320
Burns, Robert (1759–1796)	
Bannockburn	144
A Red, Red Rose	171
For a' that, and a' that	171
John Anderson, my Jo	173
Afton Water	174
Ye Banks and Braes	175
My Heart's in the Highlands	176
Auld Lang Syne	185
Butterworth, Hezekiah (1839–)	
The Thanksgiving in Boston Harbor	233
Byron, George Noel Gordon, Lord (1788–1824)	
The Field of Waterloo	98
Campbell, Thomas (1777–1844)	
Battle of the Baltic	90
Ye Mariners of England	93
Carey, Henry (d. 1743), probable author of	
God Save the King	65
Sally in our Alley	136
Carryl, Guy Wetmore (1873–)	
When the Great Gray Ships Come In	337
Cherry, Andrew (1762–1812)	
The Green Little Shamrock of Ireland	187

Index of Authors and Poems

	PAGE
Clarke, Joseph I. C. (1846–)	
The Fighting Race	332
Collins, William (1721–1759)	
Ode, Written in the Year 1746 (from *Odes on Several Subjects*)	90
Crawford, Julia (*c.* 1800–1850)	
Kathleen Mavourneen	215
Cunningham, Allan (1784–1842)	
A Wet Sheet and a Flowing Sea	141
Davis, Thomas Osborne (1814–1845)	
The Geraldines	202
Dibdin, Charles (1745–1814)	
Poor Tom Bowling	142
Dobson, Henry Austin (1840–)	
A Ballad of Heroes	iii
Douglas, William of Fingland (and Lady John Scott)	
Annie Laurie (*c.* 1700)	166
Doyle, Sir Francis Hastings (1810–1888)	
The Loss of the "Birkenhead"	114
Drake, Joseph Rodman (1795–1820)	
The American Flag	259
Drayton, Michael (1563–1631)	
The Ballad of Agincourt	70
Dufferin, Helena Selina Blackwood, Lady (1807–1867)	
The Lament of the Irish Emigrant	216
O Bay of Dublin	220
Dwight, Timothy (1752–1817)	
"Columbia, Columbia, to Glory Arise"	240
Elliot, Jane (1727–1805)	
The Flowers of the Forest; or, The Battle of Floden. Part I.	146
Emerson, Ralph Waldo (1803–1882), Concord Hymn	236
Emmett, Daniel Decatur (1815–), Dixie's Land	354
English, Thomas Dunn (1819–)	
Ben Bolt	349
Ferguson, Sir Samuel (1810–1886)	
The Coolun	213
Finch, Francis Miles (1827–)	
The Blue and the Gray	318
Foster, Stephen Collins (1826–1864)	
My Old Kentucky Home	351

	PAGE
Foster, Stephen Collins (*continued*)	
Massa's in de Cold Ground	352
Old Folks at Home	353
Freneau, Philip (1752–1832)	
Eutaw Springs	244
Geoghegan, Arthur Gerald (1809–1889)	
After Aughrim	195
Gibbons, James Sloane (1810–1892)	
Three Hundred Thousand More	288
Gilder, Joseph B. (1858–)	
The Parting of the Ways	339
Glen, William (d. 1824) probable author of	
Wae's Me for Prince Charlie	163
Harte, Francis Bret (1839–1902)	
The Reveille	270
Hayne, Paul Hamilton (1830–1886)	
Vicksburg	277
Hemans, Felicia (1793–1835)	
The Landing of the Pilgrim Fathers	230
Hogg, James (1770–1835)	
The Lament of Flora Macdonald	162
When the Kye Comes Hame	180
Holmes, Oliver Wendell (1809–1894)	
"Old Ironsides"	254
Hopkinson, Joseph (1770–1842)	
Hail, Columbia	249
Howe, Julia Ward (1819–)	
Battle-Hymn of the Republic	268
Ingram, John Kells (*c.* 1827–)	
The Memory of the Dead (or, Ninety-Eight)	200
Jonson, Ben (1573–1637)	
To Celia	133
Key, Francis Scott (1780–1843)	
The Star-Spangled Banner	256
Kipling, Rudyard (1865–)	
Recessional	126
Kittredge, Walter (1832–)	
Tenting on the Old Camp Ground	346
Lathrop, George Parsons (1851–1898)	
Keenan's Charge	279

Index of Authors and Poems

	PAGE
Longfellow, Henry Wadsworth (1807–1882)	
Santa Filomena	118
The "Cumberland"	271
The Republic (from *The Building of the Ship*)	324
Lowell, James Russell (1819–1891)	
Lincoln (from the *Commemoration Ode*)	322
Lowell, Robert Traill Spence (1816–1891)	
The Relief of Lucknow (1857)	121
Macaulay, Thomas Babington, Lord (1800–1859)	
The Battle of Naseby	82
Mahony, Francis (pseud., Father Prout) (1805–1866)	
The Bells of Shandon	214
Mangan, James Clarence (1803–1849)	
Dark Rosaleen	190
McCarthy, H., or Annie Chambers Ketchum (d. 1904)	
The Bonnie Blue Flag	305
McGee, Thomas D'Arcy (1825–1868)	
The Irish Wife	188
McMaster, Guy Humphrey (1829–1887)	
Carmen Bellicosum	245
McNally, Leonard (1752–)	
The Lass of Richmond Hill	140
Meredith, William Tuckey (1839–)	
Farragut	291
Mickle, William Julius (1735–1788), and James Beattie (1735–1803)	
There's Nae Luck about the House	168
Miller, Cincinnatus Hiner (Joaquin) (1841–)	
Columbus	228
The Defence of the Alamo	262
Moore, Thomas (1779–1852)	
The Harp that once through Tara's Halls	209
The Meeting of the Waters	209
Believe me, if all those endearing young charms	210
The Last Rose of Summer	211
Oft, in the stilly night	212
Morris, William (1834–1896)	
The March of the Workers (1885)	124
Nairne, Carolina Oliphant, Lady (1766–1845)	
The Land o' the Leal	184

	PAGE
O'Hara, Theodore (1820–1867)	
The Bivouac of the Dead	263
O'Leary, Ellen (1831–1889)	
To God and Ireland True	225
O'Rourke, Edmund (pseud., Edmund Falconer)	
Killarney	221
Osgood, Kate Putnam (1841–)	
Driving Home the Cows	315
Paine, Albert Bigelow (1861–)	
The New Memorial Day	335
Palmer, John Williamson (1825–1896)	
The Maryland Battalion	238
Stonewall Jackson's Way	308
Parker, Martin (c. 1630)	
You Gentlemen of England	134
Payne, John Howard (1791–1852)	
Home, Sweet Home	347
Pierpont, John (1785–1866)	
The Pilgrim Fathers	231
Warren's Address	237
Pike, Albert (1809–1891)	
Dixie	300
Ramsay, Allan (1686–1758)	
Lochaber	167
Randall, James Ryder (1839–)	
My Maryland	302
Read, Thomas Buchanan (1822–1872)	
Sheridan's Ride	294
The Brave at Home	317
Riley, James Whitcomb (1853–)	
The Old Man and Jim	296
Roche, James Jeffrey (1847–)	
The "Constitution's" Last Fight	251
Rooney, John Jerome (1866–)	
The Men behind the Guns	330
Root, George Frederick (1820–1895)	
The Battle-Cry of Freedom	269
Tramp, Tramp, Tramp	290
Rutherford, Alison (Mrs. Patrick Cockburn) (1710–1794)	
The Flowers of the Forest. Part II	148

Index of Authors and Poems

PAGE

Ryan, Abram Joseph (1839–1886)
    The Conquered Banner 310

Scott, Lady John (see under William Douglas)

Scott, Sir Walter (1771–1832)
    This is my Own, my Native Land 143
    Gathering Song of Donald the Black 145
    Blue Bonnets over the Border 149
    The Bonnets o' Bonnie Dundee 157
    Jock of Hazeldean 176
    Lochinvar 178

Shakespeare, William (1564–1616)
    England (from *Richard II*) 66
    Henry the Fifth's Address to his Soldiers before Harfleur . 67
    Henry the Fifth before Agincourt 68
    Who is Sylvia? 132
    Take, O, Take those Lips Away 132
    Blow, Blow, Thou Winter Wind 133

Shaw, D. T.
    Columbia, the Gem of the Ocean 258

Shepherd, Nathaniel Graham (1835–1869)
    Roll-Call 299

Sidney, Sir Philip (1554–1586)
    My True-Love hath my Heart 131

"Sliabh Cuilinn" (perhaps John O'Hagan) (1822–)
    Dear Land 218

Smith, Samuel Francis (1808–1895)
    America 227

Stanton, Frank Lebby (1857–)
    Answering to Roll-Call 329
    The War-Ship "Dixie" 331

Stedman, Edmund Clarence (1833–)
    Kearney at Seven Pines 273
    Gettysburg 282

Sullivan, Timothy Daniel (1827–)
    Song from the Backwoods 223

Tannahill, Robert (1774–1810)
    Jessie, the Flower o' Dumblane 182

Taylor, James Bayard (1825–1878)
    The Song of the Camp 119
    America 327

Tennyson, Alfred, Lord (1809–1892)
    The " Revenge " 74
    Ode on the Death of the Duke of Wellington . . . 105
    The Charge of the Light Brigade 116

Thomson, James (1700–1748)
    Rule, Britannia (from *Alfred*, a Masque written with James Mallet, 1740) 88

Thornbury, George Walter (1828–1876)
    The Sally from Coventry (from *Songs of Cavaliers and Roundheads*, 1857) 81
    The Three Troopers (from the *Jacobite Ballads*) . . . 85

Timrod, Henry (1829–1867)
    Ode to the Confederate Dead 312

Townsend, Mary Ashley (1832–)
    A Georgia Volunteer 306

Tuckerman, Henry Theodore (1813–1871)
    Washington's Statue 248

Wallace, William Ross (1819–)
    The Sword of Bunker Hill 247

Whitman, Walt (1819–1892)
    O Captain! My Captain! 320

Whittier, John Greenleaf (1807–1892)
    Barbara Frietchie 274
    Centennial Hymn 325

Wolfe, Charles (1791–1823)
    The Burial of Sir John Moore 97

Wordsworth, William (1770–1850)
    Character of the Happy Warrior 94

Work, Henry Clay (1832–1884)
    Marching through Georgia 293

INDEX OF TITLES AND FIRST LINES

	PAGE
Abraham Lincoln	320
A cheer and salute for the Admiral, and here's to the Captain bold	330
After Aughrim	195
Afton Water	174
A life on the ocean wave	348
All in the merry month of May	128
All quiet along the Potomac	344
America	227
America	327
American Flag, The	259
Am I the slave they say	205
And are ye sure the news is true	168
Annie Laurie	166
Answering to Roll-Call	329
As I was walking all alane	56
At anchor in Hampton Roads we lay	271
At Eutaw Springs the valiant died	244
At Flores in the Azores, Sir Richard Grenville lay	74
Auld Lang Syne	185
A wee bird cam' to our ha' door	163
A wet sheet and a flowing sea	141
A Yankee ship and a Yankee crew	251
Ay, tear her tattered ensign down	254
Bailiff's Daughter of Islington, The	129
Ballad of Agincourt, The	70
Ballad of Heroes, A	iii
Bannockburn	144
Barbara Allen	128
Barbara Frietchie	274
Battle-Cry of Freedom	269
Battle-Hymn of the Republic	268
Battle of the Baltic	90
Battle of the Boyne, The	193
Battle of Floden, The (see *Flowers of the Forest*)	146
Battle of Naseby, The	82
Battle of Otterbourne, The	3
Because you passed, and now are not	iii
Behind him lay the gray Azores	228
Believe me, if all those endearing young charms	210
Bells of Shandon, The	214
Ben Bolt	349
Bessie Bell and Mary Gray	55
Bivouac of the Dead, The	263
Blow, blow, thou winter wind	133
Blue and the Gray, The	318
Blue Bell of Scotland, The	165
Blue Bonnets over the Border	149
Bonnets o' Bonnie Dundee, The	157

Bonnie Banks o' Loch Lomond, The	183
Bonnie Blue Flag, The	305
Bonnie George Campbell	54
Brave at Home, The	317
Break not his sweet repose	314
Breathes there the man, with soul so dead	143
Bring the good old bugle, boys! we'll sing another song	293
British Grenadiers, The	87
Burial of Sir John Moore, The	97
Bury the Great Duke	105
By Killarney's lakes and fells	221
By the flow of the inland river	318
By the rude bridge that arched the flood	236
By yon bonnie banks and by yon bonnie braes	183
Campbells are comin', The	164
Carmen Bellicosum	245
Centennial Hymn	325
Character of the Happy Warrior	94
Charge of the Light Brigade, The	116
Close his eyes; his work is done	313
Columbia, Columbia, to glory arise	240
Columbia, the Gem of the Ocean	258
Columbus	228
Come all ye jolly shepherds	180
Come hither, Evan Cameron	150
Come, listen to another song	159
Come listen to me, you gallants so free	34
Come, stack arms, men! Pile on the rails	308
Concord Hymn	236
Conquered Banner, The	310
"Constitution's" Last Fight, The	251
Coolun, The	213
"Corporal Green!" the Orderly cried	299
"Cumberland," The	271
Dark Rosaleen	190
Dear Land	218
Deep in Canadian woods we've met	223
Defence of the Alamo, The	262
Demon Lover, The	60
Dirge for a Soldier	313
Dixie	300, 354
Do you remember long ago	195
Don't you remember sweet Alice, Ben Bolt	349
Douglas Tragedy, The	50
Drink to me only with thine eyes	133
Driving Home the Cows	315
Edom o' Gordon	18
England	66
Eutaw Springs	244
Execution of Montrose, The	150
Fair stood the wind for France	70
Farewell to Lochaber, and farewell, my Jean	167
Far over yon hills of the heather sae green	162
Farragut	291
Far up the lonely mountainside	306
Father and I went down to camp	340

Index of Titles and First Lines

	PAGE
Field of Waterloo, The	98
Fighting Race, The	332
Flag Goes By, The	336
Flowers of the Forest, The	146
Flow gently, sweet Afton, among thy green braes	174
For a' that, and a' that	171
For Cuba	328
Foreseen in the vision of sages	327
For sixty days and upwards	277
Furl that Banner, for 't is weary	310
Gathering Song of Donald the Black	145
Georgia Volunteer, A	306
Geraldines, The	202
Gettysburg	282
Girl I Left behind Me, The	207
Give a Rouse	80
"Give us a song!" the soldiers cried	119
God bless our native land	261
God of our fathers, known of old	126
God Save the King	65
God save our gracious King	65
Goethe in Weimar sleeps, and Greece	102
Green Little Shamrock of Ireland, The	187
Hail, Columbia! happy land	249
Half a league, half a league	116
Hark! I hear the tramp of thousands	270
Harp that once through Tara's Halls, The	209
Hats off	336
He lay upon his dying bed	247
Helen of Kirconnell	57

	PAGE
Henry the Fifth's Address to his Soldiers before Harfleur	67
Here, a sheer hulk, lies poor Tom Bowling	142
He which hath no stomach to this fight	68
High upon Highlands	54
Home, Sweet Home	347
How sleep the brave who sink to rest	90
Hunting of the Cheviot, The	8
I 'm sittin' on the stile, Mary	216
I 'm wearin' awa', Jean	184
In good King Charles's golden days	138
In the prison cell I sit	290
In their ragged regimentals	245
Into the Devil tavern	85
Irish Wife, The	188
I sit beside my darling's grave	225
Is there, for honest poverty	171
It fell about the Lammas tide	3
It fell about the Martinmas	18
I've heard them lilting	146
I wad I were where Helen lies	57
I would not give my Irish wife	188
Jessie, the Flower o' Dumblane	182
Jock of Hazeldean	176
John Anderson, my Jo	173
John Brown's Body	267
July the first, in Oldridge town, there was a grievous battle	193
Just for a handful of silver he left us	101
Kathleen Mavourneen	215
Kearney at Seven Pines	273
Keenan's Charge	279
Killarney	221

	PAGE
King Charles, and who'll do him right now	80
King Henry the Fifth before Agincourt	68
Lament of Flora Macdonald, The	162
Lament of the Irish Emigrant, The	216
Land o' the Leal, The	184
Landing of the Pilgrim Fathers, The	230
Lass of Richmond Hill, The	140
Last Rose of Summer, The	211
Life may be given in many ways	322
Life on the Ocean Wave, A	348
Lincoln	322
Lochaber No More	167
Lochinvar	178
Lord Randal	53
Loss of the "Birkenhead," The	114
Lost Leader, The	101
March of the Workers, The	124
March, march, Ettrick and Teviotdale	149
Marching through Georgia	293
Maryland Battalion, The	238
Maryland, My	302
Massa's in de Cold Ground	352
Maxwelton braes are bonnie	166
Meeting of the Waters, The	209
Memorial Verses on the Death of Wordsworth	102
Memory of the Dead, The	200
Men behind the Guns, The	330
Mid pleasures and palaces though we may roam	347
Mine eyes have seen the glory of the coming of the Lord	268

	PAGE
My country, 't is of thee	227
My heart's in the Highlands	176
My true-love hath my heart, and I have his	131
Nathan Hale	342
New Memorial Day, The	335
No precedent, ye say	328
Not a drum was heard, not a funeral note	97
O bay of Dublin! my heart you're troublin'	220
O Bessie Bell and Mary Gray	55
O Captain! My Captain	320
O Columbia, the gem of the ocean	258
Ode on the Death of the Duke of Wellington	105
Ode to the Confederate Dead	312
Ode, Written in the Year 1746	90
Of all the girls that are so smart	136
Of Nelson and the North	90
Oft, in the stilly night	212
Oh, had you seen the Coolun	213
Oh, say, can you see, by the dawn's early light	256
Oh, slow to smite and swift to spare	320
Oh, that last day in Lucknow fort	121
Oh, the roses we plucked for the blue	335
Oh! where? and oh, where is your Highland laddie gone	165
Oh! wherefore come ye forth in triumph from the north	82
Old Folks at Home	353
"Old Ironsides"	254
Old Kentucky Home, My	351

Index of Titles and First Lines

	PAGE
Three Troopers, The	85
'T is the last rose of summer	211
To Celia	133
To eastward ringing, to westward winging, o'er mapless miles of sea	337
To God and Ireland True	225
To the Cambrio-Britons and their Harp	70
To the Lords of Convention 'twas Claverhouse who spoke	157
Tramp, Tramp, Tramp	290
Twa Corbies, The	56
Union, The	324
Untrammelled Giant of the West	339
Up from the meadows rich with corn	274
Up from the South at break of day	294
Vicar of Bray, The	138
Vicksburg	277
Wae 's me for Prince Charlie	163
Warren's Address	237
War-Ship "Dixie," The	331
Warship of 1812, The	255
Washington's Statue	248
Wave, wave your glorious battle-flags, brave soldiers of the North	282
Way down upon de Swanee Ribber	353
We are a band of brothers, and native to the soil	305
We are coming, Father Abraham	288
Wearing of the Green, The	198
Wellington, Duke of, Ode on the Death of	105
We're tenting to-night on the old camp ground	346
What is the Voice I hear	356
What is this, the sound and rumor? What is this that all men hear	124
When Britain first, at Heaven's command	88
When comes the day all hearts to weigh	218
Whene'er a noble deed is wrought	118
When Freedom from her mountain height	259
When Robin Hood and Little John	47
When Robin Hood was about twenty years old	24
When the Great Gray Ships Come In	337
When the Kye Comes Hame	180
Who fears to speak of Ninety-Eight	200
Who is Silvia? what is she	132
Who is the happy Warrior? Who is he	94
Why weep ye by the tide, ladie	176
Wife of Usher's Well, The	58
With deep affection and recollection	214
Wordsworth, Memorial Verses on Death of	107
Yankee Doodle	340
Ye Banks and Braes o' Bonnie Doon	175
Ye Mariners of England	95
Yes, we'll rally 'round the flag, boys, we'll rally once again	269
You Gentlemen of England	134

Index of Titles and First Lines

	PAGE		PAGE
Old Man and Jim, The	296	"Revenge," The	74
Old man never had much to say	296	Right on our flank the crimson sun went down	114
Old Scottish Cavalier, The	159	"Rise up, rise up, now, Lord Douglas," she says	50
O my Dark Rosaleen	190	Robin Hood and Allin a Dale	34
O, my luve's like a red, red rose	171	Robin Hood and the King	38
On Richmond Hill there lives a lass	140	Robin Hood and Little John	24
Once more unto the breach, dear friends, once more	67	Robin Hood Rescuing the Widow's Three Sons	29
O Paddy dear, and did you hear the news that's going round	198	Robin Hood's Death and Burial	47
Our band is few but true and tried	241	Roll-Call	299
Our fathers' God! from out whose hand	325	Round de meadows am a-ringing	352
Out of the clover and blue-eyed grass	315	Rule, Britannia	88
O where hae ye been, Lord Randal, my son	53	Sally from Coventry, The	81
O, where hae ye been, my lang-lost love	60	Sally in our Alley	136
O, young Lochinvar is come out of the west	178	Santa Ana came storming, as a storm might come	262
Parting of the Ways, The	339	Santa Filomena	118
"Passion o' me!" cried Sir Richard Tyrone	81	Scots, wha hae wi' Wallace bled	144
Pibroch of Donuil Dhu, pibroch of Donuil	145	Shan Van Vocht, The	196
Pilgrim Fathers, The	231	Sheridan's Ride	294
Poor Tom Bowling	142	She was no armored cruiser of twice six thousand tons	255
"Praise ye the Lord!" the psalm to-day	233	Should auld acquaintance be forgot	185
"Read out the names!" and Burke sat back	332	Sir Patrick Spens	1
Recessional	126	Sleep sweetly in your humble graves	312
Red, Red Rose, A	171	Soggarth Aroon	205
Relief of Lucknow, The	121	Soldier's Grave, A	314
Reveille, The	270	Some talk of Alexander, and some of Hercules	87
		Song from the Backwoods	223
		Song of Marion's Men	241
		Song of the Camp, The	119

	PAGE		PAGE
Sons of the Self-Same Race	356	The muffled drum's sad roll has beat	263
So that soldierly legend is still on its journey	273	The Persë owt off Northombarlonde	8
Southrons, hear your country call you	300	The Pilgrim Fathers,— where are they	231
Spruce Macaronis, and pretty to see	238	The quarry whence thy form majestic sprung	248
Stand! the ground's your own, my braves	237	The sainted isle of old	196
Star-Spangled Banner, The	256	The sun had set	279
Stonewall Jackson's Way	308	The sun has gane down o'er the lofty Benlomond	182
Stop! for thy tread is on an Empire's dust	98	The sun shines bright in the old Kentucky home	351
Sword of Bunker Hill, The	247	There are twelve months in all the year	29
Take, O, take those lips away	132	There is not in the wide world a valley so sweet	209
Tenting on the Old Camp Ground	346	There lived a wife at Usher's Well	58
Thanksgiving in Boston Harbor, The	233	There's a dear little plant that grows in our isle	187
The breaking waves dashed high	230	There's Nae Luck about the House	168
The breezes went steadily thro' the tall pines	342	There was a youth, and a well-beloved youth	129
The Campbells are comin', Oho, Oho	164	They've named a cruiser *Dixie*,— that's whut the papers say	331
The dames of France are fond and free	207	This is my Own, my Native Land	143
The despot's heel is on thy shore	302	This one fought with Jackson, and faced the fight with Lee	329
The Geraldines! the Geraldines!—'t is full a thousand years	202	This royal throne of kings, this scepter'd isle	66
The harp that once through Tara's halls	209	Thou, too, sail on, O Ship of State	324
The king sits in Dumferling toune	1	Three Hundred Thousand More	288
The kynge came to Notynghame	38		
The maid who binds her warrior's sash	317		